AF624008

HANDBOOK OF
HOSPITALITY AND TOURISM

HANDBOOK OF

HOSPITALITY AND TOURISM

Edited by

Praveen Sethi

ANMOL PUBLICATIONS PVT. LTD.
NEW DELHI - 110 002 (INDIA)

ANMOL PUBLICATIONS PVT. LTD.
4374/4B, Ansari Road, Daryaganj
New Delhi - 110 002
Ph.: 23261597, 23278000
Visit us at: www.anmolpublications.com

Handbook of Hospitality and Tourism
© 2005

ISBN 81-261-0441-4

PRINTED IN INDIA

Published by J.L. Kumar for Anmol Publications Pvt. Ltd., New Delhi - 110 002 and Printed at Mehra Offset Press, Delhi.

Contents

Contents

Preface

Tourism is basically an economic activity on the part of the host country. Its main advantage is that it generates employment, income and foreign exchange inflows.

The term 'hospitality and tourism' now enjoys wide circulation as a label for describing business activities and an area of academic study encompassing hotel, catering and restaurant operations. Indeed, so accepted is the term that there exists little elaboration of its meaning and, more significantly, no systematic attempt at comprehending what is implied conceptually by the word 'hospitality'.

In order to demonstrate the problematic nature of hospitality as a concept it is necessary to point to the distinction between 'ancient' and 'modern' hospitality common to historical accounts of the phenomenon. In what is in any case a limited literature, the distinction is explored here by reference to two commentaries, published some sixty years apart, of the origins and historical development of hospitality.

Editor

1
Hospitality Industry

The term 'hospitality management' now enjoys wide circulation as a label for describing business activities and an area of academic study encompassing hotel, catering and restaurant operations. Indeed, so accepted is the term that there exists little elaboration of its meaning and, more significantly, no systematic attempt at comprehending what is implied conceptually by the word 'hospitality'. According to Ambrose Bierce's *Devil's Dictionary*, hospitality is 'The virtue which induces us to feed and lodge certain persons who are not in need of food and lodging'. Eschewing this comic view (and there are many others), recourse to the more conventional undergraduate tactic of reference to a standard dictionary yields: 'friendly and liberal reception of guests or strangers'; 'friendly and generous entertainment of guests'; and 'hospitable treatment or reception'. In the latter case, that of the *Longman Concise English Dictionary*, reference is drawn back to the root 'hospitable' which in addition to the definition 'offering a generous and cordial welcome (to guests and strangers)' also lists 'offering a pleasant or sustaining environment'. At one level then it seems that 'hospitality' is a very simple and precise term in so far as the last of these attempts to clarify meaning alerts us to the possibility of disassociating the personal aspects of hospitality (generosity, cordiality) from the impersonal (the provision of a hospitable environment).

It is such a distinction that in fact points to a certain

elusiveness in a more considered use of the term, particularly in conjunction with the word 'management' the resulting compound of which may be regarded as an oxymoron. The objective of this paper is to dissect the concept of hospitality and to draw out some implications of the term or an understanding of hospitality management.

Two conceptions of hospitality

In order to demonstrate the problematic nature of hospitality as a concept it is necessary to point to the distinction between 'ancient' and 'modern' hospitality common to historical accounts of the phenomenon. In what is in any case a limited literature, the distinction is explored here by reference to two commentaries, published some sixty years apart, of the origins and historical development of hospitality. The necessary artificiality of this approach is more than compensated for by the clarity with which each account outlines the conceptual difficulties attendant on discussions of hospitality.

Muhlmann in his contribution on 'hospitality' to the *Encyclopaedia of the Social Sciences* concentrates primarily on primitive and archaic societies. Hospitality is seen as essentially organic, as a vital and integral part of such societies revealing much about their cultural values and beliefs. According to Muhlmann, the factors which promote hospitality in these contexts are (a) the fear of strangers, (b) religious rules governing hospitality, (c) the need for trade, (d) the desire to display personal wealth and largesse, and (e) the desire to exchange news. Strangers are feared because they appear as bearers of' magical and/or mystical powers. Hospitality 'represents a kind of guarantee of reciprocity—one protects the stranger in order to be protected from him'. In religious terms, Muhlmann notes that amongst Greeks and

Romans hospitality was religiously sanctioned, certain gods watching over strangers and religious convention requiring the entertainment and care of those so protected. In the Middle Ages, monasteries performed hospitable functions by taking in travellers and others, often providing specially built accommodation in the form of hospices. Gift exchange between guest and host represents, for Muhlmann, an early form of trade in which the proper behaviour of people in exchanging gifts served as a lubricant to the development of closer trade links predicated on more rational means of exchange. The display function in hospitality is not new: it is particularly associated with the proffering of food and indeed, the excess of such hospitality is neatly parodied as early as Petronius' account of Trimalchio's feast in *The Satyricon* written in the first century AD. In the desire (and need) to receive and exchange news are found I he seeds of the nation state and diplomacy as understood in the modern sense, needs that remained simple for only a short time before requiring a degree of institutionalisation that entailed greater formality in hospitality.

This last point is important for it leads Muhlmann to argue that the hospitality of ancient and primitive societies bear little resemblance to that of the modern world:

> The germ of the decay of hospitality is inherent in the institution itself in that it inevitably extends frontiers and the domain of peace and promotes trade; as a result there arise public legal principles, which go beyond the personal and the familiar and take the place of hospitality.... Primitive hospitality was addressed to the public enemy; in the modern world the distinction between friend and enemy in the political sense is irrelevant. The old hospitality ; as a social or religious obligation; that of modern times rest., with the discretion of the individual. The old hospitality was in integral part of the culture,

> often a junction of law, custom, religion and trade; that of modern times is incidental and casts little light on cultural life.

At first sight this can be adjudged a somewhat jaundiced and pessimistic view. Fear of the stranger is still an important element of host-guest relationships, albeit in modified form, as contemporary analyses of tourism have shown. Magical and mystical powers are not the problem of modern hospitality. Rather, strangers, in the form of tourists, bring with them the threat of social and environmental damage and the erosion of the values and traditions of host communities. At the same time, for many tourist destinations, the dependency on tourism as *trade* is very clearly marked in terms of (at least) the economic exchange which in many cases fosters the dependency of hosts upon guests.

However, Muhlmann's complaint is that, in essence, the organic and spiritual qualities of hospitality have disappeared, replaced in the public sphere by a formally rational system of (usually monetary) exchange whereby hospitality is provided in particular institutional forms (hotels, restaurants) that are essentially impersonal. For the most part, hospitality is no longer about the personal giving of the host's own food and accommodation but a matter of impersonal financial exchange. To use the jargon of contemporary leisure and tourism studies, hospitality has been commoditised.

Similar views to those proposed by Muhlmann are advanced by Heal in her study of hospitality in early modern England. She argues that hospitality in modern society lacks centrality in our value systems:

> For modern Western man hospitality is preponderantly a private form of behaviour, exercised as a Matter of personal preference within a limited circle of friendship and connection. As such it is also considered a social luxury, to be pursued

> when circumstances are favourable, but abandoned without serious loss of status when they prove adverse.

In early modern England Heal argues, hospitality was both a form of social duty and social control: open hospitality was accepted as part of the social system but at the same time there was a need to regulate both the potential disorder it could create and the burdensome costs that could be generated by the provision of hospitality. This was achieved in an abstract sense by stressing the boundaries of duty. A man's first duty was to his family and household and then other kin, neighbours, friends and finally strangers and enemies.

The view of hospitality that derives from the work of Muhlmann, Heal and others is one that sees hospitality as radiating from the household, developing, as societies develop, into a more institutionalised phenomenon that nevertheless retains its characteristic as a highly personal form of social behaviour. As Heal states in the context of her study of early modern England, the concept of hospitality was: 'bound to that of reciprocity, of the exchange of gifts and rewards to which value not simply articulated in money terms attaches... when Englishmen wrote of hospitality, they used a language of exchange in which reciprocates were not assigned a monetary value'. The arguments advanced by Muhlmann and Heal could be construed as verging on the highly romanticised, seemingly suggesting that hospitality has been 'polluted' since, in the public sphere, its provision became a form of rational economic exchange rather than a social duty. There is some evidence to support this view. A number of other studies suggest either directly or more implicitly that until the beginnings of the modem hotel industry, the provision of impersonal forms of hospitality was never regarded as more than a necessary evil, as subordinate to (or sometimes incorporated in) the personal hospitality of the powerful host whether in individual or corporate form.

Having said this, there is no logical reason to suppose that the privatisation and rationalisation of social relationships attendant on industrialisation makes the provision of commercial hospitality in all respects a form of exchange calculated solely in monetary terms, it is equally possible that the quality of hospitality has changed little but the mode of exchange—the mechanisms of giving and receiving—has. This is clearly not the view of Muhlmann and Heal but it is one that in their preoccupation with the historical they do little to refute. The view of both authors is, seemingly, that the mode of exchange invariably dictates the quality of an economic and social experience. Put crudely, once hospitality is paid for it is no longer hospitality, and forms of hospitality untainted by monetary exchange are assumed to be in some way superior. This view is highly romanticised and nostalgic and, more significantly, produced without detailed reference to analysis of the commercial provision of hospitality. As a result, attention is directed to the earlier point concerning modes of exchange and processes of giving and receiving.

Gifts, exchanges and hospitality

Such issues are traditionally and most explicitly dealt with by 'exchange theory' which has its roots in Mauss's classic work *The Gift* a book retaining its influence despite alternative contemporary reformulations of the nature of reciprocity and exchange associated with American writers such as Blau and Romans. The latter view social exchange and economic and market exchange as very similar: individuals behave in a hedonistic and utilitarian fashion, engaging in social interaction on the basis that such interaction will yield returns. Mutual reciprocity exists but the basis of exchange is calculative and involves little trust or shared values. This view has been criticised as making unfounded psychological assumptions about individuals, particularly in respect of the extent to which people are self-seeking and calculative. Also questioned is the extent to which it is possible to posit a distinction between social and economic forms of exchange, Social exchange may occur without economic exchange (though not necessarily without the expectation or future economic exchange), but whether the reverse is true is more doubtful. Many forms of socioeconomic exchange are regulated by third parties, often the state via the medium of law, such that any absence of trust an reciprocity and the failure of exchange to meet the expectations of the parties to it is catered for by the provision of bureaucratic mechanisms of recourse that offer one or both parties the prospect of restitution.

Plainly put, it is not sensible to conceive of economic exchange without social exchange, a view recognised in point of fact by some recent defenders of modern exchange theory as well as its critics. In the tradition of exchange theory still firmly rooted in Mauss's anthropological commentary, the interrelationship between social and economic exchange taken to involve shared values and trust. Models of exchange may vary and will have varied consequences for the nature of reciprocity but the social dimensions to reciprocity are not dependent on the mode of economic exchange. The phenomenon of hospitality, like many other cultural phenomena, retains vestiges of its pre-industrial form as defined by Muhlmann and Heal.

This and many of the other issues discussed above are analysed at length in a paper by Burgess which, incomprehensively, has attracted little attention, given the fundamental issues with which it deals. It is possible to concentrate on only a small part of Burgess's work here, but his principal arguments derive from the proposition that gift exchange is a valuable metaphor for studying hospitality and hospitable behaviour. His views may be usefully summarised as follows.

- Though any gift may have symbolic and/or utility value, those who give seek to enhance the value of their gifts by transferring some part of the self to the recipient, the object of such behaviour being to establish symbolic bonds between the parties which may communicate *inter alia*, degrees of formality, warmth and sincerity in a relationship.
- Gifts convey information about, and confer identity upon, those who give, just as the nature of the hospitality on offer in a particular context establishes the commitment and involvement of the host in the provision of hospitality.
- Gift exchange, like hospitality, entails an assessment of the needs and desires of the recipient by the giver and this is often directed to achieving the best possible outcome in terms of establishing bonds of trust.
- Gift exchange, like hospitality, is directed towards establishing an interaction order whereby the nature of the exchange entails certain implicit rules guiding the behaviour of parties to it
- The reciprocity involved in social exchange is such that parties to the act assume a shared responsibility for its outcome.

The interesting implication of Burgess's arguments is—as suggested in the previous section—that whilst the economic dimensions to reciprocity are not unimportant, the social aspects of the process of exchange enjoy priority in interactional relationships. Further, the use of gift exchange as a metaphor for hospitality and hospitable behaviour highlights the extent to which modern hospitality continues to evidence features of pre and non-industrial societies. Burgess himself provides some interesting in-sights on the latter, but is less direct in exemplifying his major themes in a contemporary context. However, it is easy enough to provide a selection of brief illustrations of the five themes listed above.

As Burgess notes, many providers of hospitality impress their own personal stamp upon hospitality services. They may adopt a 'host role' working within their own organisation and interacting with guests in an effort to convey something of the 'self' and imprint their own personality upon the operation. In corporate organisations, similar functions are performed by the proprietors' representatives, specifically managers.

Irrespective of the economic dimension to exchange, it is often the case that elements of the hospitality package remain uncertain or ill-defined. For example, Stringer in his study of the British bed-and-breakfast business notes that many tourists experience difficulties in staying in another person's home and there was 'occasional sensitivity as to whether guests were genuinely welcome'. Successful reciprocity in a hospitality organisation is predicated on the willingness of the host to clearly define the parameters of the act of exchange and to respond to guests' uncertainties in this area.

Modern marketing theory has at its heart the (perhaps idealised) notion that satisfying the wants and needs of consumers is paramount. This applies no less to the provision of hospitality where, however, hosts may be required to be more immediately responsive to the often mercurial demands of guests, since it is the immediate response, the solution of an individual guest's particular problem that is both expected and serves to establish personal bonds between parties to the exchange.

A hotelier may have many guests but a crucial and tacit dimension of the hospitality relationships is that service is rendered to each individual.

To say that social interaction is rule-bound is to articulate a truism. Several studies of behaviour in hospitality organisations have concerned themselves with rules that govern the behaviour of parties to acts of exchange. These rules, which are more or less flexible depending on context, are primarily concerned with how to both give and receive, and circumscribe acceptable and unacceptable behaviour, serving to ensure that exchange and reciprocity are kept within acceptable boundaries. Examples would include mutual respect for public and private areas of the organisation participation in the rituals of the organisation by the guest, and the maintenance of prevailing standards of decorum.

The intention to give (whether or not in return for economic consideration) is premissed on certain assumptions concerning the shared role of giver and recipient in ensuring that an act of exchange is successful. In purchasing a good—a tangible item—it is often the case as noted earlier that third party regulation of exchange—via the medium of the law exists to support the exchange. Thus the recipient is expected to treat the item purchased in an appropriate way in return for which the provider offers a guarantee of the item's functional integrity. In many instances, providers of goods offer guarantees beyond statutory rights of the 'If this product fails to satisfy...' type. Similar legal guarantees exist in respect of the purchase of services. However, with hospitality services, where functional aspects of the object of exchange are more difficult to define, both negative and positive feedback is more immediate and providers often have mechanisms to redress grievances in a more rapid and direct way. In the case of both goods and services therefore, elements of trust are built into a relationship that transcend legal obligations. The point is an important one. Muhlmann's view, reported in the first section above, that 'public legal principles' replace hospitality in modern societies overstates the issue. Public legal principles are an adjunct to exchange utilised as a last resort. Many of those who supply goods and services attempt to offer a personal guarantee of their products and restitution of grievances is sought at an early stage of the post-exchange event where this breaks down. However, just as providers seek to offer repair mechanisms for acts of reciprocity that break down then so do recipients face obligations to ensure such acts are successful in their outcome, by not using products for purposes for which they were not intended. Translated to the provision of hospitality, the obligations of the guest include forbearance from unreasonable claims and complaints against the host and the services the latter provides, and practical engagement with the rules and conventions of the hospitality unit in such a manner as to ensure its smooth running.

Hospitality and hospitality management

Any discussion of the concept of hospitality, is, in the absence of an academic literary tradition of any substance necessarily abstract in its conception. However, from the foregoing discussion, two principal points emerge.

The differences between industrial and pre-industrial hospitality are not so great as would be apparent from the accounts of those who view rational economic exchange as in some way diluting the nature of hospitality. Indeed, the economic dimension to reciprocity in modern economies could be viewed as a formalisation of that which was always implicit in such acts.

Modern commercial hospitality is defined relative to at least two reference points: the historical conventions of public and commercial hospitality, and private hospitable behaviour. Commercial hospitality embraces elements of both and the inherently social nature of hospitality in a symbolic sense is preserved even within a system of reciprocity characterised by rational economic exchange.

If this analysis is broadly correct, then hospitality management is about the management of reciprocity and exchange. This does not mean that such management has to be successful, though it will almost certainly be directed towards successful outcomes. The rosy view of archaic and pre-industrial hospitality explored earlier in the paper emphasises the importance of highly personalised forms of hospitality to the lubrication of anything from inter familial to interstate diplomacy. What it ignores in its preoccupation with attitudes to the nature of hospitality is the manner in which hospitality is delivered, the actions of those physically engaged in the planning, coordination and execution of hospitality services. There is also a convenient failure to explore failures in hospitality, historically speaking, and the consequences of such failures.

Failures to address the mechanisms by which hospitality is delivered is a major weakness of those views that regard contemporary hospitality offered commercially as being depersonalised and lacking social significance. The contemporary provision of commercial hospitality continues to exhibit highly personalised qualities. Indeed modern commercial hospitality is no less organic in form and delivery than that of the precommercial age. Mystique direction towards cushioning (if not overwhelming) the recipients of hospitality is a feature of the commercial hospitality organisation. Such mystique, represented by attempts at the tailoring of service to each individual guest's needs within essentially impersonal organisational structures may be regarded as serving to deliberately obfuscate the economic basis of exchange. The fact that hospitality is purchased is far less significant than the fact that what is purchased remains undefined beyond a specification of essential terms—for example, bed-and-breakfast, full board and so on.

Within set parameters, hospitality managers are allowed a great deal of latitude and flexibility in providing hospitality, precisely because the economic basis to exchange is only a minor part of the total hospitality package. As Nailon argues, the hospitality manager is engaged in the manipulation of a variety of resources—those in the external environment and those that form part of the management, technical and human resource infrastructure of the organisation. Nailon's account serves to remind us that the modern hospitality organisation is directed ideologically to the satisfaction of what are perceived as individual needs and wants in a social setting. This is reflected in the extensive body of evidence that outlines the nature of the hospitality manager's role set as essentially social, as 'meeter and greeter' of guests, as peripatetic controllers of their units, as flexible operators in terms of their labour management practices.

Hospitality management training and practice retains strong attachments to 'ideal' forms of delivery of hospitality services that emphasise the social dimension to reciprocity. At the same time, as Burgess notes, a difficulty for commercial hospitality is the extent to which these ideals are distorted (or at least mediated) by cultural conventions that in the UK at least have required a certain distance between host and guest. This is an important point yet its significance should not be exaggerated. Barriers and boundaries are defining features of acts of reciprocity and exchange. In the case of hospitality, attention to the abstract features of the phenomenon, though important, should not blind us to the extent to which the management of other forms of exchange is directed however haphazardly or successfully to achieving highly personalised social transactions.

In this context, a meaning for hospitality management beyond the merely mechanistic begins to emerge. Both outside and within the hospitality management research community the term has generated some unease. Heal sees the term 'hospitality management' as constituting a paradox, as exhibiting a tension between generosity and exploitation in the marketplace, as perhaps verging on the oxymoronic. Close scrutiny of the nature of exchange and reciprocity in social relations makes this view appear superficial. In this paper an attempt has been made to explore a little more deeply the validity of the concept of 'hospitality management' relative to the phenomenon of hospitality more generally. Burgess ended his exploration of the issue by implying a need for more detailed analysis of the concept at the abstract, theoretical level. This is a sensible prescription and one, furthermore, that might yield sufficiently valuable in-sights that can be put to good use in advancing research in the field more generally as well as repelling criticisms—both real and those arising from academic snobbery-directed at the legitimacy of hospitality management as an independent field of enquiry.

2

Tourism Planning

The purpose of this chapter is to describe the state of the art of planning for tourism development to sketch the progress of planning concepts and applications for tourism with emphasis on recent changes. Although planning for specific sites, such as for resorts, has taken place for centuries, great changes have taken place in tourism planning concepts and applications in only the last few decades. As nations, provinces, cities, and investors now seek the rewards of tourism, these changes are opening up new opportunities. More areas are recognizing that better planning can prevent most negative environmental and social impacts at the same time that economic benefits can be enhanced. Even though much of the scope of this paper relates to the North American experience, many of the principles and ideas are applicable elsewhere.

Because the topic of tourism planning is confused by ambiguity of the terms 'tourism' and 'planning', it is necessary at the outset to clarify meanings. For purposes here, tourism includes all travel (business and pleasure) except commuting from home to work. Included are the categories of visitor, tourist and excursionist as recommended by the World Tourism Organization. It encompasses all the physical development and management required to provide for the traveler's interests and needs. The term planning, however, is even more ambiguous. Within tourism, it popularly has many meanings: site and building planning, market forecasting, political planning, and market planning. The focus here is placed on physical planning, land use, and design. In the context of state of the art, some forms of tourism planning and design have taken place for centuries. Even in ancient times, ships and coaches were designed for sea going and land-based travelers who sought objectives of trade or mere curiosity. The brief travel history by Bridges cites the planning and building of travel services and facilities by ancient Romans and Egyptians. These plans and developments were created in response to travel market demand partly for commerce but also for health and to visit seaside resorts and major shrines, such as temples, statues and pyramids.

For centuries, the dominant form of tourism planning has been for facilities and services. This form continues to encompass individual building sites, travel routes and mechanisms for passenger transportation. Planning at a larger scale—community and region—seems to be a much more recent phenomenon. Even seaside and mountain resorts that emerged in the mid-nineteenth century tended to grow from individual site increments rather than from regional or area plans.

This site-scale emphasis was the logical outcome of the complex nature of tourism and the growth of specialization. It was logical for business enterprise to narrow its focus on only the site and its development for financial success. It was logical for governmental agencies, based upon their legal mandates and individual policies, to concern themselves primarily with tourism related plans and developments within their own jurisdictions such as for parks and transportation. Equally specialized was the development of the planning and design professions. Probably the oldest was architecture, created primarily as a building design profession. Then, with Frederick Law Olmsted's land design work, especially for urban and natural resource parks, landscape architecture was created as a separate but related profession. Engineering developed with a strong focus on mechanical and structural design. Planning, as a profession, stemmed primarily in response to urban growth issues, land use, and allocation of public facilities. Educational institutions responded with the creation of distinct and autonomous professional programs. For reasons of public safety the professions of architecture, landscape architecture, engineering, and planning became legalized, requiring separate examination licensing and regulation. Related to tourism design has been the great growth of specialized educational programs in hotel, restaurant, travel agency, and park management.

These well-defined planning, design, and management disciplines have been utilized by many developers within all tourism sectors. Today, three sectors have become the major decision makers regarding investment, development and management of the many pieces that make up tourism. Worldwide, an important role in land ownership, development and management is performed by governmental agencies. Examples include transportation routes, airlines, parks, recreation areas, natural resource preserves, and basic infrastructure, such as water supply, waste disposal, police and fire protection. Throughout the world, the voluntary and nonprofit sector has become a major stakeholder in tourism. Lands, facilities and programs by nonprofit organizations offer many opportunities for tourism such as festivals, events, historic restoration and reuse, youth and adult camping, and religious pilgrimages. More conspicuous in developed nations is the profit-making private enterprise sector that plans, builds and operates hotels, motels, food services, travel agencies, airlines, resorts, tour companies, and theme parks. All three sectors have increased their interest in better tourism planning in the last few decades. Although nations vary in the balance of roles of these three sectors, all three can be found nearly everywhere.

This background is presented only to show that for a great many years the fields of design and planning have had—and for good reasons—a narrow and specialized focus rather than application to larger scales, such as the community, area or region. In spite of this background, significant changes in tourism design and planning have taken place in recent decades. These changes have not resulted from great inventions or startling research of planning. Instead, several factors have converged, resulting in a new paradigm.

Factors influencing planning

In only the last few decades, several new trends have dramatically influenced planning applications to tourism. The strong preoccupation with promotion by national, provincial, state and city tourism agencies is now being modified. Many of these tourism leaders are changing their budget balances to include new functions of research, education and planning. In the field of tourism planning, the following are among the leading factors fostering change.

For a long time, new tourism development was largely planned according to land and building patterns of the past and generalized assumptions regarding markets. New resorts were elaborations of past resorts; new motels like old motels; and new restaurants like former ones. More recently, this approach of supply-side imitation has been modified greatly in an attempt to meet new market needs.

Travel market research is revealing new classifications of travelers, demonstrating that not all market segments seek the same thing. Ritchie has pointed out that new market trends are creating new challenges—cultural and natural resource interests, better human relationships and desire for specialized travel products. Creative and innovative planning and design approaches are now changing in order to develop attractions, facilities, and services that are better reflections of segmented market needs. For example, new franchise food establishments such as McDonald's frequently modify a standard architectural design in an historic district to harmonize with historic buildings, meeting new cultural needs of travelers.

Hobbs has reported a stronger market demand for quality, now being reflected in the design and planning for all tourism development. The ordinary, hackneyed and commonplace no longer satisfy travel market demand. Privatization Throughout the world, democratic governments and market economies have been replacing command economies. Tourism-related businesses are growing in numbers. Airlines, hotels, resorts and attractions formerly developed and operated by governments are being opened up to private entrepreneurs. With increased demands upon governmental funds, many park and recreation services used by travelers are being turned over to private enterprise. Even in areas where governmental subsidy continues, private business directors are exercising greater control of planning and design of their facilities and services. Advocates of a 'Quality/Value Managed' private tourism plan cite market satisfaction rather than governmental control as a major opportunity before today's travel organizers. The US experience with deregulation of the airline industry has demonstrated improved service quality, safety and better fares

Decentralized private development is proving to be more responsive to changes in travel market needs and interests than centralized bureaucratic control. But, the new form of privatization includes many public-private cooperative ventures rather than pure *laissez-faire*.

Universally, environmental concerns are stimulating greater interest in tourism planning and are expressed in two major ways. First, tourism destinations are more aware today of environmental quality threats from all sources. Municipal and industrial waste continues to cause air, water, and land contamination. Depletion of forests, reduction of wildlife, air pollution and soil erosion continue to destroy resource potential for tourism. Gradually tourism proponents are beginning to recognize these threats and are expressing their concerns in political and physical plans.

Second, it is now well documented that tourism, if improperly planned and managed, can produce its own negative environmental impacts. A 2000-delegate five-day conference produces about 600 pounds of aluminum cans and paper waste equal to 170 trees. Beach resorts often were built too close to the water's edge and have been damaged by beach erosion. Many waterfront hotels have contaminated their own swimming, boating and fishing waters with untreated sewage. For example, a majority study of the Mediterranean region emphasizes the lack of an overall environmental tourism policy with regulations needed to halt erosive trends. New resort, hotel and destination plans are reflecting the need for greater care in site selection, land use planning, and handling of potential environmental threats.

Many specialists and practitioners are now seeking planning and development processes within the ideology of 'sustainable development'. Nations, provinces and destinations are becoming more aware of the need to set sustainable development as a goal for tourism. Slater in a Canadian conference on tourism and sustainable development stated, 'All these initiatives— reducing and recycling waste, adopting energy efficient practices, providing complete and credible information, etc.—are all important steps to a more sustainable industry'.

Today's professional approach to tourism design and planning has broken dramatically from the past. Today a multifaceted planning-design team is replacing the individual specialty approach of the past. Such a team often includes architects, landscape architects, planners, and engineers. Some projects require additional specialists on the team such as historians, geologists, archeologists, wildlife specialists, and marine biologists.

Another major change is a new role for professional designers and planners—acting as a catalyst for new solutions. These professionals are moving from an elitist approach to greater involvement of all parties involved in and impacted by design decisions. This role that includes public involvement is more costly and takes more time but produces solutions that are more acceptable to all parties in both the short and long run. Such involvement is resolving many conflicts of the past. For example, planners resolved a twenty-year stalemate on a highway controversy in New Hampshire, USA. Plans for an Interstate Highway through a scenic mountain landmark area were stopped by environmentalists. This issue was finally resolved by means of planning leadership that brought opposing factions together. The solution: congressional action that allowed modified interstate standards (lower speed limit, narrow shoulders, narrow median) and protected scenic beauty. This catalytic action resulted in a plan that was agreeable to both highway engineers and public environmental groups.

The traditional focus on site scale design and planning is now being modified by increased emphasis on the community/destination and regional scales. Even though many of the planning principles and processes are similar for all three scales, they are emerging as distinctive in their application.

Regional (national, provincial, state) tourism planning, although slow to develop, is now appearing more frequently. Preoccupation with promotion is now being modified by budgeting some resources for research and planning. As more research has revealed the social, economic and environmental impacts of tourism, the need for broad-scale planning has become more evident.

Among the earliest reported efforts for regional tourism planning were those by Gunn, Kiemstedt and Lawson and Baud-Bovy. Concepts by Gunn arose following several years of technical advisory work for tourist and resort businesses in the state of Michigan, beginning in 1945. (This work was sponsored by the Tourist and Resort Extension Service, Michigan State University.) After a few years of business counseling experience, it became clear that individual tourist business success was as dependent upon external as internal factors and that a broader-scale approach was needed. Study, revealed the need for new concepts and processes for both environmental and economic goals.

Opportunity for an experimental application of these concepts came three decades ago with a project resulting in a seminal regional tourism plan, *Guidelines for — Tourism Recreation in Michigan's Upper Peninsula,* an area of 10 584 000 acres and a population of approximately 300000. Innovative was a planning process that involved a university, planning professionals, and local citizen committees for all fifteen counties of the region. The implementation of this process took about three years of interaction, study, and creative work. It involved three major steps: (1) study of resources, economic development, tourism sectors, and travel markets; (2) synthesis of study findings; and (3) derivation of conclusions and recommendations. The project revealed several basic principles for regional tourism planning in addition to specific recommendations for growth in that region. These principles have proven their universal value in recent years and include the following:

- Economic impact comes first through service businesses —hotels, motels, restaurants, and shops. But these are facilitators, not total causes of tourism.
- Demand for these services results from visitors who travel to an area and take part in attractions—things to see and do (for business and pleasure). Attractions are the primary causes of travel.
- Attractions are owned, designed, built and managed land areas and structures that serve two functions: they have attracting power, drawing people to special locations, and they provide visitor satisfactions.
- Attractions depend greatly upon locations with abundant and high quality natural and cultural resources and access from nearby communities and market sources.
- Tourism is a functioning system composed of a demand (market) and supply side (attractions, transportation, services, information, promotion).

These principles gave rise to the tourism planning reality that not all geographical areas have equal potential. The geographer-planner Fagence has stated that: 'locations, regions, resources, amenities and infrastructure have an unequal potential and capacity for particular forms, types and scales of development'. For tourism, this means that a region will contain areas that vary greatly in potential. The concept of 'destination zone' attempts to define those areas that have greatest potential. The Upper Peninsula study resulted in delineating ten destination zones. In the ensuing years, most of the recommendations of this plan for zone development and resource protection have been implemented. Reflection suggests that a major reason for success was a process that combined local input with specialized study and concepts by professional designers and planners.

A destination zone can be conceived as having three major parts that need to be integrated: areas with attraction potential, a community that has adequate infrastructure and attraction potential, and can support new travel services, and transportation and access from market sources. Thus, a destination zone encompasses not only a community but its surrounding area as well. (Further discussion is provided in 'Destination scale' below).

It is conceivable, then, that the major thrust of a regional tourism plan should be the identification of key destination zone potential. With such new understanding in each potential zone, tourism development leaders can initiate their own local planning processes for expansion. Conversely, areas with little potential should not be given investment stimulation. A regional geographic assessment process, aided by computer geographic information systems (GIS), has been developed by Gunn and applied to several regions in the United States in recent years: Texas, Oklahoma, Upcountry South Carolina, Delaware and Illinois. The South Carolina example is used here to illustrate the process.

The study area was a six-country portion of northwestern South Carolina, 3849 square miles in size and adjacent to the Blue Ridge Mountains of North Carolina. The major purpose of the project was to identify destination zones and potential development appropriate to the environment and suited to markets and to the production of tourism growth. The study included four major phases: (1) research of 'program' and' 'physical' factors, (2) derivation of conclusions from research, (3) location of prime zones of potential, and (4) suggested development projects in zones and identification of other opportunities. Program study included review of secondary data for information on (1) travel markets, (2) information systems, (3) promotional programs, (4) socio-environmental issues, and (5) planning and action agencies with ability to implement. Physical factor study was prepared for two groups of resources—natural and cultural. These physical factors were summarized in narratives and drawn on generalized maps.

Overall results from this regional study provided the following conclusions:

- Significant tourism development is already in place.
- Region has opportunity to compete well with others.
- Growth and popularity depend upon further planning and design.
- New cooperation of decision makers within and among zones is needed.
- Stronger linkage between rural attractions and cities is needed.
- Greater outside cooperation would help region.
- Small scale and slow growth is most adaptable to region.
- Needed are several important new steps: market research, training, education, public cooperation, regional and zone leadership and integration, and greater protection of resources.

Some observations on this process should be

emphasized. Following this regional approach, it is the responsibility of all tourism forces at the regional level and within the delineated zones to take further steps. For example, existing tourism capacities and limits to environmental stress must be determined. Existing political and tourism organizations may need to realign their boundaries or enter into new cooperative arrangements to follow through. Each zone contains one or more communities as focal points for expansion of services such as lodging and food. If several communities lie within a zone this suggests the need for cooperation in developing common themes. This process is proving its effectiveness in laying a foundation for regional tourism policy and development.

Many other regions have become engaged in some form of regional planning for tourism development in the last few decades. A survey by WTO (World Tourism Organization) in 1980 revealed that 348 regional and 266 intraregional plans had been prepared at that time. Japan reports that its planning division of the Department of Tourism is active in the following functions:

- Overall coordination and planning of tourist administration.
- Supervision of the Japan National Tourist Organization.
- Improvement of reception services for foreign visitors.
- Research and study on tourism.
- Subsidies to the tourist industry.
- Matters relating to the acquisition of stocks by foreign investors in the field of tourism.
- Collection and compilation of tourist-related documents.

- Handling of general affairs for the Council for Tourism Policy.

Special emphasis was placed on important natural and cultural resource areas. By 1989, 39 'Special Areas' (of cultural significance) had been designated and planned for tourism. Australia has established a national plan that includes: marketing and coordination; research and statistics; economic and business issues; transport and facilitation; training, employment and standards; environment and social issues; and accommodation and market growth.

Another current GIS approach to the assessment of tourism potential is the 'Coastal Tourism Resource Inventory Project' (CTRIP) (ARA Consulting Group, 1991) for British Columbia, Canada. The purposes are: (1) to develop and implement a rigorous and credible tourism resource mapping methodology and (2) to ensure that the inventory provides a cost-effective tool to support tourism planning. It consists of two phases. The first phase is to develop, test and refine the inventory methodology. The second phase is to prepare a tourism resource inventory for the entire coastline of British Columbia.

Rather than generalizing for total tourism potential, this project focuses on eight categories of visitor activity, identified by consensus of consultants, operators, and recreationists:

sportfishing, overnight	kayaking
sportfishing, day charters	scuba diving
coastal overnight cruising	marinas
coastal cruising, day	cruise ships

For each category, specific site criteria were identified and used in resource evaluation. This step is followed by GIS overlays of factor maps specifically suited to the end-use category. Although this is in the experimental stage, it again shows the value of resource study and computer mapping tools for new tourism planning methodology.

Exemplary is regional tourism planning led by the Tourist Board (STB). In cooperation with 32 Tourist Boards, the STB provides planning and financial assistance for expanded development, including new golf courses, old town rejuvenation, fishing, the arts, cycling, access and transport. A new tourism Management Initiative includes plans for: newly designated tourist routes, priority destination area needs, town and village measures for improvement, scenic viewpoints, environmental awareness and protection, and facility design guidelines.

Although not yet supported by a great groundswell of interest, tourism planning at the regional scale is the topic of more conferences, the concern of more policymakers, the subject of more technical study (such as use of GIS), and a beginning of serious implementation. Regional tourism planning is especially effective in creating national policy on transportation, marketing, interagency cooperation, and environmental and social issues related to tourism.

Even more popular has become planning and design at the destination scale—a community and surrounding area. Proper functioning of a destination includes three major parts: attractions, community, services and transportation. Tourism functions require integrated planning of the surrounding area and the city. Many recreational and cultural activities take place in rural areas as well as in cities, requiring cooperation among all political jurisdictions and private organizations.

Recently, several guides to planning and developing destinations have been prepared in the United States. The book, *The Community Tourism Industry Imperative: the Necessity, the Opportunities, its Potential* contains twelve chapters of guidance information for individuals and organizations that wish to develop destination zones. The province of Alberta prepared its Community Tourism Action Plan Manual as a guide for organizations and a 24-step process for tourism planning and development. As of 1990, 250 of 429 eligible Alberta communities have developed their plans following this guide. The US Travel and Tourism Administration, in recognition of dwindling rural economies, has developed a tourism planning and development guide, *Rural Tourism Development Training Guide*. These and others are indicative of the new interest in making a more concerted planning effort at the destination scale than in the past.

Two important examples of planning at the destination scale are included in New Challenges in Recreation and Tourism Planning. The Sils/Segl communities and surrounding areas in Switzerland have been planned to foster protection of mountain scenery of the Canton of Grisons by concentrating building areas. In France, Tarlet has reported on destination tourism progress in recent years. A major plan for the Aquitaine coast surrounding Bordeaux was prepared in 1967 and has met with reasonable success in years since. The tourism economy has improved at the same time that basic resource assets have been protected. Tarlet reports that planning of mountain tourist zones has met with mixed success. Many jobs have been created, new highways have improved access and the area has been revitalized. At the same time, some landscapes have been damaged, market studies were insufficient and sometimes development has not been adequately integrated with loco communities.

Among destination plans, there appears to be no uniform approach. Some are prepared by government& tourism agencies whereas others are the product of public private cooperation. The Pacific Area Travel Association has sponsored several consultant task force projects at this scale. For example, a week of intensive study and evaluation of tourism in Moorea, French Polynesia, by a task force of four specialists resulted in specific recommendations for improvement. The study methodology included air and land reconnaissance, visits to tourism installations, interviews with proprietors, meetings with governmental officials and community representatives, and review of documents. Consensus was reached by the study team on 14 specific conclusions and recommendations including the establishment of a central sewage treatment plant to avoid beach and water pollution. The tourism sector was asked to provide better tourist access and interpretation for the significant natural and cultural resource areas, such as the beautiful central mountains and over 30 Polynesian archeological sites. Because hotel occupancy was already marginal (below 50%), the task force recommended denial of a proposed mega-resort that would do damage to the fragile environment. Since the report was issued, this proposal has been refused by official local action. An excellent example of effective destination planning is the plan for Viborg County, Denmark.

The physical plan is described as a comprehensive land use and area plan that includes: directive on urban development patterns, infrastructure, and protection of wetlands and natural resources. The plan resulted from collaboration among the County Council, mayors of municipalities, and tourist association representatives. Essentials of the plan also include product development, marketing and information, education, public planning and administration, and organization and economy. The plan is integrated with plans of the Danish Tourist Board. Another worthy example of destination planning in Denmark is the plan for the region of Flyn.

Comparatively recent is the proliferation of destination tourism planning. Now there is greater sensitivity to visitor capacity management, integration of tourism with the local society and economy, and protection of natural and cultural resources as foundations for more and better traveler experiences. New organizational mechanisms that foster collaboration on planning are appearing. More areas are seeing the value of planning that utilizes input from local citizens as well as planning specialists and consultants.

Site scale

Perhaps the greatest change emerging at the site scale is a new design paradigm that includes a combination of professional expertise and greater insight into social, behavioral, economic and environmental aspects of each tourism project. This change implies less design elitism and more public participation in the design process. There is greater recognition that each site design and development is part of an environmental whole rather than an isolated entity. Certainly, the special talent and experience of professional designers is as essential as ever. But, the enduring test of a design is not merely a designer client agreement but rather a satisfying and valuable experience by the visitor.

Critical to this new approach to design at the site scale is new awareness of place and placemaking. Each place has its own characteristics that provide a special foundation for development requiring protection of assets and unique design rather than thoughtless and uniform modification of land resources. From this design approach, new attractions and other tourism developments are being established that are endemic to place. This principle of local uniqueness creates development that is more competitive than a homogenized tourism landscape.

Another new design principle involves eco-design ethics. The burgeoning market interest in natural resource features is now requiring much greater design and management sensitivity to the environment. This new approach is not mere altruism—it is good tourism economics. For example, the collaboration between owner and architect for Maho Bay Camps, US Virgin Islands, has produced a popular, profitable and environmentally sound facility. The owner-developer argues that it is more profitable to work with nature than against it and that when well-designed and managed, the environment can be a valuable marketing tool.

An increasingly important design trend is greater involvement of those impacted by new development. In British Columbia, Canada, a 'Co-Design Approach' has been applied to coastal planning. Several focus groups identified specific themes that led to design principles:

- se of natural landscaping with indigenous species;
- a marine architectural theme; and
- walkways to connect downtown with waterfront.

Artists then interpreted these into graphics, followed by specific plans for tourism that are likely to be implemented.

The Western Australian Tourism Commission (n.d.) has published *Public Involvement in Tourism Development: What Does it Mean for the Developer*? This guide states that all tourism developers have the obligation of letting the public know about plans by means of open houses, workshops, community liaison, and media releases.

Greater collaborative design and planning among professionals and many involved parties is taking place. An example is the Victoria & Alfred Waterfront, Cape Town, South Africa. Hotel investors, civic officials, architects, planners and citizen groups have collaborated on major waterfront redevelopment for both local citizens and visitors. Of the first phase investment (R63 million) R35 million has been spent in infrastructure alone—roads, water supply, waste drainage, landscaping, and relocation of nonconforming structures. These plans have received many honors and awards for their innovative approach.

Greater public-private planning between tourism interests and national park administrators is taking place. An example is the site planning project for Orange Valley Resort, Antigua. The focus is on a resort complex but collaboration on plans for an adjacent national park is an important element of the project. Proposed for the national park are three zones: natural reserve, recreation zone, and a development zone (272 acres, 12% of total). The master plan objective is to create a world-class resort that is fully integrated into Antiguan way of life at the same time that it provides for visitors and adds to the economy. The plan concentrates buildings and facilities on 'hardened' sites and manages rare and fragile environmental assets for long-range resource protection.

The major change in site scale planning and development is greater integration with the physical, political and social setting. Local citizens and governmental agencies are now beginning to cooperate with owners and designers in the creation of plans. Better design is demonstrating that tourism development and environmentalism are compatible, even essential to each other. There is a growing trend toward more localized, small-scale and slow-paced development rather than externally imposed, large-scale and high-impact development. The special qualities of places are being protected as new site designs are prepared for tourist facilities, services and attractions.

3

Tourism Trends to Next Millennium

The total Australian resident shortterm departures (ARSTDS) experienced a 5.45% average annual growth (AAG) rate between 1980 and 1992. The growth rate of ARSTDS picked up substantiaily in 1992 after a very disappointing 1991. More specifically, the number of such departures in 1992 totalled 2276300 persons, an 8.43016 growth over 1991. This follows a decline of 3.26% in 1991, which was largely due to the Gulf War. It is also apparent that over the course of the last 13 years both America and Asia have surpassed the Old Continent in terms of AAG rates. Asia by achieving an AAG rate of 7.86% has moved from its position as the third most popular destination region in 1980 (behind Europe and Oceania) to the most popular in 1992. On the other hand, America's AAG rate of 7.26% in relation to Europe's modest 2.87% may result in America becoming the second most popular destination for Australians in the next few years if these trends were to persist.

However, looking at the very latest figures in 1992, it is worth noting that ARSTDS to Europe experienced a 12.310/6 growth over 1991, which compares quite favourably to Asia's 7.41% and America's 8.54% achieved over the same period of time. This may be an auspicious sign for the European destinations which have been suffering badly from the Australian tourists' turnaround towards Asian, American and Oceanian destinations during the 1980s.

It is also evident that travel to the Old Continent hit a snag in 1991 when there was a substantial 13.46% decline over 1990. This decline followed rather large increases of 10.29% in 1989 and 9.85% in 1990 and was due to the Gulf War and, of course, the continuing recession in Australia.

At an individual country level the United Kingdom (combined with Ireland) ranks as the third largest single destination for Australians and is by far the top European destination—accounting for almost half of the Australian visitation to Europe—despite a moderate 2.5% AAG rate over the last 12 years. Other significant European destinations for Australians are The Netherlands, France, Germany, Italy and Greece.

From these destinations France has been experiencing a high AAG rate of almost 10% while ARSTDS to Italy and Greece have simply flattened out with a very low AAG rate of 1.2% for Italy and zero AAG rate for Greece. Of course, it is also worth noting that both Italy and Greece (especially Italy) experienced substantial increases in 1992 in relation to 1991 following the end of the Gulf War. The AAG rates to the German Democratic Republic and The Netherlands have been 3.77% and 2% respectively, although as a proportion of the total ARSTDS to Europe the ARSTDS to these nations as well as Italy and Greece have remained rather stable.

In this paper, we generate a model which seeks to explain what determines ARSTDS to the Old Continent as a whole as well as to some of the major European destinations. The main aim is to discover and quantify relationships between ARSTDS and the determinant factors such as time, movements in the real value of the Australian dollar, disposable income and Australian tourists' attitudes towards European destinations in relation to other destinations that compete for the

Australian tourist dollar. Work of this kind can set the scene for undertaking accurate forecasting in an industry where uncertainty about the level of anticipated demand for tourist services represents one of the main obstacles in the process of developing planning procedures. Forecasting can provide at least some indications of the expected level of demand which consequently enables businesses to plan and control their resources accordingly.

The rest of this chapter is organised as follows. The next section discusses the rationale for the choice of the adopted model in the context of the current literature. The functional form of the model and the estimation technique are then presented and some interesting empirical results are discussed, for Europe as well as for some individual European countries. Finally some concluding remarks are offered.

In the tourism literature the most frequently used dependent, variables are the total number of visits, visits per capita, and total or per capita tourist expenditure. Data on an annual basis have been the most common data that appear in the literature. This is because explicit international tourism data are published mainly on an annual basis in most international publications. In addition, the use of yearly data provides the convenience of avoiding the effect of seasonality. In this paper, however, quarterly data of ARSTDS to Europe were used, in order to quantify not only demand determinants but also the seasonal effect on air travel to Europe. International travel is expensive and has been generally classified among luxury goods and services. Undoubtedly, the level of income determines the likelihood that an individual will undertake an overseas trip.

Theoretically, the larger the real per capita GDP of a

country is, the more likely the citizens are to spend on pleasure and entertainment and consequently, the more likely is the undertaking of an overseas trip. Indeed, the majority of tourism studies have shown that the demand for tourism is invariably highly income-elastic. However, there were cases in which an inverse relationship between real per capita income and arrivals at a destination had emerged. For example, Chadee and Mieczkowski found an inverse relationship between US income and US tourist arrivals from the USA to Canada. They justified their findings by making the assumption that Canada had been a quasi-domestic destination for Americans and they further concluded that in the face of a rise in US real per capita income US travellers were likely to visit other international destinations. The same situation emerged in the Var *et al.* study when they examined the relationship between Canadian per capita income and arrivals of Canadians to Turkey.

Nevertheless, the findings of the abovementioned studies cannot constitute a rule as far as the relationship between per capita income and arrivals is concerned. Indeed, other empirical studies have shown that whenever the real per capita income is being used as proxy for the disposable income, the respective regression coefficient is positive and usually more than unity.

The appropriate form of the price variable is by no means clear according to Witt and Martin. The cost that tourists bear for undertaking an overseas trip can be classified into two categories: firstly, the associated cost prior to the departure from the origin country and secondly the cost that emerges while at the tourist destination. The determination of the cost that comes into the second category is a complex one. This is because there is a need to estimate many influential factors that determine this cost component (i.e., time spent at the destination, quality of services, amenities used) and this can become a very troublesome task.

Most studies in this area use retail price indexes of the origin and the destination countries and/or exchange rates as proxies for the cost that tourists bear or the prices that tourists are likely to pay while at the destination. The dilemma that one faces in including the exchange rate and/or relative prices[2] has been addressed by many researchers, who have expressed their views from different perspectives. Gray in agreement with Loeb argues:

> Prices are seldom completely known in advance by travellers so that the price level foreseen by the potential traveller will depend predominantly upon the rate of exchange of his domestic currency and hearsay evidence. Thus, while the influence of the price variable is undoubtedly complex, the rate of the exchange rate can be expected to be a prime indicator of expected prices.

In addition, Artus states: 'The consequences of a change in the exchange rate are immediately perceived by potential foreign travellers. On the other hand these persons are not well informed about recent price developments in foreign countries'. However, the inclusion of relative prices (as a variable) in determining tourism demand for a particular destination was adopted by other researchers and bolstered by Loeb who attempted to express international tourism demand (in the form of travel exports) as a function of the exchange rate, real per capita income and relative prices. His findings provided evidence that: 'relative prices, and not just exchange rates and real per capita income are an important contributing factor to real travel exports'.

The use of relative prices (in the form of CPIs of the origin and destination countries) was also adopted and critically analysed by Witt and Martin. In their attempt to investigate the choice of an appropriate variable that would represent the tourists' cost of living, their results were found to be in agreement with those of Loeb's. They stated that the empirical results that stemmed from their study did not 'provide evidence of clear superiority (between CPIs and exchange rates), but rather indicate that the consumer price index either alone or together with the exchange rate, is a reasonable proxy for the cost of tourism. In their conclusion, they stressed that the exchange rate on its own is not an acceptable proxy.

Overall, it can be said that both variables have been found to be significant determinants of tourism demand at a destination. There is no clear evidence to exclude one or the other. Consequently, in the context of our model it will be assumed that both relative prices and nominal exchange rates are expected to exert an influence on ARSTDS to Europe.

As the data series that will be examined is a time series one (quarterly), the inclusion of variables that account for the seasonal and time effects, in the estimated model, is essential. The trend component, represents the long-run movement that ARSTDS usually follow along with the economy's long-run growth. This component can also be affected by changes in travellers' preferences and in their real disposable incomes as well as by population shifts. Of course, seasonality is the cyclical behaviour that takes place on a regular, shortterm basis. Baron has addressed the importance of studying the underlying patterns in trend and seasonality in the tourism industry which is heavily affected by them.

Overall, we will consider the Australian real per capita GDP as proxy for the Australian tourist's disposable income, the real exchange rate (i.e., changes in relative prices including the impact of exchange rates) between the origin and the destination country, time, seasonality and competing destinations as the main determinants of ARSTDS to Europe. Indeed, it is widely accepted that as far as the destination area is concerned, these factors influence the tourist's opinion quite significantly.

Functional form and estimation techniques

Having taken into consideration what the literature review suggests, an international travel model would take the following general form:

$$ARSTDS = FRPCGDP, RER, ARSTDSOA, ARSTDSAM, TIME, S_1 S_2, S_3) \quad (1)$$

where Australian resident shortterm departure (ARSTDS) is the dependent variable of the regression model and is measured by the total number of traveller that intend to stay overseas less than a year and Europe or a specific European country is the main destination that they will visit.' Real per capita gross domestic product (RPCGDP) is the total gross domestic product (GDP) of Australia divided by the product of the respective quarter's Australian consumer price index (ACPI) multiplied by the population of Australia in that particular quarter. The estimation of the RPGDP data points has been undertaken by using the following formula:

$$RPCGDP = (GDP/POP)/ACPI \quad (2)$$

Real exchange rate (RER) is the real cost of tourism in Europe in terms of Australian dollars. It is estimated by making use of the following formula:

$$REF = (NER_{AUD,FC} ACPI)/FCPI \quad (3)$$

where $NER_{AUD,FC}$ is the nominal exchange rate between the Australian dollar and the foreign currency (which is expressed in units of the foreign currency per Australian dollar), and FCPI is the foreign consumer price index. Indeed, assuming that the FCPI represents adequately the cost of tourism in a foreign country, the product of the ACPI multiplied by the NER when divided by the FCPI will give the real purchasing power of the Australian dollar at the European destination under consideration. Therefore when the RER decreases the Australian traveller would probably revise downwards his/her plans for a visit and therefore the number of ARSTDS would decline. The reverse would happen if there was a rise in the RER, As we have already mentioned, the inclusion of the variables ARSTDSAM and ARSTDSOA is aimed at capturing the association of the total ARSTDS to Europe in relation to other competing destinations such as America (ARSTDSAM) and Asia/ Oceania (ARSTDSOA). TIME is the time trend variable. Seasonal dummy variables (S_1, S_2, S_3) are included in order to account for the effect of seasonality on ARSTDS to Europe. An inspection of the graph of ARSTDS to Europe suggests that the seasonal pattern was fairly stable during the sample period.

In econometric modelling the most widely used technique for estimating tourism demand is the ordinary least squares (OLS) method. However, there are variations in the functional forms of models that have been derived in the area of tourism. The log-linear models have been widely used by researchers of international tourism whenever an attempt was made to use an econometric model.

We argue that ARSTDS are unlikely to adjust instantaneously to changes in RPCGDP and RER, and found that a one quarter lag of both variables performed best. On the other hand, ARSTDSOA and ARSTDSAM, being substitutes, ought to have their impact contemporaneously.

In this chapter, we reject the use of a simpler linear

model because, in the all-Europe model, autocorrelation was encountered; after reestimation using the Cochrane-Orcutt technique, the model exhibited heteroscedasticity.

In the period under review, the economic regressors are strongly trended, and three of the four are highly correlated. We therefore enter these variables as first differences in the model. The basic model we test is

$$\begin{aligned} LARSTDS = {} & \beta_0 + \beta_1 S_1 + \beta_2 S_2 + \beta_3 S_3 + +\beta_4 \, TIME \\ & + \beta_5 \Delta LRPCGDP_{-1} + \beta_6 \Delta LRER_{-1} \\ & \beta_7 \Delta LARSTDSOA + \beta_8 \Delta LARSTDSAM + \varepsilon \end{aligned}$$

where

LARSTDS	=logarithm of ARSTDS
Si =	seasonal dummy (Si =in quarter i, 0 otherwise)
TIME	= time trend (TIME = 1,2,.....)
$\Delta LRPCGDP_{-1}$	= change in the logarithm of Australian real GDP per capital lagged by one quarter
$\Delta LRER_{-1}$	= change in the logarithm of the real exchange rate lagged by one quarter
ΔLARSTDSOA	=change in the logarithm of ARSTDS to Oceania and Asia
ΔLARSTDSAM	=change in the logarithm of ARSTDS to America
ε	=random error term

On the assumptions that tourism from Australia to Europe is a superior good and obeys the law of demand, and that travel to Oceania, Asia and America are substitute goods, the hypothesised signs of the coefficients are β_5 $\beta_6 > 0$ and β_7, $\beta_8 < 0$. For example, the number of the ARSTDS to Europe is expected to increase (decrease) if there is a rise (fall) in the real exchange rate (i.e., in RER), *ceteris paribus*. The same is true with respect to changes in the real per capita gross domestic product (i.e., RPCGDP). On the other hand, one would expect a decline (rise) in the total ARSTDS to Europe in the presence of a rise (decline) in the total ARSTDS to competing destinations such as America, Asia and Oceania.

Finally, and before proceeding to the next section which presents the empirical results, it should be noted that the Australian Bureau of Statistics (ABS) publications on tourist arrivals and departures was the main source for gathering data for departures to Europe. The quarterly publication of the International Monetary Fund provided data on exchange rates and consumer price indexes of European countries and Australia, while ABS publications provided data on the Australian gross domestic product and consumer price index and the population of Australia. The period covered by the database is from January 1980 to April 1992.

We describe here the results obtained from the all-Europe model. The results for particular countries, which are broadly similar. All models were estimated using the Microfit3 program.

In models where autocorrelation presented problems, they were reestimated using the Cochrane-Orcutt technique. Where this has been necessary, the diagnostic statistics are based on OLS tests of the models using Cochrane-Orcutt transformations of the variables. In all cases the diagnostics are satisfactory; however, we have chosen not to delete variables whose *t* values were not significant at the 0.05 level.

Interpretation of the coefficients of the economic variables is, at first sight, fairly difficult, since we are dealing with differences of logarithms. It is easy to show, however, that the first differences of the logarithmic regressors are the logarithms of ratios between successive periods.' Although we are not able to interpret the coefficients as simple elasticities with respect to, say RER, we can nevertheless draw some meaningful conclusions. If the ratio of RER to its previous level increases by 1% the corresponding coefficient indicates the average change in ARSTDS, *ceteris paribus.*

The coefficient of real per capita income term, $\Delta LRPCGDP_{-1}$, has the expected sign, and a value of 2.2227. This implies that ARSTDS to Europe would be approximately 2.2% higher, on average and other things being equal, were the ratio 1.01 instead of 1.00 in the preceding quarter, in other words if the growth rate in real per capita income was 1% per quarter. This result is in agreement with the majority of the studies which have attempted to construct a suitable model for forecasting tourism demand.

We had no readily available basis for constructing a real exchange rate for the whole of Europe, and experimentation with the use of the Trade Weighted Index proved unsatisfactory. We used the pound sterling as a proxy and found that the coefficient of $\Delta LRER_{-1}$ had the expected sign, and a value of 0.29835. This implies that ARSTDS to Europe would be approximately 0.3% higher, on average and other things being equal, were the ratio 1.01 instead of 1.00 in the preceding quarter, in other words if the growth rate in the real exchange rate was 1 % per quarter. During the sample period this term had a downward trend, hence the real exchange rate effect was largely negative.

The coefficient of the ARSTDS to Oceania and Asia

term, ΔLARSTDSOA, has the expected sign, and a value of 0.31096. This implies that ARSTDS to Europe would be approximately 0.3% lower, on average and other things being equal, were the ratio 1.01 instead of 1.00 in the same quarter, in other words if the growth rate in ARSTDS to Oceania and Asia income was 1% per quarter. Since during the sample period this growth has generally been positive, we conclude that Australian tourism to Oceania and Asia has had a negative impact on tourism to Europe.

The coefficient of the ARSTDS to America term, ΔLARSTDSOA, did not have the expected sign, and had a value of 0.26020. This is puzzling because this variable is significant at the 0.01 level. It also has the wrong sign in the models for individual countries. Since Australian tourists are unable to nominate more than one main destination, it is not conceivable that ARSTDS to Europe and America are complementary goods, which might have explained the result. We offer the following speculation regarding this anomalous finding. People travelling through Europe and America as part of a single trip, may nominate their main destination arbitrarily; hence essentially the same factors have caused them to visit both places.

The trend coefficient was 0.010442 which indicates a trend rate of growth of approximately 1.05% per quarter or 4.27% per annum.

The coefficient of the March quarter dummy was −0.22225. This corresponds to a seasonal index of 0.8007, where the December quarter index is defined to be 1.0000. Seasonal factors appear to cause an approximate reduction of 20% in the March quarter, compared with the December quarter.

The coefficients for the June and September quarters were almost equal, and hence were replaced by a single dummy, S_{23} which was defined to be 1 in the June and September quarters, and 0 otherwise. The coefficient of S_{23} was 0.46276 which corresponds to a seasonal index of 1.5885, thus seasonal factors appear to have caused almost a 60% increase in ARSTDS to Europe in the June and September quarters, compared with the December quarter.

Next we used the all-Europe model to make some forecasts for the five years following the sample period. Since accurate forecasts of the values of the economic regressors is not possible, we construct several scenarios, all of which involve constant growth rates. The most likely scenario is that growth rates will continue at roughly the same average rates as those observed in the sample period.

The forecasts are not particularly sensitive to the scenarios used, or in other words the forecasts are determined largely by the trend and seasonal factors. Very large changes in the economic regressors would be required to bring about substantial differences in the forecasts, assuming of course that there are no structural breaks in the model during the forecast period.

4

Tourism Innovation

The aim of this chapter is to pinpoint areas of research of particular relevance to management of tourism. A major feature of tourism research is that it is closely related to practice. Indeed, the borderline between research and innovation in the industry is blurred. This is a major strength of much of the work reviewed below. However, the weakness of some of the research is that it is imperfectly grounded in any theoretical perspective, which leads to descriptive work and the lack of real analytical bite. Attempts to remedy this defect are under way and there is a trend to tighter frameworks, more careful definitions and quantification of key dimensions. Research in tourism is by nature interdisciplinary (or transdisciplinary). However, academic and subject boundaries being as impermeable as they are, a considerable amount of work has been carried on within traditional subject boundaries. An attempt is made here to break down these barriers by using a task or problem-oriented schema rather than a discipline-based one. However, it will be recognized that most 'impact' studies of tourism are made by economists just as most studies of the cultural changes wrought by tourism are the province of sociologists.

Naturally, a considerable amount of time and effort has been given to attempts to define the nature and scope of 'services' and 'the service industries'. A composite view of what constitutes a service includes: intangibility, perishability, customization, simultaneity of production and consumption, consumer participation in production and use without ownership. Every one of these by itself is insufficient to differentiate a service from a non-service, and the concept remains rather elusive except in a multifaceted definition. Further, most companies producing physical goods also produce services, and many service companies such as airlines are heavily equipment based. Differentiation cannot proceed then, except very crudely, by counting firms.

Most research in tourism is multidimensional, that is to say it is rarely a pure type. Thus, 'impact studies' will also include elements of the tourism planning system, descriptive elements and management issues. This is a healthy sign in that the research area has not become too compartmentalized.

There has been a recent upsurge of interest in the service industries as a subject of research, particularly their internationalization. The founding of a journal, *The Service Industries Journal,* has been an important focus for dissemination of information.

Much has been made of the increasing proportion of services in the Gross Domestic Product of advanced countries, so much so that it has become commonplace. However, the interdependency between manufacturing and services must also be emphasized.

Tourism ranges from highly equipment-intensive service businesses, such as airlines and hotels, to much more people-based companies, such as tour operators, and information-based operations, such as travel agents. Even within these sectors differentiation occurs. For instance, the centralized reservation system of international hotels and airlines is based on the collection, manipulation and transmission of large quantities of information.

Research on advances in technology, particularly information technology, in the tourism sector thus goes hand-in-hand with advances in the use of this technology.

An increasing amount of research is being conducted on service industry multinational firms. The 1989 UNCTC study is an example of a rapidly growing research focus. Multinational firms in the tourism industry feature greatly in this work. A review of this research is made by John Dunning. Largely, this strand of research has concentrated on the methods by which multinational firms in tourism service foreign markets and the study of particular modes of market servicing such as franchising. The relationship between this work and practical international corporate planning is strong.

Thus, tourism as a set of interrelated service industries is one of the leading research areas for the study of the uniqueness of the services sector.

The peculiarities of service industries lead to particular management problems, which are also the focus of research.

In order to delineate an area of academic research, it is necessary to describe the phenomena to be encompassed. Much of the work in tourism to date has been descriptive, at least in the early exploratory stages of new projects and prior to the development of concepts.

A great deal of work has been carried out of the case study type. This involves the examination of one destination or facility (accommodation, hotel or attraction) and less usually one origin (country, region or town exporting tourists). Subsets of descriptive studies include urban tourism, rural tourism, tourism in difficult areas, island tourism.

Several case studies of urban tourism and a related concept, tourism in difficult areas, have illuminated the potential and problems in using tourism as (part of) a strategy to regenerate declining cities. These studies relate strongly to policy prescriptions, to methods of planning and to visitor motivations. They have played a most useful role in moving tourism research away from excessive concentration on 'sun and sea' tourist destinations. Studies such as that of Jansen-Verbeke present a model of city tourism relating the main product (inner city environment) to the tourist and promoters. The Jansen-Verbeke study also presents a profile of inner city visitors, including activity patterns, the importance of product characteristics and the role of promotion in attracting visitors to inner city areas.

A descriptive study of historic Dutch cities moves rapidly into analytical work on the motivations for inner city tourism and to policy implications. Similarly, the case study approach of Buckley and Witt on 'difficult areas' examines the promotion and planning role of local government bodies.

The degree of sophistication of the responsible bodies varies enormously, even in the restricted sample covered and there are policy lessons to be learned. The 1989 case study also examines the question of viability what attractions, infrastructive and accommodation does a city or an area' need to be a discrete, viable destination? Where one town or city does not have the minimum critical mass, a policy of cooperation regionally is suggested. This approach is taken further by Vandermey, who presents a preliminary conceptual model of an urban tourism system.

Urban tourism research has been a prime example of policy oriented research, beginning with a descriptive base but building on this to develop a conceptual system.

Many examples of research that outline the tourism potential of 'outworn industrial areas' such as those above and Travis's study of the South Wales valleys have gone hand-in-hand with the implementation of innovative policies by local and national governments and tourist boards. Indeed, a guide for local authorities was produced by the English Tourist Board in 1980. The example of US cities in this regard has been path-breaking, notably Baltimore's inner harbour and Lowell's historic textile mills. Urban tourism research has shown that, by innovating, regional and local bodies can use tourism as part of a regeneration strategy. They have also sounded a warning that tourism is not, and cannot be, a panacea for all economic ills.

Research on rural tourism has illustrated an essential element of 'balance' in tourist development. Indeed, much of it has had an implicit cost-benefit calculus. Tourism in rural areas has played a positive role in raising rural incomes and introducing 'growth poles' into backward, low-income agricultural areas, thus preventing or slowing out-migration. However, it has had disruptive effects on the rural environment, on local cultures and life styles, on agricultural patterns and even productivity. Consequently, the litany of the rural tourism researcher is to call for planning.

It is clear that infrastructural development is essential if tourists are to be transported to and accommodated and amused in the rural area, As this is usually the province of public bodies, then such bodies have a degree of control over access. The key concern is largely that the very thing that rural tourists require a bucolic environment is not destroyed by the sheer weight of tourists. Unique attractions, which exist in an essentially rural environment, such as the cave dwellings of Spain, France and Turkey, and Stonehenge in England, pose particularly difficult problems of balance, access and destruction of the environment. However, it should be noted that not all the economic effects are positive. Often rising land values make it impossible for (young) local people to buy or maintain property, and the purchases of holiday homes by tourists can destroy local communities.

Several examples of case studies of rural tourism are contained in Bouquet and Winter including the Isles of Scilly, the Valle d'Aosta, Cornwall, Brittany, and the Great Barrier Reef in Queensland, Australia. The primary aim of this collection is to offset the economic (income-generating) aspects of rural tourism against the social and cultural costs. Environmental concerns, which loom large in rural tourism research, are examined in the section on environmental consequences of tourism.

A subset of case study research has examined island tourism. A feature of islands is that it is possible to spatially delineate effects on the community under study and to examine feedback effects. Leakages from the island economy can be more easily identified. A considerable amount of this work has been carried out in the Caribbean and is related to issues of the impact of tourism on development.

The issues of development also impinge on the marketing of tourism in small island states, where tourism is often the major sector of the economy. Issues of dependence on tourists, on the perceived negative effects and of benefits largely flowing abroad need to be taken into account in development policies.

The importance and scope of the tourist industry is illustrated by OECD's study of the evolution of tourism in member countries, Tourism Policy and International Tourism, which examines the labour market in the hotel industries, the international tourist flows and the economic importance of international tourism in member countries. The OECD, of course, represents all the major developed market economies of the world, and the statistical annex is a particularly useful presentation of data on international tourist flows.

Studies of the impact of tourist development on a particular destination or destinations have been the largest single element of tourism research. Much of this work is predominantly the work of economists and has concentrated on the effect on incomes and employment, possibly to the exclusion of social and environmental factors. This neglect is much less true of more recent work. The major concerns of impact studies are the estimation of the impact of tourism on income levels and on employment generation. To this end, tourism multiplier analysis has developed.

Tourism multipliers

The direct spending of a tourist on transport, accommodation, food, amenities and other services will have a direct effect on incomes in the destination. Part of this expenditure will be re-spent by its recipients on meeting their needs. Thus, a second round of spending is generated. This second round expenditure generates a third, fourth and fifth, and so on, until the final round becomes negligible. The ratio between the initial spending and the final accumulated total expenditure is termed the multiplier effect. In each round leakages occur on savings and on imports, which have no further expenditure generating effect. The size of these leakages, governed by the propensity to save and to import, determine the ultimate size of the multiplier effect. Tourist expenditure thus has a *direct* effect, an *indirect* effect through the increased expenditure of the tourist sector and an *induced* effect, arising from the increase in income levels resulting from the direct plus indirect effect.

Multipliers have been calculated for national economies, regions, cities and towns, using a variety of methodologies. A summary is given in Fletcher and Snee, and individual examples are found in Pallard for Antigua in the Caribbean and Sadler, Archer and Owen for Anglesey, Wales. Naturally, the larger the area covered, the larger is the multiplier, because the import leakage is correspondingly smaller. National multipliers for large countries range between 1.2 and nearly 2, for small island states from 0.56 to just over 1 and for cities and towns from 0. 15 to 0. 3. Calculation of multipliers has become a major element in policy analysis. If the ultimate economic benefit of tourism is the extra income generated for the destination, then it is essential to have a quantitative estimation of this benefit. The policy use goes further, however, because it is with employment multipliers that, in an age of less than full employment, policymakers are concerned.

The employment multiplier shows how many full-time jobs (or full-time-equivalent jobs) increased tourist expenditures generate. It requires additional detailed information on the precise amounts of spending and additional assumptions on the rate of conversion of spending to (new) jobs.

An important adjunct to multiplier effects is input-output analysis. Input-output analysis is a general equilibrium technique, which maps the structure of an economy by quantifying the inputs from different sectors into final demand. For a given increase in final demand, by tracing the impact through an Input-output table, the effect on each subsector can be estimated. Thus, for a given projected increase in tourist demand, the effect on the construction industry, for example, can be estimated. This provides a flexible planning tool. The use of the technique in general is described by Archer and Fletcher and Snee. A study of Gibraltar using the technique has been conducted by Fletcher, Snee and MacLeod.

The impact of day trips

The excursionist, as distinct from the tourist, is a visitor who stays less than a maximum of 24 hours in his/her destination. The effect of such visitors is often underestimated. The amount of international excursions is growing within Europe and in North America. Developments in international travel, including the Channel Tunnel, will rapidly expand this sector of the international tourism market. The impact (largely uninational but not exclusively so) of day trips in many countries is examined in AIEST.

Cost-benefit studies

Cost-benefit analysis is a generic name for a set of techniques used to evaluate the viability or impact of new expenditures or developments. Its essential elements are: a complete inventory of all the effects, good and bad, of the development and a valuation of these effects. In practice, of course, it is difficult to capture and evaluate every effect.

Cost-benefit analysis can be used as a straightforward financial tool. All costs are listed and rated by market prices and all revenues are accounted for in the same way. If the net present value is greater than or equal to zero, then the project is viable; if not, it should not be undertaken. Thus, a commercial valuation of a project over a given time period with a given discount (interest) rate can be arrived at. Under normal circumstances, such as the establishment of a new hotel, estimates will have to be made of certain key parameters, such as the projected costs of fixtures and fittings, and forecasts of demand will have to be made. Under these circumstances, cost-benefit analysis provides a framework into which to fit all the known facts and assumptions and a decision rule on outcome. However, it is in the area of social cost-benefit analysis that the technique can be most useful. Social cost-benefit analysis allows non-commercial factors to be built into project appraisal. This is achieved by weighting certain benefits and costs at values other than market prices. Such accounting or shadow prices are intended to reflect more accurately the opportunity costs in situations where market prices are distorted by monopoly, or government intervention, including taxes and subsidies, exchange controls or tariff and non-tariff barriers to trade. This may be a particularly acute problem in less developed countries, particularly those following an import substitution policy. In these cases, world prices of traded goods may be used and non-traded goods, such as electricity, can be valued by breaking them down into equivalent trade goods. Labour can be valued at the prevailing wage rate or at its opportunity cost, that is, the value it would provide if it were not employed in the tourism project. This is derived from the Little-Mirrlees method of project evaluation.

It is further possible to include the impact on saving and on income distribution by adding weighting factors to projects, which generate extra savings or lessen income maldistribution. Where foreign exchange is scarce, net earnings of foreign exchange can be given extra weight. The use of cost-benefit analysis in planning tourism projects is widespread. It is a versatile technique which allows (government) objectives to be built directly into the calculations. It also allows decisions to be made where market prices would dictate otherwise. For this reason, all deviations from market prices (shadow prices) must be carefully justified. Several examples of its use are listed in Curry.

The development effects of tourism

A major area of controversy and of research interest is

the question whether tourism contributes to development or hinders (distorts) development. This is an issue not only for less developed countries but also for advanced industrialized societies. Needless to say, conflicting results have emerged from research on this topic. Tourism has been described as 'a passport to development' and has been attacked as distorting development into desirable outcomes. There is no doubt that the conclusion depends upon the nature of the destination, the type of tourism and the way tourism is managed (or not managed), but it remains true that at least sometimes the outcome depends on the predilections of the researcher. Even with the most sophisticated research techniques, judgements remain important.

The nature of the destination will influence the development impact through factors such as: the alternative income earning opportunities facing the indigenous population, the geographical spread or concentration of tourist modes, the demographic features of the host country (density, age structure, cultural background), ecological and environmental background, infrastructural provision and political structure. The type of tourism will also influence development: the level of spending of the tourists, the form of tourism (business, holiday), the national groups involved, the type of tourism ('sun and sea', cultural tourism) and seasonality factors. Neither of these two factors are given nor immutable. 'Me host environment can be altered by investment, by planning and controls and by (government) incentives, subsidies or penalties differentially applied. The type of tourism can be altered by promotion, prohibition and planning.

The most important economic impact on development arises from tourist spending, which, through the multiplier, can play an important role in stimulating the host economy. This will have effects in increasing income and creating or preserving employment, particularly given the labour intensive nature of tourism. Other effects have been noted. These include the 'demonstration effect' of tourism, which presents the local community with models of behaviour different to their traditional mode and, therefore, may distort behaviour. This may be both negative and positive. Negative effects have been adduced to include an increased desire for luxury goods, which also has a negative balance of payments effect in many developing countries because of the high import content. Other influences are changes in political structures, the impact on family life (because of the increased demand for female labour), on morals (particularly where sex tourism is a major element, an example being Thailand), on local culture and communities, and migration. A difficulty of such a research agenda is that many of the 'impacts' attributed to tourism are the result of *any* economic development.

A further element of impact is that upon income distribution within the host country. The rapid development of many tourist modes has induced spatial differences in income levels and, where divisions exist on ethnic lines within countries, it can produce benefits for one tribal or ethnic group when others remain stationary, thus inducing political tensions. The influence on the class structure has also been the subject of research. There are many studies of the development impact of tourism and, because of the importance of the subject, there will be many more. Future research needs to be more careful in specifying the precise area of benefit and costs. With rigorous and transparent cost-benefit analysis, where the value judgements and assumptions are all carefully specified, more progress will be made. We should beware of seemingly unbiased research, which is really a cloak either for increased state intervention or for laissez-faire policies. Either policy might be justified in certain circumstances, but consumers of research and policy-makers need to be crystal clear on what those circumstances are.

Transport studies

Transport plays an important role in the tourism industry. It is, of course, a major object of study in its own right. Despite this, or possibly because of it, the subset of transport studies that directly relates to tourism is relatively neglected. Research in transport studies covers transport policy and planning, traffic models, traffic control (including route choice and route guidance), assessment and planning issues, public transport (supply and demand uses), studies of regulatory and organizational change, and accident and safety studies. Many of the techniques developed in transport studies are of direct relevance to tourism research, notably information technology applications, survey design issues (including preference experiments) and the general use of quantitative models. The high level of development of mathematical models in transport studies is exemplified by *Transportation Science*, the quarterly journal of the Transportation Science Section of the Operations Research Society of America, which publishes mathematical models and heuristics of transportation systems, including strategic planning models. It is clear that tourism transport plays a major role in determining the effects of tourism on the origin and destination countries. An outline of this is given by Heraty in examining the local effects of tourism transport on less developed countries. Improvements in transport infrastructure are specified: airport-hotel transfer, sightseeing and ground tours, provision for individual travel, and transport for cruise ship passengers where this is important. Studies of major transport companies such as airlines are an important input into the tourist literature. An example is the comparative review of Singapore Airlines and British Airways by Sikorski. It is a major task of research to bring together the work done in transport studies with that more specialized work on tourism. In fact, many of the relevant studies in transport are privately commissioned and often not widely disseminated.

Descriptive statistics on tourism

In order for quantitative estimates of the extent, impact and nature of tourism to be made and for effective forecasting, the body of data on tourism has to be improved. Essentially, this is the task of central government in each tourism generating and destination country. International tourist arrivals and receipts data for receiving countries and outbound tourism data for generating countries are collected and compiled by the World Tourism Organization (WTO), which enables a satisfactory and compatible data base to be generated. However, the WTO data are only as good as the basic information supplied by individual countries, and this varies wildly. Most information is provided by grossing-up sample surveys, based on a very small sample in many cases. Consequently, subsets of data may be grossly misleading. The more micro the level of analysis, the more likely are errors to exist. There is a constant demand for improvements in national statistics, because intracountry tourism is less likely to be accurately measured than international tourism. Consequently, the size, shape and future development of the tourist industry may be greatly misspecified. There is a continued need for improvement of information, particularly as the industry grows in importance. Much of the research conducted relies on published, secondary data and its accuracy must command constant attention. There are many countries in the world where the quality of data is actually decreasing because of lack of resources devoted to the statistical services.

Tourism forecasting

Tourism development and planning takes place in an uncertain world. One of the key uncertainties, from the point of view of suppliers of tourism services, is the level and nature of future demand. For practitioners, this is a crucial variable. Both the econometric approach and non-causal quantitative techniques have been developed to enable tourist arrivals and a breakdown by types of tourism to be more accurately foreseen. In addition, models have been developed which enable major events to be factored into models. Techniques such as the Delphi method, which relies essentially on achieving a consensus of informed experts, are an important tool, particularly when the factors driving developments are imperfectly understood. With the demand for better forecasts and better calibrated predictions in the area of tourism (demand) forecasting, it is reasonable to expect further developments in the forecasting area.

Information studies in tourism

Given the difficulties of obtaining accurate data in many areas of tourism, the growth of research in information studies and in data bases is encouraging. Such research is beginning to provide the foundation for more accurate research and, therefore, policymaking and management practice.

Important data bases now exist covering:

1. General tourism resources, including bibliographic sources, search mechanisms, and abstracting services.
2. Statistical and quantitative databases, including air travel and other industry indicators.

The growth of information systems and the means

of access through the spread of microcomputers gives an opportunity for important developments in research and immediacy of access to research. The expansion of computer software also enables the study of modelling, information networks and market information.

The environmental consequences of tourism

With the growing worldwide concern for environmental issues, it is not surprising that there is an increasing amount of research related to the tourism industry's environmental and ecological effects. Much of this research is policy driven and a large part of it is financed by bodies that are not neutral but committed to an environmentalist position. As with many of the other research issues reviewed, the impact of tourism in the environmental area depends on the quantity and nature of the tourism in question. Again, much of the concern is with the effects of mass tourism, but, almost uniquely, the environmental impact of small numbers of tourists into virgin areas can have a disproportionately negative effect on the environment and wildlife.

The countervailing forces are important also. There are many occasions where environmental change has been prevented by the earnings (or possibility of earnings) that the tourism industry brings. In addition, it is necessary to distinguish between the environmental effects of tourism and other continuing pressures. Aesthetic and ecological degradation must be distinguished. There remains a great requirement for further case study work and for synthesizing efforts. Despite the shift to 'green' politics in recent years, environmental issues are often treated as a residual. There is a pressing need for environmental, ecological and even aesthetic factors to be built into comprehensive cost-benefit analyses of tourism projects.

Spatial issues in tourism

A great deal of fundamental research in tourism has been carried out by geographers, or analysts with a geographical background. The spatial issues of tourism are obvious and important, as tourism involves the spatial movement of large numbers of people. The movement of people also necessitates the movement of resources and results in a changed pattern of economic activity. The spatial impact of tourism has a concentrated aspect in and around the destination, and a ripple effect on nearby areas plus a further effect on the origin. The development of concepts such as the tourism system and the tourism environment draw for much of their inspiration on spatial analysis. The locational aspects are emphasized in concepts of tourism destination zone, tourism destination area and areas of regional impact. These concepts have evolved into a system of spatial planning which is an essential aspect of tourism planning for destination regions. Much of this work is the province of consultants and specialist consultancy firms rather than of individual researchers, and so much of it has a proprietary (and competitive) element. The major virtue of research on tourism destination areas is that it enables an integrated, adaptive and action-oriented strategy to enable spatial planning of rapid tourist development. The seminal work has been carried out by Gunn, working in a North American context, but the theoretical base has been adapted to planning internationally. It allows the integration of physical planning and, through this, environmental elements into a holistic approach. The development impact of tourism has also been enhanced by spatial work conducted by geographers, often in collaboration with specialists in other disciplines. The analogy of tourism with international migration, albeit an imperfect analogy because of the temporary nature of tourism, allows the adaptation of models of migration to tourist flows. In an age of 'mass' tourism, the impact of the constantly replenishing flow of tourists has a similar impact to a migratory inflow.

The social and cultural impact of tourism

All too often, the social and cultural impact of economic changes are treated as residuals. If there was a danger of this occurring in tourism research, it is no longer true. As many studies have found benefits in terms of income and employment generation, it has been left to sociologists to take up the mantle of 'the dismal science' and point out many of the dis-benefits in terms of social costs. As Allcock points out, much early work was conducted as an attack on tourism without a solid sociological base. Several concepts have now been developed to begin to encompass the social effects of tourism. One important concept is the 'demonstration effect', which, it is suggested, often corrupts local people and presents models of lifestyles that they cannot hope to attain, thus breeding discontent and the possibility of corruption and crime. There can also be knock on effects of local class and status structures and disruptions to traditional hierarchies. Political and spatial relationships will also be reorganized. Family structures, the role of women, the cohesion of the local community, moral problems and microeconomic structures have all been shown, in individual cases, to be affected by tourist development. However, few of these sociological studies have been conducted on a comparative basis and generalization of the results is difficult. Many of the studies see destination areas as passive recipients of external change imposed from without. Many elements attributed to tourism should more accurately be attributed to more general factors and to any kind of development. There is also concern that the sociology of tourism should not be theoretically isolated from the development of the discipline as a whole.

Leisure and recreation

Tourism, leisure and recreation are clearly interrelated concepts, and it is in the study of leisure that sociologists have made considerable research progress. Class differences in patterns of leisure, patterns of leisure change over time and the positioning of tourism within a wider social and cultural context have all been contributions. The distinction between work and leisure and the structuring of leisure time place tourism in a wider cultural context. The management of leisure services is well covered by Gratton and Taylor.

Motivation of the tourist

The social psychology of the tourist is the fundamental factor in buyer behaviour and demand patterns in tourism, and it is fair to suggest that it has been studied more in the commercial context, by market researchers, than in the pure research sense. Terms such as the quest for excitement' and the 'quest for authenticity' are coined to explain some of the primary human motivations in undertaking tourism. The process of privatization (that is, attempts to appropriate public goods as private ones) has also been seen as a key element. It is fair to say that coherent and comprehensive social psychological models are not yet available. Despite this, each of the attempts above to encompass tourist motivations conceptually has a great deal to teach us in the fundamental restructuring of basic motivations, which needs to be a research priority. Otherwise, our understanding of consumer behaviour in tourism will remain superficial. There are encouraging signs that this is beginning to happen, as is shown in the analysis by Chon, applied to the recreational traveller.

Consumer behaviour in tourism

Research on consumer behaviour in tourism has largely a market research focus. The main input is from analyses of tourist responses to standard preprogrammed questionnaires. It therefore qualifies rather more as innovation than research. In this framework tourists, or rather tourist motivations, are treated as a'black box'. In goes the stimulus (perhaps an advertising campaign), and out comes the response (perhaps an increase in purchases of the heavily promoted product). The underlying elements in this result, the motivation for the behaviour observed, is unknown or assumed away. The great amount of data collected by market research organizations represents a largely untapped resource for the testing of hypotheses on consumer response. The fault lies not in data availability but in the structuring of hypotheses to examine basic motivation. This leads back to the previous section, where a deficiency was noted in the understanding of the social psychology of tourism.

This is not to say that, at the level of understanding purchasing patterns in the short run, there are deficiencies. Clearly, the excellence of much consumer research in the tourism industry enables patterns to be predicted with a reasonable degree of accuracy. What is lacking is a longer-term understanding of fundamental motivation. Large-scale switches in demand over the medium term, such as the trend towards environmentally friendly purchases, can only be understood when fundamental concepts are developed and refined. A major problem with consumer motivation research is that much of it is privately commissioned and is often not made available to the general enquirer.

The politics of tourism

There can be little doubt that the politics of tourism, in the sense of resolving conflicts that arise from tourist development and the process of reconciling (or failing to reconcile) opposing points of view, are crucial to the development of the industry and the phenomena of international tourism. Apart from the area of policy studies. This aspect has received relatively little attention. There is a great deal of scope for a political science analysis of the disparate scope of international tourism. Many aspects, touched on in other sections of this review, require careful study by political scientists. Conflicts within the destination country, the impact of foreigners both as tourists and developers, conflicts in the origin country (staying in the home country generates more domestic income) and between countries are all themes that surface again and again. At conferences on tourism, interested parties have axes to grind and viewpoints that are diametrically opposed the developer and local residents, the foreign investor and environmental groups, trade unionists and entrepreneurs are some examples. The political process is crucial and is worthy of further analysis.

Policy analysis in tourism

Policy analysis and evaluation is a major element of tourism research. The consequences of tourist development ex post are an important indicator of likely *ex ante* benefits and costs of similar development. Much of tourism research can be seen as policy review work. This is likely to be influential for decision-makers and for future innovations in the industry. It will be seen from previous parts of this chapter that some elements of the outcome of tourist developments are likely to be more effectively evaluated than others. It is a frequent complaint that the more easily quantifiable elements, such as employment creation, are more likely to be given weight against elements less easy to quantify, such as environmental damage. The level of sophistication of policy analysis in international tourism is increasing, but it remains dependent on developments in the core disciplines and their successful integration.

Management research in tourism

Much of this book is concerned with developments in management technique, skills and outlook as they apply to the international tourism industry. It is in this area that great progress has been made. The application of state of the art management skills and techniques is, of course, differentially distributed throughout the industry. Access to research in this case is also differential much of it is in English, with French and Spanish also important. It has also influenced the larger and more international companies rather more than small insular operations. Very few operators of small hotels, attractions, transport facilities and catering establishments have been exposed to management research on tourism. This is largely a problem of dissemination (and of training). A two-tier profession is emerging, with highly trained, aware up-to-date professional management in the large company transnational sector and traditional techniques prevailing in smaller companies. The focus of much research, also, has been on large companies. The role of management in the small company involved in international tourism is a research lacuna.

Within the management discipline, it is perhaps particularly the marketing area that has been most extensively developed. Comprehensive texts such as that of Middleton draw on a great deal of marketing research and provide a good vehicle for dissemination. There has been less of this kind of activity in finance, organizational behaviour, personnel and operations management. At the research level, though, the management disciplines have been active and, as funding for basic research from the industry itself increases, this research will feed into practice through more widespread dissemination in the near future.

Research on training in tourism

It is almost universally agreed that training is crucial to the Competitiveness and indeed survival of the international tourism industry. As quality competition is so important to competitive strategy, the skills of the individuals in the component service industry (hotels, catering, transport) become key elements in the struggle for market position. In many countries, the lack of training in the industry has been identified as a key strategic weakness.

Therefore, many countries have established or expanded their training programmes for the tourist sector. Because this is a relatively new phenomenon, there has been little analysis, as yet, of the efficiency or effectiveness of these programmes. Hence, there is little policy analysis to establish which training programmes produce the best results or what design the next generation of programmes should have. This is clearly an urgent task for the international tourism industry, its constituent bodies and national and regional governments. Apart from overall policy and analysis, more micro-oriented research is required on the content of training programmes, teaching methods, curriculum development and access methods.

Research in hotel and catering studies

In some ways, work on the hotel and catering sector has been the poor relation of tourism research. Much of the work done has been teaching-related and this heuristic role has permeated research activity. Work that does exist takes a descriptive view of industry structure or methods of operation within the industry. This type of work is aimed at the practitioner and is extremely valuable in raising standards and awareness.

There is a need to increase basic research on hotels and catering. Many of the fundamental and integrative concepts outlined above have yet to be applied to the hotel and catering sectors of the industry, and research remains almost entirely related to management operations.

It is a major strength of research work in tourism that it has been and continues to be task-driven. There is more than a sense of partiality in much of the work. Indeed, tourism research is defined by its interest in a related cluster of industries rather than by a disciplinary, ethical or theoretical base. However, this bias, if bias there be, is not one-sided.

Environmental groups have conducted research, showing the negative impact of tourism in the way that organizations in the tourist industry sponsor work that shows the good side of tourism. It is also a fair point that tourism research lacks a theoretical base, but it is perhaps unrealistic to expect such a variegated set of phenomena to have a single theoretical underpinning. Rather, we would expect the study of the international tourism industry (or industries) to be developing a number of theoretical underpinnings, and this is proving to be the case. In the forthcoming period we can expect a competition of paradigms and we should not expect any one research agenda to prevail. Tourism research, like tourism itself, will remain dynamic, variegated and at times internally conflictual. Its strengths of practicality, policy orientation and relevance are likely to be accentuated. It remains to be seen if its weaknesses can be ameliorated.

The research will continue to feed innovation to the industry and to be stimulated by it. There is a sense of closer community between those who work in the tourism industry and those who research it than is the case in almost any other-field.

However, many of the issues are new and it takes time to identify, describe, conceptualize and test hypotheses on new phenomena.

Research agenda in international tourism

The strengths of tourism research are its trans-disciplinarity and relevance to actual operation in the industry. Its weaknesses are its partiality and its lack of core theory. Key research issues are listed below:

- More comprehensive integration of tourism within a theoretical analysis of the services sector as a whole.
- A movement onwards from descriptive studies of destinations to analytical approaches to impact.
- More comprehensive cost-benefit analyses, based on a holistic approach to the economic, sociological, environmental and political impact of international tourism.
- The integration of leisure and recreation, hotel and catering studies with tourism into a related framework of analysis.
- More fundamental understanding of the social psychology of tourists.
- Development from policy analysis to a political science of tourism.
- A feedback of concepts from management studies in tourism to tourism research.

5

Tourism Promotion

The receipts from international tourism can provide a valuable source of earnings for many countries both developed as well as developing. Although tourism, is sensitive to the level of economic activity in the tourist generating countries, it provides a more stable earnings than primary products. The income from tourism has tended to increase at a higher rate than merchandise export in a number of countries. There is now almost an assured channel of financial flows from the richer countries to the not so richer, and developing ones, raising the latter's export earnings and rate or economic growth. Tourism is thus a most important source of income for many countries. For instance, there were more visitor arrivals in Spain in 1981 (40 million) according to official Spanish sources than the actual population of the country (36 million). Newly emerging countries in such areas as the Caribbean depend very heavily on tourist income, which often represents the major part of the gross domestic product (G.D.P). Even developed nations like Canada, which derived over 11 per cent of its gross domestic product from international visitors in the year 1975, rely heavily on the income from tourism. Tourism thus forms a very important source of income, especially of foreign exchange for several countries. Although the amount contributed in foreign currency per tourist varies greatly from one place to another, the importance of receipts from tourism in the balance of payments, and of tourist activities in the national avenue, has become considerable for many countries. The major economic benefit in promoting the tourism industry has therefore tended to be the earning of foreign exchange. Income from foreign tourism in the form of foreign exchange earnings adds to the national income and, as an invisible export, may offset a loss on the visible trading account and be of critical importance in the overall financial reckoning. This is more true in case of developing countries. For many developing countries, particularly the small countries, which are mainly dependent upon primary products such as a few basic cash crops, tourism often offers a, more reliable form of income. In the case of some European countries, notably Spain, Portugal, Austria, Yugoslavia and Greece, the invisible earnings from tourism are of a major significance and have a very strong positive effect on the balance of payments. Tourism is thus a very useful means of earning the much needed foreign currency. It is almost without a rival as an earning source for many developed as well as developing countries. These earnings assume a great significance in the balance of payment calculations.

The balance of payments shows the relationship between a country's total payments to all other countries and its total receipts from them. In other words, it may be defined as a statement of income and expenditure on international account. Payments and receipts on international account are of three kinds: (i) the visible balance of trade (relating to tile import and export of goods); (ii) invisible items (relating to the services such as shipping and insurance); (iii) capital transfers. The receipts from foreign tourism form an "Invisible export", similar to other "Invisibles" which come from transportation and shipping, banking and insurance. income on investments, etc. Because most [illegible]ies from time to time have serious problems with the balance of their international payments, much attention comes to be focused on tourism because of its potentially important contribution to, and also effect upon the balance of payments.

The receipts from international tourism however, are not always net. Sometimes expenditures are involved which must be set against them. Net foreign exchange receipts from tourism are reduced principally by the import cost of goods and services used by visitors foreign exchange costs of capital investment in tourist amenities and promotion and publicity expenditure abroad. Peters has said: "Certain imports associated with tourist expenditure must be deducted.... the importation of material and equipment for constructing hotels and other amenities, and necessary supplies to run them; foreign currency costs of imports for consumption by international tourists; remittances of interests and profits on overseas investment in tourism enterprises, mainly hotel construction; foreign currency costs of conducting a tourism development programme, including marketing expenditure overseas".

Reliance of imports to meet tourist's needs does not however, deny developing countries the opportunity of earning foreign exchange in supplying such goods and services. Imports are, to a large extent, as essential to the operation of the tourist sector as to that of other sectors. The important question is whether the value added domestically on an export good or service is maximized. Maximization of import substitution without due regard to the effect on overall tourism receipts (i.e. demand) may be counter-productive. Secondly, differences in the pattern and level of reliance on imported goods and services, capital equipment and manpower are very wide depending upon the level of development of a country. In some cases this reliance is simply due to a lack of resources that will be transformed into items to be sold to the industry. In others, the industry has not yet drawn on such, supply potential, for which it may be an important stimulus. There is a general need for careful programmes of positive import substitution.

The multiplier effect

It is evident from the above paragraphs that earnings from tourism occupy an important place in the national income of a country. Without taking into account receipts from domestic tourism, international tourism receipts alone contribute a great deal. The flow of money generated by tourist spendings multiplies as it passes through various sections of the economy. In addition to an important source of income, tourism provides a number of other economic benefits, which vary in importance from one country to another and also depending upon the nature and scale of tourism. The benefits from infrastructure investments, justified primarily for tourism--airports, roads, water supply and other public utilities--may be widely shared by the other sectors of the economy. Tourist facilities such as hotels, restaurants, museums, clubs, sports complexes, public transport, national parks are used also by domestic tourists and visitors, businessmen and residents, yet a significant portion of the costs may be borne by international tourists. Tourists also contribute to tax revenue both directly through sales taxes and indirectly through property, profits and income taxes. Tourism provides employment, brings infrastructural improvements and may help regional development. Each of these economic aspects can be dealt with separately, but they are all closely related and are considered together. Let us first look at the income aspect of tourism. Tourism as a source of income is not easy to measure, at least with any degree of accuracy. This is because of the multiplier effect. The flow of money generated by tourist spending multiplies as it passes through various sections of the economy through the operation of the multiplier effect. The multiplier is an income concept. The multiplier theory emerges from the work of Kahn and Keynes. It can be systematically explained as follows: from an initial impulse, such as investment or expenditure, there springs one or more primary effects such as income, savings, etc. These primary effects in their turn, and in the course of a second period, produce secondary effects of the same type as the first. The process is repeated several times in a given lapse of time. The multiplier makes it possible to calculate the sum of the various primary, secondary and tertiary effects of the same type and hence the relation between the total of the effects of the same nature and the primary effect. This relation is represented by the multiplier, which is then applied to the primary effect in order to arrive at the total effect.

The multiplier mechanism has also been applied to tourism and in particular to tourist expenditure. The nature of the tourism multiplier and its effect may be described as follows: The money paid by a tourist in, say, paying his hotel bill will be used by the hotel management to provide for the costs which it had incurred in meeting the demands of the visitor, e.g., such goods and services as food, drink, furnishing, laundering, electricity, and entertainment. The recipients, in turn, use the money they have thus received to meet their financial commitments and so on. In other words, tourist expenditure not only supports the tourist industry directly but helps indirectly to support many other industries which supply goods and services to the tourist industry. In this way money spent by tourists may be said to be used several times and to spread into various sectors of the economy. In sum, the money paid by the tourist, after a long series of transfers over a given period of time, passes through all sectors of the national economy, stimulating each in turn throughout the process.

Every time the money changes bands it provides 'new' income and the continuing series of conversions of the money spent by the tourists form what the economists term the multiplier effect. The more often the conversion occurs, the greater its beneficial effect on the economy of the recipient country. However, this transfer of money is not absolute as there are `leakages' which occur. Such leakages may occur as a result of for instance, by importing foreign goods, paying interest on foreign investments, etc. Any leakages of these kinds will reduce the stream of expenditure which in consequence will limit and reduce the multiplier effect. Income generated by foreign tourist expenditure in countries possessing more advanced economics, which generally are more self-sufficient and less in need of foreign imports, will tend to have higher multipliers than countries which are less self-sufficient and need to support their tourist industries by substantial imports. If the developing countries are to gain maximum economic benefits from tourism, they should control very strictly those imported items for tourist consumption and to keep foreign investment expenditure to a reasonable level. The benefits, otherwise, accruing from tourism will be reduced or even cancelled by the leakages.

The most important leakage would appear to arise from expenditures on importation of agricultural products like food and drink. In a primary macro-economic approach to the prospects opened up by tourism establishment in a developing country, it is regarded as advantageous that a good portion of tourist consumption should consist of food products. It is estimated that the major part of these products can be found in those countries, whose economic structure is largely agricultural in character. In this sense tourist consumption, derived from international flow, can offer an assured outlet to a production which is already active within the country, without raising problems connected with export of such products in the international markets. Home grown products could thus be substituted for imported foodstuffs and a significant saving effected.

Such savings would help to increase the tourism multiplier, which in turn would help the host country to derive maximum economic benefits from its tourist industry. This aspect of the question is all the more important in that the multiplier effect maintains its efficacy as long as no importation takes place. It follows that if the national economy is to derive the maximum benefit from the impact, of international and national tourism, there is an elementary obligation to find all those products needed for tourist consumption. The dynamics of agricultural production in recent years appear to confirm the ability of developing countries to produce the major part of their agricultural products required for tourist consumption without resorting to massive imports. The tourist economy of any country, if it is to remain healthy, must rely upon local agricultural production and this elementary condition seems today to be on the way to realization in the majority of developing countries.

Development of infrastructure

Development and improvement of infrastructure is another important benefit. The benefits from infrastructure investments, justified primarily for tourism airports, roads, water supply and other public utilities--may be widely shared by the other sectors of the economy. In addition to development of new infrastructure, the improvements in the existing infrastructure which are undertaken in order to attract tourists is also of crucial importance. These improve-ments may confer benefits upon the resident population by providing them with amenities which, hitherto, they had not enjoyed. Furthermore, the provision of infrastructure may provide the basis or serve as an encouragement for greater economic diversification. A variety of secondary industries may be promoted which may not serve the needs of tourism. Thus, indirectly, tourist expenditure may be responsible for stimulating other economic activities.

One of the characteristics of underdevelopment is that of deficiencies in the basic infrastructures, which lie at the root of a series of serious problems related to the development of tourism. Construction of primary infrastructures represents the foundation of any future economic growth even though they are not directly productive. The tourist industry illustrates the elementary need for basic infrastructures. It has today the important benefit of being able to profit from the existing infrastructures and thus to make a decisive contribution to the growth of the national economy. The traffic arising from international and national, tourism, moreover, represents a reward for the capital invested and can now contribute to the financial efforts required for maintenance. The satisfactory degree of development achieved in this specific sector now permits major tourist progress, while giving further proof of the complementary character of tourism in relation to other economic sectors. Creation of basic infrastructures for tourist usage will also be of service to the other sectors of the economy like industry and agriculture. The outcome of this is better equilibrium of general economic growth.

Regional development

Another important domestic effect relates to the regional aspects of tourist expenditure. Such expenditure is of special significance in marginal areas, which are relatively isolated, economically underdeveloped, and have unemployment problems. The United Nations

Conference on International Travel and Tourism held in Rome in 963 noted that tourism was important not as a source of foreign exchange, but also as a factor in the location of industry and in the development of less developed regions. It further stated that in some cases the development of tourism may be the only means of promoting the economic advancement of less-developed areas lacking in other resources.

The underdeveloped regions of the country can greatly benefit from tourism development. Many of the economically backward regions contain areas of high scenic beauty and of cultural attractions. These areas if developed for use by tourists can bring a lot of prosperity to the local people. Tourism development in these regions may become a significant factor in redressing regional imbalances in employment and income. Tourist expenditure at a particular tourist area greatly helps the development of the areas around it. Many countries both developed as well as developing have realized this aspect of tourism development and are creating and developing tourist facilities in underdeveloped regions with a view to bringing prosperity there.

Khajuraho in India which is now an internationally famous tourist spot is an example of one such region. To illustrate, Khajuraho, a remote and unknown small village about twenty years ago, is now on the world tourist map attracting thousands of tourists both domestic as well as international. Today, Indian Airlines (domestic carrier) flies a jet plane between capital city of New Delhi and Khajuraho and seats are not easy to come by. Thousands of tourists visit the place by air, rail and road transport every month to see the architectural beauty of temples and erotic sculptures whose creators were the Chandela kings, who held sway in North India from the 9th to the 13th centuries. Today 22 glorious temples remain, with perhaps the most classic Indian architecture, wreathed in seemingly living sculpture. Together they represent the finest expression of the art of medieval India.

The area around Khajuraho is now pulsating with life. The place has provided employment to hundreds of local people in hotels and shops. There is already a thriving clay model industry devoted to making replicas of the famous temple sculptures. A number of shops dealing with items of presentation, handlooms and handicrafts have created jobs for many. As a result of this, local people are recipients of additional income which has resulted in their increased prosperity. The subsequent development of areas around Khajuraho will provide additional employment opportunities resulting in general prosperity of the people.

But for the development of tourism in the area, Khajuraho, would have remained a remote unknown village. Many such areas of tourist interest where industrial development is out of question because of distance from markets, lack of raw materials and transportation facilities, scarcity of power, water etc., can greatly benefit if developed properly. These areas if developed for tourism can provide lot of prosperity in the region and can provide jobs for a large number of unskilled workers. It can generate work for the construction industry and a wide range of other supporting industries. What is more, it can be a source of prosperity to the local population.

There is no dearth of areas which could after they are developed for tourism become great assets to the region in particular and to the country as a whole. French government has created a series of new resorts particularly to bring prosperity to the areas which traditionally have been underdeveloped. The Italian government is likewise attempting to develop tourism in Southern Italy in order to help redress the economic imbalances which have long existed between the north and the south. Tourism is to be regarded not as an area of peripheral investment but as one of primary investment whose benefits will help in creating employment opportunities and in the regeneration of backward regions.

Effects on employment

Another major direct economic effect of tourism relates to employment. The problems of unemployment and underemployment are more acute in the developing countries. Why, then, do the developing countries not concentrate their major efforts on a tertiary economic activity such as tourism, which calls for manpower on a large scale? The problems which the industrialized countries face in recruiting manpower for the tourist industry confirm that, in any productive process consisting of services, human labour remains the basic need. None of the technological progress achieved has succeeded in rendering the human factor less indispensable in this sector, and this is true to an absolutely indisputable extent if we draw a comparison with other productive sectors. The high social impact of the tourist industry is well known, for it has repercussions in every other national economic sector through the multiplier effect, which is particularly marked in those services that are complementary to the tourist accommodation industry.

The tourist industry is a highly labour intensive service industry and hence is a valuable source of employment. It employs large number of people and provides a wide range of jobs which extend from the unskilled to the highly specialised. In addition to those involved in management there are a large number of specialist personnel required to work as accountants, housekeepers, waiters, cooks and entertainers, who in turn need large number of semiskilled workers such as porters, chambermaids, kitchen staff, gardeners, etc. In addition, it should be emphasised that tourism is also responsible for creating employment outside the industry in its more narrowly defined sense and in this respect those who supply goods and services to those directly involved in tourism equally are beneficiaries from tourism. Such indirect employment includes, for example, those involved in the furnishing and equipment industries, souvenir industries and farming and food supply.

Construction industry is another very big source of employment. The basic infrastructure--roads, airports, water supply and other public utilities and also construction of hotels and other accommodation units create jobs for thousands of workers both unskilled and skilled. The entire important sector of basic infrastructures represents appreciable source of employment of manpower. In many of the developing countries, where chronic unemployment often exists, the promotion of tourism can be a great encouragement to economic development and, especially, employment. When discussing about employment, it is necessary to consider the seasonal nature of the tourism industry. Where general diversification alternatives are scarce, a combination of heavy dependence on tourism and highly marked seasonality calls for measures to develop off-season traffic.

Tourism and economic value of cultural resources

It may appear strange to discuss cultural tourism in this era of mass tourism. As an example of this conception of tourism a statement by J. Fourastie may be quoted here: "It is necessary for us to learn to look, to behold, to meditate, to question--actions virtually unknown if we are to judge by the bands of tourists who are content with a brief glance which will allow them to affix the mention 'seen' to the greatest number of countries or monuments. We can then hear them say 11 have done Italy, Greece, Mexico'--as if it were sufficient to pass through a place to know it. A man who has seen ten Cathedrals once has not seen a single one, a man who has seen the same Cathedral fen times may perhaps have seen something".

Nevertheless, the first appearance of tourism in the world had a cultural motivation, and tourism has always stood as a unique vehicle for the cultural propagation that is necessary to a deeper understanding of peoples. Tourism, with its basic element of movement, stands for the possibility of communication between differing civilizations and it has served in this sense since its first emergence. Tourism has always been an essential medium for broadening the limits of human know ledge. From the very early times, a mainspring of the urge to travel has been that based on the cultural interest. Even today we can witness large masses of people travelling to foreign countries to become acquainted with the usages and customs, to visit the museums and to admire works of art. As Medlik says: "When the tourist comes in contact with the place he visits and its population, a social exchange takes place. His social background affects the social structure and mode of life of his destination; he is in turn affected by it and sometimes carries back home with him new habits and ways of life". Every type of civilization, from the most sophisticated and advanced to the most primitive, is a source of attraction and curiosity for mankind.

Tourism remains basically a cultural phenomenon. One way of hastening the beneficial effects resulting from tourism is to bring the cultural heritage into the economic circuit, thus justifying the investments made at the cost of the national community for its preservation. Taking a strictly [illegible] view the cultural heritage of a nation may [illegible] considering that the preservation of its culture is one of the basic responsibilities of any community. But considering the financial obstacles especially for the developing countries, this may appear to be a rational approach. Hence mass tourism can contribute unique benefits to the exploiting of the cultural heritage of a nation and can serve indirectly to improve the individual cultural level of both nationals and foreigners, while at the same time developing into national wealth. The circle thus closes: cultural and tourist economy, instead of standing in opposition, derive reciprocal advantage from one another.

An Italian illustrated review, the Milan *'Tempo'*, sometime back published a full-page advertising display featuring a middle-aged lady of unmistakably foreign origin, wearing a flowered hat, sunglasses and gloves and laden with an assortment of parcels. The caption in the advertising display reads: "A foreign tourist stands admiringly before a work of art. She came to Italy for this purpose. She bought six pairs of shoes in Milan, nine tablecloths in Florence and seven dresses in Rome. Our artistic heritage is an inexhaustible source of culture and wealth. Let us protect it!" There is an affirmation in the above publicity slogan as to how cultural resources are brought into the economic circuit of the country.

Cultural resources have another specific characteristic which can act as a positive element in the developing countries. Those developing countries that possess an ancient civilization or an original culture can benefit greatly from tourism as many people would like to experience the exotic. Thee will be a great urge on the part of the tourist to visit and become acquainted with the ancient civilization. The greater part, if not the totality, of the developing countries possesses clearly determined and original characteristics capable of attracting flows of tourists from industrialized countries who are in quest of novel human knowledge. The main justification for cultural tourism is in fact not solely the cultural heritage alone. It also means the prospect of contact with other civilizations, their original and varied customs and tradition with their distinct characteristics. The entire process creates a powerful lever on motivation towards travel. A factor favourable to the developing countries is the unequalled and characteristic novelty of the different civilizations, ancient or recent, so revealed, which can only add a further and decisive motivation for undertaking the journey.

A two-way exchange is thus achieved between the industrialized and the developing countries. This two-way exchange is expressed in the following terms by Boyer: "We can say that the tourist process provides or should provide for exchanges between economic values (from the countries which send out tourists) and cultural values (from the countries that receive tourists)". It may be added that Boyer is clearly referring to the industrialized countries as generators of tourists, and to the developing countries as receivers of tourists. The characteristic benefit resulting from cultural tourism for the national economies and the balance of payments of the developing countries are quite significant.

Tourism and international understanding

Improving international understanding is another major area where tourism can play and has played a major role. Tourism can be a vehicle for international understanding by way of bringing diverse people face to face. It has been cited as a major contributor to international goodwill and as a prime means of developing social and cultural understanding among all peoples of the world. The interaction of a large number of people with the local population of the country visited results in making friends and goes among way in increasing friendships. Tourism can greatly enrich and promote friendship and goodwill.

People belonging to different countries, practising different life-styles and speaking different languages come together to make friends. There is a mingling of cultures which has positive, effects. Tourism helps to break down prejudices, barriers and suspicions that exist between nations. The very best way of getting to know another country is to go there, and when vast numbers travel, the narrow, rigid boundaries that keep people in compartments naturally tend to shrink and a positive move towards better international understanding begins to operate.

Tourism thus is not only an economic activity of importance inasmuch as it earns a country the foreign exchange. It is an important medium of social and cultural development and also of promoting lasting goodwill and friendship among the nations of the world. It also helps in the regional development of the country and acts as a means of social education and better understanding among the peoples in different regions of the country. In the long run the, most important contribution of tourism is developing understanding among varied cultures and life-styles.

The world Tourism conference which was held at Manila, Philippines in October, 1980 considered the nature of tourism phenomenon in all its aspects and the role tourism is bound to play in a dynamic and vastly changing world. Convened by the World Tourism Organisation the conference also considered the responsibility of various states for the development and enhancement as more than a purely economic activity of nations and peoples. The significance of tourism to developing countries came up for detailed discussion during the conference. The participants in the World Tourism Conference attached particular importance to its effects on the developing countries. The Conference from the beginning pronounced, itself on this subject. It stated its conviction "that the world tourism can contribute to the establishment of a new international economic order that will help to eliminate the widening economic gap between developed and developing countries and ensure the steady acceleration of economic and social development and progress, in particular of the developing countries."

Manila Declaration on World Tourism considered almost all the aspects of the tourism phenomenon. Besides the economic aspects, social, cultural, spiritual aspects also were considered. The conference was also convinced that world tourism can be a vital force for world peace and can provide the.moral and intellectual basis for international understanding and interde-pendence.

The declaration states:

(1) Tourism is considered an activity essential to the life of nations because of its direct effects on the social, cultural, educational and economic sectors of national societies and their international relations. Its development is linked to the social and economic development of nations and can only be possible if man has access to creative rest and holidays and enjoys the freedom to travel, within the framework of free time and leisure whose profoundly human character it underlines. Its very existence and development depend entirely on the existence of a state of lasting peace, to which tourism itself is required to contribute.

(2) On the threshold of the Twenty-first century and in view of the problems facing mankind, it seems timely and necessary to analyse the phenomenon of tourism, in relation fundamentally to the dimensions it has assumed since the granting to workers of the right to annual paid holidays moved tourism from a

restricted elitist activity to a wider activity integrated into social and economic life.

(3) As a result of people's aspirations to tourism, the initiatives taken by States regarding legislation and institutions, the permanent activities of voluntary bodies representing the various strata of the population and the technical contribution made by specialized professionals, modern tourism has come to play an important role within the range of human activities. States have recognized this fact and the great majority of them have entrusted the World Tourism organization with the task of ensuring the harmonious and sustained development of tourism, in cooperation, in appropriate cases, with the Specialized Agencies of the United Nations and the other international organizations concerned.

(4) The right to use of leisure, and in particular the right to access to holidays and to freedom of travel and tourism, a natural consequence of the right to work, is recognized as an aspect of the fulfilment of the human needs by the Universal Declaration of Human Rights as well as by the legislation of many States. It entails for society the duty of providing for its citizens the best practical, effective and nondiscriminatory access to this type of activity. Such an effort must be in harmony with the priorities, institutions and traditions of each individual country.

(5) There are many constraints on the development of tourism, nation and groups of nations should determine and study those constraints, and adopt measures aimed at attenuating their negative influence.

(6) The share tourism represents in national economies and in international trade makes it a significant factor in world development. Its consistent major role in

national economic activity, in international transactions and in securing balance of payments equilibrium makes it one of the main activities of the world economy.

(7) Within each country, domestic tourism contributes to an improved balance of the national economy through a redistribution of the national income. Domestic tourism also hightens the awareness of common interest and contributes to the development of activities favourable to the general economy of the country. Thus, the development of tourism from abroad should be accompanied by a similar effort to expand domestic tourism,

(8) The economic returns of tourism, however real and significant they may be, do not and cannot constitute the only criterion for the decision by States to encourage this activity. The right to holidays, the opportunity for the citizen to get to know his own environment, a deeper awareness of his national identity and of the solidarity that links him to his compatriots and the sense of belonging to a culture and to a people are all major reasons for stimulating the individual's participation in domestic and international tourism through access to holidays and travel.

(9) The importance that millions of our contemporaries attach to tourism in the use of their free time and in their concept of the quality of life makes it a need that governments should take into account and support.

(10) Social tourism is an objective which society must pursue in the interest of those citizens who are least privileged in the exercise of their rights to rest.

(11) Through its effects on the physical and mental health of individuals practising) it, tourism is a factor that

favours social stability, improves the working capacity of communities and promotes individual as well as collective well-being.

(12) Through the wide range of services needed to satisfy its requirements, tourism creates new activities of considerable importance which are a source of new employment. In this respect, tourism constitutes a positive element for social development in all the countries where it is practised irrespective of their level of development.

(13) With respect to international relations and the search for peace, based on justice and respect of individual and national aspirations, tourism stands out as a positive and ever-present factor in promoting mutual knowledge and understanding and as a basis for reaching a greater level of respect and confidence among all the peoples of the world.

(14) Modern tourism results from the adoption of a social policy which led to the workers gaining annual paid holidays and represents the recognition of a fundamental right of the human being to rest and leisure. It has become a factor contributing to social stability, mutual understanding among individuals and peoples and individual betterment. In addition to its well-known economic aspects, it has acquired a cultural and moral dimension which must be fostered and protected against the harmful distortions which can be brought about by economic factors. Public authorities and the travel trade should accordingly participate in development of tourism by formulating guidelines aimed at encouraging appropriate investments.

(15) Youth tourism requires the most active attention since young people have less adequate income than others for travelling or taking holidays. A positive

policy should provide youth with the utmost encouragement and facilities. The same attention should be provided for the elderly and handicapped.

(16) In the universal efforts to establish a new international economic order, tourism can under appropriate conditions, play a positive role in furthering equilibrium, cooperation, mutual understanding and solidarity among all countries.

(17) Nations should promote improved conditions of employment for workers engaged in tourism and confirm and protect their right to establish professional trade unions and collective bargaining.

(18) Tourism resources available in various countries consist at the same time of space, facilities and values. These are resources whose use cannot be left uncontrolled without running the risk of their deterioration, or even their destruction. The satisfaction of tourism requirements must not be prejudicial to the social and economic interests of the population in tourist areas, to the environment or, above all to natural resources, which are the fundamental attraction of tourism, and historical and cultural sites. All tourism resources are part of the heritage of mankind. National communities and the entire international community must take the necessary steps to ensure their preservation. The conservation of historical, cultural and religious sites represents at all times, and notably in time of conflict, one of the fundamental responsibilities of states.

(19) International cooperation in the field of tourism is an endeavour in which the characteristics of peoples and basic interests of individual states must be respected. In this field, the central and decisive role

of the World Tourism Organization as a concept-utilizing and harmonizing body is obvious.

(20) Bilateral and multilateral technical and financial cooperation cannot be looked upon as an act of assistance since it constitutes the pooling of the means necessary for the utilization of resources for the benefit of all parties.

(21) In the practice of tourism, spiritual elements must take precedence over technical and material elements. The spiritual elements are essentially as follows:

(a) the total fulfilment of the human being;

(b) a constantly increasing contribution to education;

(e) equality of destiny of nations;

(d) the liberation of man in a spirit of respect for his identity and dignity;

(e) the affirmation of the originality of cultures and respect for the moral heritage of peoples.

(22)Preparation for tourism should be integrated with the training of the citizen for his civic responsibilities. In this respect, governments should mobilize the means of education and information at their disposal and should facilitate the work of individuals and bodies involved in this endeavour. Preparation for tourism, for holidays and for travel could usefully form part of the process of youth education and training. For these reasons, the integration of tourism into youth education constitutes a basic element favourable to the permanent strengthening of peace.

(23)Any long-term analysis of mankind's social, cultural and economic development should take due account of national and international tourist and recreational activities. These activities now form an integral part of the life of modem national and international societies. Bearing in mind the acknowledged values of tourism which are inseparable from it, the authorities will have to give more increased attention to the development of national and international tourist and recreational activity, based on an ever-wider participation of peoples in holidays and travel as well as the movement of persons for numerous other purposes, with a view to ensuring the orderly growth of tourism in a manner consistent with the other basic needs of society.

(24) The States and other participants in the Conference, together with the World Tourism Organisation, are strongly urged to take into account the guidelines, viewpoints and recommendations emanating from the Conference so that they can contribute, on the basis of their experience and in the context of their day-to-day activities, to the practical implementation of the objectives set with a view a to broadening the process of development of world tourism and breathing new life into it.

(25) The Conference urges the World Tourism Organization to take all necessary measures, through its own inter machinery and, where appropriate, in coòperation with other international, inter-government and nongovernmental bodies, so as to permit the global implementation of the principles, concepts and guidelines contained in this final document.

Tourism promotion is one of the important elements of the marketing mix as well as an important tool for marketing. As applied to the tourism industry, the most important function of marketing is to bring about an awareness of the product in the minds of existing as well as prospective consumers in the overall market areas.

This awareness about a particular product or a service is to be brought about through a medium and the medium in this case is the 'message'. Through an appropriate message the detailed information about the product is passed on to the consumers.

The message about a product, however, is to reach a consumer. It is to be communicated. There are several channels through which the message is to be communicated. These include both print as well as electronic media, direct mail and persuasion, sales support and public relations.

All the above activity form a part of overall tourism promotion. The term promotion is interpreted and defined in several ways. Basically, the purpose of promotion is to inform, to persuade, to encourage or more specifically to influence the potential customers or trade intermediaries like travel agents, tour operators, reservation services, hotel and charter brokers, through communication channels to think and act in a certain manner.

Systematic communication both with the actual and potential customers as well as with trade intermediaries is very essential with a view to bridging the gap between the producer of goods and services on the one hand and the customer on the other. This is necessary as like in any other industry, successful marketing in tourism cannot rely only on a product of the right kind, or a market related pricing policy or reliable and effective distribution network alone.

The basic function of all tourism promotional activities is to have an effective and meaningful communication with the consumer and the trade intermediaries. How is this awareness to be brought about in the minds of consumers and intermediaries in the market areas? This is possible through certain identifiable methods which are being practised by all the marketing organisations. The awareness is brought about through certain methods/marketing tools. These are as follows:

A. Advertising

B. Sales support activities

C. Public Relations

All the above tools are, however, complementary to each other. It is the proper and judicious blend of these which is essential for the successful promotion of a programme or a product.

Advertising

Advertising is a non-personal communication of a sales message to actual or potential purchasers of a product by a person or an organisation selling a product or a service. The sales message is delivered through a paid medium for the purpose of influencing the buying behaviour of those purchasers. The term may be defined as "any activity designed to spread information with a view to promoting the sales of marketable goods and services." As such, it operates in two ways: firstly, by spreading information among consumers, about the possibilities of consumption, and secondly, by seeking to influence their judgement in favour of the particular goods which are the subject of the advertisement. Use of certain paid media space is, however, a prerequisite.

Advertisement can, therefore, also be defined as "a paid public message designed to describe or praise a product." Unless a communication has as its purpose a sale of a product or service, it is not properly considered to be advertising. For example, the publication of a message in a newspaper by a philanthropic organisation soliciting funds is not an advertising activity. It is only a public announcement as there is, no sale of a product involved.

Origin of advertising

The history of advertising is quite *ancient and* interesting. The original advertisements, perhaps, were announcements written on public walls several thousands of years before the birth of Christ, offering various commodities for sale. As economic forces expanded with the rapid growth of population and the discovery of new worlds, so did the advertising activity prosper. Since the effect of advertising is directly proportionate to the strength of the channel of *communication or* medium carrying the message to prospective purchasers, it was not until the late seventeenth century that the subject took on any great importance. Printing process from movable type had been in existence, for about 200 years, and primitive 'newspapers' were beginning to flourish.

As the various media were being developed particularly newspapers and magazines, merchants were able to offer their products to larger group of consumers, and expenditures for advertising increased correspondingly. Thereafter, the advances made in the sphere of photography, photoengraving, and printing served to bring advertising into focus as a major economic force. Finally, the spurt in mass media magazines and newspapers with circulation in several millions, radio broadcasting facilities capable of influencing millions of people simultaneously have raised the business of advertising to a major importance in the world's economy. Added to all this the introduction of television gave a real boost to advertising in recent times.

Setting objectives

Setting objectives of advertising by an organisation is very important. An advertising objective is a clear and concise description of exactly what the advertising programme is intended to accomplish in a given period of time. Very often the management is not sure exactly why it is spending money and time on advertising without realising what it expects to achieve from this in return.

Advertising is an investment and like all investments it should produce measurable results. Measuring results vis-a-vis inputs put in terms of investment is, therefore, very important and a crucial aspect which each *organisation needs* take care of. The first and the foremost reason for setting advertising objectives is, therefore, to measure the return on one's advertising investment.

The second reason is that with the availability of so many alternative methods for marketing products available and with both consumers and customers becoming more and more value-conscious every day, organisations must seek the most efficient way of marketing the goods and services if they are to remain competitive. There is another important reason for setting objectives. An advertising campaign is the product of the combined work of an entire team of specialists. The team consists not only of top management marketing, advertising and product managers, but also of agency copywriters, media personnel, art directors, TV producers, etc. It is, therefore, important that all these people are concentrating on a single product and putting their concerted efforts in the same direction. Without written and concise objectives all this would be difficult to achieve. Objectives, therefore, serve the purpose of coordinating, and integrating marketing and advertising efforts.

Professor Robert Buzzell of the Harvard Business School, in a written submission to the Federal Trade Commission during hearings on modem advertising practices in July 1971, gives the following example of possible advertising objectives for a manufacturer's consumer product advertising:

To increase sales directly by:

(i) encouraging potential purchasers to visit dealers or distributors;

(ii) announcing special sales, contests or other promotions;

(iii) securing new dealers or distributors,

(iv) inducing professional persons e.g. to recommend a product;

(v) distributing coupons to be redeemed on purchases;

To create awareness and interest in the company's product by:

(i) informing potential buyers about product features;

(ii) announcing the availability of new products;

(iii) demonstrating the benefits of a produces use;

(iv) comparing a product with competing product;

(v) showing how a product should be used;

(vi) informing potential buyers about the company's technical skills, production facilities, technical services, etc;

(vii) informing purchasers about where products can be obtained;

(viii) announcing changes in prices, packages, labels, etc.;

(x) publicising a new brand name or symbol.

The above advertising objectives for manufacturer's consumer product advertising can be applied for the tourism product advertising to achieve best possible results. The broad objectives in tourism advertising include making the tourist product as widely known as possible and to make it as attractive as possible for the prospective consumers.

Advantages

There are several inherent advantages in this method.

The biggest advantage is its *wide coverage.* Advertising is especially appropriate for communication with a large number of perspective purchasers of a commodity or a service. A uniform sales message is directed towards all prospective purchasers. An advertisement can be placed before a large number of prospective customers as compared with the efforts of a salesman. *Frequency* is another advantage. It can make its appeal frequently, whereas the calls of salesmen are usually not so frequent. Another advantage is its accessibility. It may reach prospects whom salesmen would find difficult to interview, owing to lack of interest, or inaccessibility to salesmen. Advertisement may reach such prospects through many types of media and under a variety of circumstances, and may thus attract their attention and arouse their interest. Lower cost is another major advantage. Large numbers can be reached economically, Le, at a lower cost per contact than in any other technique available.

Advertising may be used to do a variety of selling tasks. A great deal of advertising attempts to win acceptance for the product. Such advertising may produce few specific demands for the advertised brands, yet when retailers display or show advertised goods they sell more readily than non-advertised ones. Therefore, retailers often hesitate to handle non-advertised goods unless they are obtainable at low prices. Advertising thus directly stimulates sales to retailers. Advertising may at times be used to make the complete sale. Some direct mail and periodical advertising attempts to make sales by requesting readers to forward orders accompanied by the necessary payment. When the number of potential buyers is small and when they are widely scattered it could be extremely costly to reach them through salesmen. Advertising then becomes the most economic means of doing the entire sales job.

Planning the advertising

While planning the advertising, the agency must give careful consideration to the actual make-up of the advertisement. The headline copy, illustrations, colour scheme, size, layout, and method of printing or reproducing the advertisement must be planned very carefully, This is necessary in order to gain attention of the customer, maintain his interest in the message, question of periodicity of advertisement. How frequently to advertise? For instance, is it better to use a full-page advertisement once a month or a quarter-page weekly? A frequently presented thought is likely to force itself into our consciousness. People are inclined to believe statements they hear or see repeatedly and hence the logic of frequent repetition of advertisements. In starting a special campaign the advertisements should not be spaced regularly. Early in the campaign they should be used close together, while later on they can be issued at much longer intervals. This is desirable because consumers forget rapidly at first and much more slowly later on. After the facts are retained by the prospects, the advertisements can be presented at much longer intervals.

Media selection

The advertiser should give careful attention in planning to the selection of the medium or media especially adopted to his needs. The selection will depend upon the factors like the area to be covered, the type of audience to be reached, the appeals to be made and upon the services and facilities of the particular medium in relation to costs. The important factors which, influence the media selection are: (i) media habits of the target audience, 00 product characteristics: for example, TV may be the appropriate media for those products which may require a demonstration of their operation for effective impact on the target audience; and (iii) cost of the media.

Message selection

The massage selected for use in the advertisement should be such that it retains the interest in the minds of the customers about the product. The customer must maintain his interest in the message, and secure the action desired by the seller of the product. The objective is to present the advertiser's message in such a way that the illustration may lead the reader to favourable considerations of the advertisement, The important characteristics of an effective message are:

(i) *Information: it* should be adequate for a decision,

(ii) *Interest: it* should be able to catch the attention of the largest audience.

(iii) *Authenticity: it* should avoid exaggerated claims,

(iv) *Persuasion:* it should be capable of creating a favourable conviction in the target audience, and

(v) Memory value: it should have something in it which can help the target audience to remember it.

Cost

agency must relate the estimated cost of the objectives planned and the contribution expected from advertising. Can the advertiser carry on a campaign large enough to make it effective? Are the funds available or will they become available through the sale of the product. How much does the agency spend for the advertising? The various methods commonly used are:

(i) *Affordable method: here,* the advertising budget is set on the basis of what the agency can afford;

(ii) *Percentage of sales method:* in this case, the agency sets the advertising budget on the basis of specific percentage of sales,

(iii) *Competitive parity method:* here the company sets its budget to match those of its major competitors;

(iv) *Objective and task method:* in this the advertising budget represents the outlay required to perform the various tasks which are necessary to achieve the properly defined advertising objectives of the company. This method is considered the most rational.

Determining advertising effectiveness

In today's world, advertisement through any media has become extremely expensive. In view of this it becomes very important for the agency to ensure that the money spent on it does bring returns by way of increased sales. This could be done by way of evaluating or testing the effectiveness of advertising. Testing methods may be used to evaluate the results of an advertising campaign. By evaluating and analysing the effectiveness of advertisements that have been used, future advertisements may be improved. In addition, tests may be applied before advertisement has been run. Pretesting of an advertisement prevents expenditure that would not be profitable and leads to expenditures that give the best results. In determining advertising effectiveness the commonly used methods are given below:

(i) *Inquiries:* Answer back coupons, with some inducement, are incorporated in many advertisements, The amount of response is an indication of the effectiveness of the concerned advertisement.

(ii) *Recall tests:* Here the respondents are shown the magazine cover or any other media vehicle in which the concerned advertisement had appeared. They are then asked to tell which advertisements in that publication they remember.

(iii) *Recognition tests*: Here the respondents are shown the advertisement and asked if they have read them.

(iv) *Sales tests*: Here, the actual sales results before and after the concerned advertising are examined. The sales results in the selected 'test markets' are also compared to those in some chosen 'control markets', i.e., the markets where the concerned advertising is not done. This is done to eliminate certain factors, other than advertising, which may also have influenced the sales.

Advertising the powerful instrument of modern marketing has only recently come to be used extensively for promotion of tourism. This is a far cry from the era when colourful folders and posters were the only apparent form of travel promotion. In the field of tourism advertising is mainly used to create initial awareness and interest in the tourist service or destination to be promoted and motivates potential tourists to decide to make further equities about costs, bookings, facilities, etc. It implies indirect communication with selected target groups the potential tourists through paid messages designed to praise a particular destination or an area. For a country which is trying to attract tourists, there can be two principal forms of advertising. (i) consumer advertising, and (ii) trade advertising. To reach a wide a number of consumers, such media as newspaper advertisements, radio spots, TV prime time advertising are used. However, this form of advertisement is very expensive. For a developing nation it is extremely difficult to afford such a type of advertisement because of financial constraints. Trade advertising on the other hand which is an indirect form of advertising is a very economic method.

The trend today is towards group travel. A tourist for various reasons chooses to travel as a member of a group, as opposed to travelling individually. The result, therefore, has been that a number of very large tour operators have established their offices in such market areas. While the tour operator puts together inclusive tour packages, the tourist merely pays one package price for all services and is assured of a holiday. Such packages are then sold in retail by numerous smaller travel agents located in various market areas and the result is that a group is formed. For a country which is trying to market its product, the area towards which these efforts are aimed is thus narrowed down to the important tour operators/wholesalers The media used to achieve this is large scale advertising in travel trade journals and newspapers of international repute having travel sections.

Advertising plays a crucial role in marketing a tourist product. If the tight combination of conditions is present the effect of advertising would be to increase the demand for the particular country's tourist product. Among the factors favourable to the successful use of advertising are the rising trend of demand in the particular product and an opportunity to stimulate selective demand, i.e., preference for the particular product. This is most likely where there is a possibility of product differentials, and where consumer satisfaction depends largely on hidden qualities that cannot easily be judged at the time of purchase, or where strong emotional buying motive exists as in the case of tourism.

Steps in planning an advertising campaign

There are several stages through which any advertising campaign must evolve. It may be explained here that term product in the larger sense includes not only products such as soaps and cigarettes but also service 'products' such as tourism, insurance, etc. The following are the various stages:

Defining the product

Before one can develop any communication of advertising for a product it is essential to know what is that the product offers to consumers. This is very important. When you advertise a soap you are not advertising a cake of compound of alkali and oil in an attractive printed pack but you may be advertising beauty or deodorant protection or youthfulness and so on.

To assess, therefore, what the product means to the prospective users we have to first ascertain the benefits that the users will derive from the product. Here are a few examples of this kind of benefit derivation:

Car tyre can offer confidence;
security or safety;
Household cleaning can offer convenience, pride or hygenic conditions;
Cosmetics can offer romance,
self confidence or glamour;
Cigarettes can offer
social status, confidence;
Travel can offer rest, relaxation glamour,
confidence or status.

From these examples one can see that in most cases the user benefit is not always apparent as a product feature. But it must be remembered that people buy things for the benefits they derive when using them. We must look at the product through the mind and eyes of the user. To do this it is sometimes necessary to conduct research amongst users or prospective users to find out what it is that they get from particular products. One can at the same time assess their knowledge, attitude, and usage of competitive or substitute products so that the strengths and weaknesses of one's product are known.

This study of consumer assessment is important as in any system of communication the idea existing in the mind of the receiver will effect the interpretation of the message being received. In some cases it may prevent the message from either being noticed or perceived, let alone being received or understood.

Once we have arrived at this product benefit definition we must then study this in relation to other factors.

First, the relative importance to the consumer of the several product benefits the more important the benefit the greater its motivating values. Second, the relative position of one's own brand and substitute brands in regard to these product benefits to create a unique and memorable message, the main ideas or benefits should be as distinctive and different from others as possible.

Let us now assume that we have studied our product and its users and potential users attitude towards the product and have arrived at a definition of product benefits which we feel are most important. We have by this stage got our proposition. We now proceed to the next stage in our planning.

Defining the market segments

We have a product, we know what users expect or want from it Now we must assess how many users we have and where they are located. Most of this information will have been collected through various sources and supplied by the organisation marketing the product. The kind of information that should be available will relate to the following:

(a) *Consumer information*

(i) Type of consumer-number, sex, age, socio-economic profile;

(ii) Location of the consumer—whether they will be found in cities, small towns or rural areas or in all areas and in what proportion in each;

(iii) Geographic distribution—whether there are any regional variations in the market spread and if so, why;

(v) Shopping habits—the amount or size of individual purchases, the frequency or number of times a product is bought during a month or a year, whether bought on regular planned basis or through an impulse decision at point of sale;

(v) Decision making—often the person who actually buys the product does not always make the decision and buy or select the particular brand. It, therefore, becomes important to find out who it is who makes the decision and also the extent of the actual buyer's role in changing or influencing this decision. The reason for finding this out is to get an idea as to whom the advertising message should be directed. The person who decides is very important and in the case of joint decisions it may well be necessary to direct the advertising to two or more decision-makers.

(b) *Distribution Information:* Types of outlets, number of such outlets and the importance of each type; the location of these outlets in different cities, towns and rural markets, the dealer's part in the selling activity.

(c) *Sales Information:* The trends over the years and any significant shifts that may have occurred in different geographic areas and the reasons for these changes is a very important information. Seasonal variations that may be related to weather, festivals and other local and national reasons are also very important. In giving us all this information the manufacturer will not merely be giving us information about his product but also of competitive and substitute product against which his product will compete.

This information will provide us with a knowledge of the dimension of the market so that we will be in a position to assess which particular markets are of greater importance. This will also assist in creating the media plan to reach each market and also in creating relevant messages for each. In terms of media selection, the statistical information that will be supplied will enable to plan a campaign using media which will provide cover, reach and frequency related to the market definition.

(d) *Attitude segmentation:* This relates to segmenting the market by user motivation. For example, it has been shown that certain type of people use certain products in larger quantities and more regularly than others. In the same way some people travel more often than others. These groups are termed the heavy user group. And, in most cases it is not usual socioeconomic categorisation that distinguishes them. This may be termed as attitude segmentation or separation. The problem in such segmenting or separating into two groups is that unlike socioeconomic segmentation it is difficult to physically isolate the group. This can, however, be achieved through segmenting as it were the advertising message. It is important to note, however, that this sort of segmentation should not be overdone. Social appeals or segmented campaigns should only be developed if it is found that there are large enough groups of consumers who have attitude which would respond to such appeals. Often, however, it is not only the advertising that is segmented but the product itself is separately produced for each of the segments.

At this stage we will have progressed from product definition to a knowledge of the market, its size, location and, different segmentation patterns.

Interpreting the marketing objectives

What we have been discussing until now is information of the environment in which the advertising campaign will have to work. As we have discussed earlier, since advertising is only the communication aspect of the total marketing function we have to take into account the marketing plans of the manufacturer, both in the long-term and short-term, and relate the advertising to these.

The marketing objectives that are given by the manufacturers will detail the plans that the manufacturer has for his product in the coming year and in some cases for a few years ahead. These plans would cover items such as:

(i) The sales targets for the coming years broken down into regional targets, pack size targets, etc. as the case may be.

(ii) The distribution, merchandising and sales promotion activities planned to support the sales increase;

(iii) The role that advertising is expected to play in creating consumers;

(iv) The inhibiting factors which will work to prevent him from achieving his target, competitive products and their advertising, consumer attitudes, etc.

It is important to note that in any marketing operation the product formulation, packaging and pricing, distribution and availability at point of sale are all of vital importance. All that advertising can do is to bring consumer to the point-of-sale. But if the product is not properly made, packaged or priced or is not well merchandised or promoted at the point-of-sale and, therefore, is not visible, then it is quite possible that the sales effect of the advertising will not fructify. This brings out the importance of integrating these various activities. Once we have got clearly the marketing objectives of the client and their plans in relation to these objectives we can then see what the advertising has to communicate and to whom with a view to provide the maximum relevant support to the agreed marketing plan.

Planning the advertising campaign

We now know what we have to *sell,* to whom we have to sell, where the prospective consumers are located and also how the product will be made available to them. Our object now is to create an advertising campaign Which will reach target audience and motivate them to come to ask for and buy the product.

Let us now go to the concept of the proposition in the narrow funnel. We have not processed all the facts that the manufacturer has given us and we have perhaps had a dialogue with the consumer, through research, to ascertain his knowledge, attitude and usage of the product and its competitors. As a result we have found out the proposition that we feel would be most motivating. We have also found out where the consumer is located, how and when he buys the product. We are now in a position to get down to work on the two aspects which make up an advertising plan: (1) the Creative Strategy and (2) the Media plan.

The creative strategy: Creativity in advertising has to work within the discipline of our 'funnel'. Let us see how this happens. We have at the one end the proposition. We now have to transform the proposition into the idea which is to be communicated. In converting the proposition into the idea we have to use creativity. But this is an important point, you will notice that this is where the funnel narrows. This narrowing of the funnel is significant inasmuch as it is no use being creative without direction and relevance. For bright ideas to be useful there must also be the right ideas. It is this idea that we now have to communicate to our target group. In order to communicate it we have to bring to bear what may be called the skilled craftsmanship of advertising. Media people, production people and creative people will be involved in this area. But the most vital creative work is what is done in the narrow section of the funnel in creating an idea from the proposition. In terms of this craft aspect of the agency's activities we will have to channelise the idea into various material that will be required for the advertising campaign. This can range from press advertisements to film commercials, to radio spots, to posters and other point-of-sale material, TV spots, etc. All these items will be creative interpretation of the idea.

The Media Plan: While creativity is perhaps most closely related in an agency with the development of an idea and its interpretation into advertising material, it also plays a role in the development of a media plan. Let us know briefly the way in which an agency constructs a media plan. Media may be defined as vehicles of mass communications which are used to carry advertising messages. Very rarely, except in the case of direct mail advertising& are media developed solely as advertising communication vehicles.

One may broadly classify media into two groups:

(a) Media which are read, seen or heard by the consumer for their 'editorial 'work. These are the newspapers, magazines, the radio programmes, cinema shows, TV programmes which are read or tuned into or watched by the consumer for the editorial' material which they offer. The advertising benefits from the editorial climate of this media.

(b) Media, usually more 'reminder' type of media such as outdoor media, hoarding, transportation signs, posters, kiosks, neon signs, etc., which are noticed in passing only. They obtain consumer exposure due to the fact that the consumer's living habits cause him to pass by them. For instance, commuters in trains and buses, motorists and pedestrians on roads are all exposed to such media.

Point of sale items also fall within the same group. In preparing media plans one has to study the behaviour and exposure of consumer groups with regard to both kinds of media. We have to study both kinds of media. We have to study what media our target consumer looks at for 'editorial' pleasure and when he does so and in what frame of mind. By studying his living habits and his pattern of movement we can assess which of the second group of media he will be exposed to as a general rule. In the more advanced countries it is possible to get detailed statistics on the kind of audience that each medium has. In advanced countries this information is very detailed indeed and permits one to prepare very accurate media plans. In other countries, however, this information is still very scanty and apart from basic circulation information it is rare that one gets much else. However, through experience one gradually builds up a fund of knowledge which enables one to select appropriate media for appropriate markets. Here, apart from the circulation information a study of the quality of the medium in terms of editorial content and style is a very useful method of evaluating reader types.

Media planners have to create what is known as the media mix consisting of various types of mix comprising of various types of media. The selection of these media will depend on:

(a) The target audience that is to be reached: its reading or media exposure habit and its location and movement and shopping habits. This information will permit us in selecting such media as will reach target consumers most effectively;

(b) The product to be promoted and its use by the target audience.

For instance, if one were selling holiday travel to a businessman and one were also selling machinery to the same businessman, it would be perhaps inappropriate to release the former advertising in technical magazines though they might provide adequate coverage of this particular businessman. It would be equally inappropriate to release the latter advertising in a leisure magazine reaching the target audience.

(c) The nature of the message—whether it is a persuasive long copy story, or whether it requires demonstration of the product in action or presentation of the product in colour. All these factors would influence the media planner. Magazine would allow long copy stories, film or TV commercials, project demonstration and poster and colour press advertising would present the product in colour for easy identification.

The term mix suggests that a number of different types of media are frequently required to provide total coverage for any campaign. For example, while one might use press or TV to put across the main informative story of a product it may be necessary to utilise some outdoor and point of sale media in order to effectively remind the consumer of the product on his way to the market or at the time of buying. This interlinking of different media brings into focus the importance of designing creative material with a unified theme so that the reminder media material can bring back to mind the advertising message conveyed earlier by the informative media.

(d) Competitive activity: it is considered good media tactics to design a media plan that will let the advertising dominate competitive activity. Often, when the budget is smaller than that of the competitor the media planner recommends heavier use of fewer media so as to achieve this dominance.

(e) Budget restraint. The media planner has to assess carefully the different buys he can make within the budget and then recommend what he feels will give the best impact value for the particular campaign.

At the end of the exercise the media planner will have worked out a list of media detailing the audience that each media offers,, the number of insertions or spots to be released in each, the number of times the target audience will be reached and a cost-analysis for each media.

In order to relate this plan specifically with the targeted sales, separate analysis can also be prepared indicating the amount of coverage or number of contacts that will be exposed to advertising in each of the sales territories.

We have now a media plan which takes into account the target consumer, the creative requirement, market location and budget limitations. The Creative Strategy and Media Plan are then presented to the client. This is what is called an Advertising Presentation. At this presentation the agency relates their plans to the total marketing effort and indicates how it will fit in.

Implementing the campaign: Once the advertising campaign has been approved in terms of the creative strategy and the media plan, the agency next has to apply different 'crafts' in order to implement the campaign in the manner in which it was planned. 'These range from the preparation of press advertisement material to the production of IN and film commercials, recording of radio spots and production of point 0 sale material, etc. On the other hand *the* media buyer and scheduler has to implement the media in terms of preparing estimates, schedules and release orders for press, cinema, radio and other media. The agency takes on for the advertiser the responsibility of seeing the right time so that the total plan, as envisaged, becomes operative. Once the Campaïgn has beer released it becomes necessary to assess its impact. This brings us not only to the final stage of activity on a campaign but also brings us to the first stage of the next campaign.

Assessing the Impact and Value of a Campaign: It is not possible always to evaluate the effect of an advertising campaign in terms of sales as too many other factors are involved. This is particularly so in serv ce advertising. Therefore, the result of a campaign cannot only be shown by way of sales. But there must be some way of measuring the value of the campaign. In answer to this question it is felt that the impact of an advertising campaign should be assessed by the extent to which it results in changing the attitude of the selected target consumers, Therefore, having planned, prepared and released our campaign we start after a suitable interval to compile information on its impact value.

This study will provide information on the following:

1. *Awareness:* the extent of shift in the degree of awareness of an agency or product is highly relevant as unless people are aware of something they can neither have an attitude towards it not act in regard to it.
2. *Attitude dimensions* are also important. It is necessary to measure to what extent the right attitudes have been communicated and accepted. We will have to find out at the time of formulating the proposition what these right attitudes should be.
3. *Purchase of* the product is very important as merely having a favourable attitude towards the product is not enough. It must be one that is motivating enough to cause usage. The measure of users that are created due to the shift in attitude *therefore becomes* very important.
4. *Repurchase of* the product. It is said that advertising can

result in a first sale but it is for the product itself to perform and earn the second sale. By 'perform' of course one does not only mean preference in visible terms but in satisfaction terms as well in this case, the amount of satisfaction a traveller has derived from a visit, etc. In other words the product must live up to the expectation which the advertising has created.

Pre-testing advertising

Pretesting of advertisements is yet another technique of advertising testing. This attempts to assess the communication value of an advertisement whether press advertisement, or TV or radio spot in advance of the actual release or screening. In this way it is possible to develop advertising material which most effectively conveys the proposition idea. This pretesting technique can also assist in forecasting the change in attitude, etc. which the campaign can achieve. A set of advertisement commercials, etc., are prepared and these are shown to small groups of representative consumers. The effectiveness of the various approaches in conveying the proposition is then measured. This type of testing assists the agency to judge whether the idea created is in fact correctly communicating the motivating proposition to the target consumer. In this way we are back again at the first stage of the next campaign and the cycle begins once again.

Advertising agency

An advertising agency may be explained as an organisation consisting of one or more persons, the function of which is to provide advertising, merchandising, and other services and counsel relating to the sale of a client's goods and services. The compensation for the services is generally derived from commissions rendered by the various media, the facilities of which are purchased by the agency on behalf of the client. The major difference which distinguishes the agency from other service organisations such as publicity and public relations firms arises from the fact that the greater portion of the income of the agency is represented by commissions received not from the customer of the agency, called the 'client, but from newspapers, magazines, television and radio stations and other media from which the agency purchased time and space for the client.

The advertising agency is a service organisation which undertakes the planning and preparation of advertising, The agency service consists of interpreting to the public, or to that part of it which it is desired to reach, the advantages of a product or service. Originally agencies were media owners, service departments and not independent organisations as they are today. In the early days of advertising, agencies acted as representatives of newspapers and sold space in them to advertisers. At first, the agencies bought space in bulk, and made their profit by selling it in smaller units for as much as they could get. Later, agencies started to sell space on a commission basis, and a commission system is still the current basis for agency remuneration, agencies taking their profit from commissions granted by media owners rather than from advertisers.

Later on the agencies started a copywriting service and soon afterwards design and art services were added to their functions. By this time agencies were really working more for the advertisers than for the newspaper proprietors, and before long they became full fledged service organisations giving their clients a complete range of advertising services.

The agencies also became independent, and bought space in whichever newspaper and other advertising media they thought best served their clients interests.

Today the term agency no longer applies in the legal sense, since the agency makes contracts in its own right with its clients on the one hand and with media owners on the other. It remains a party to the advertisement contract, which it would not were it an agency in the legal sense of the word. Agencies are thus liable in law for debts to media, even though they made the booking on their client's behalf.

Selecting an agency

Selection of a suitable advertising agency is a major factor which determines the success or failure of a promotional work of an organisation. The choice of an advertising agency will depend on the size of a promotional budget, the range of services required *and above all the objective assessment of the professional* qualities of the agency.

Most of the national tourist organisations and major tourist enterprises have *appointed their own* advertising agencies. The advertising campaigns of these organisations are run through the *agencies. The national tourist offices usually hire the services of* the specialised advertising agencies in various tourist generating markets to help them in market research, audience information gathering, designing messages and getting advertising schedules in wells-elected media.

Agency procedure

When an organisation appoints an agency, the first task of the agency personnel is to find out about their clients activities and Problems. The agency would spend considerable time making a *thorough* investigation until the advertiser's problems have been properly identified and defined. The size of the appropriation and the period to be covered are also important to the agency. Normally the client will give the agency all *the* information it needs when *he gives his* advertising 'brief. The quality of work produced by the agency to a large extent depends *on the* client's Aft in giving *his* agency all the relevant information it needs in order to prepare advertising proposals on his *behalf.*

Once the agency is confident that it has a correct understanding of the situation, it can start the vital work of preparing an advertising campaign, to help the client achieve his marketing objectives.

Once the problem is clearly defined, the agency staff will start to solve it. Here the accounts executive' plays a very important role. He may start by calling, a meeting of 'Plans Board' on which there will be representatives of all the important agency departments present to consider the theme to be featured in the advertising. The media department will advise on media to be used. The 'Plans Board" discusses the clients overall marketing problem from every angle and finally agrees on a basic solution.

Each major advertising agency has various departments whose area of work are well defined. The following are the major departments of an agency and their scope of work:

(i) *The Research Department*: When the agency staff attempts to define their clients marketing problems *they may* decide that they lack sufficient information to reach a sound judgement and will take the assistance of the Research Department. A good amount of information is readily available in published form. Before any field research is undertaken there is always desk research which involves checking through existing sources of information. As soon as information collected has been checked, there are further meetings of the 'Plans Board' to consider the advertising and marketing campaign. Once this is done, the individual departments set to work to crystalise their ideas and to produce detailed proposals in accordance with the agreed broad plan.

(ii) *The Media Department:* Once the general strategy is agreed, it is now up to the media department to get down to detailed planning with the aim of spending the client funds in such a way that his advertising message Teaches prospective buyers as effectively and economically as possible. The media department then evaluates the media and selects the most suitable one in the light of clients requirements.

(iii) *The Creative Department:* The Creative Department takes i work to a more advance level. Copy is written for press advertisements or printed material and layouts prepare For posters or display material, roughs and dummies a made and storyboards drawn up for TV or cinema commercials.

(iv) *Review of Proposals:* As soon as detailed media and creative proposals are ready, the Plans Board meets again to review the progress of the work. The purpose is to check the proposals point by point to be submitted to the client b ensure that there are no discrepancies in the work of the individual departments.

(v) *Presentation of Proposals:* Once the detailed proposals have been approved by the review board, they are made read for presentation to the client. The media schedule is typed out in its final form as is the advertisement copy. The finished versions of designs are prepared by the creative staff. These are then presented to the client. Creative and media proposals are presented together. Where the presentation is on the major campaign, the agency may call on all those concerned to make a "dry run' beforehand, amounting almost to a rehearsal. Some agencies even put the entire presentation on film or video tape and screen this to the client rather than risk the possibility of error that is always present in the 'live' presentation.

(vi) *Execution of the Proposal:* Before giving an agency a 'go ahead' or a formal approval to proceed, the client checks the proposals to ensure that they are sound and that they dovetail with his company's marketing objectives. Once the agency has the client's agreement, the advertising proposals are put into effect.

Sources of income

An agency's income is derived from media in the form of commissions and from clients in the form of service fees. The proportion of income derived from these two sources varies from agency to agency depending upon the prearranged agreement made with the client in any of the following ways:

(a) Receiving commission from media and billing the client for non-commissionable expenses plus a service fee, which may be either 15 per cent or 17.65 per cent of the expenses;

(b) Charging the client a minimum fee and rebating all commissions to the client until the point is reached when commissions equal the fee, after which all commissions are retained and the fee is discontinued;

(c) Charging the client a set fee and rebating to him all commissions received, production expenses being billed to the client at cost;

(d) A cost plus arrangement whereby the agency bills the client for a specified sum to represent the agency's profit, and invoices the client for all media and production expenses at cost.

However, in actual practice the most prevalent form of compensation is the first described above which is commission plus service fee.

Public relations

The most difficult part of public relations work is attempting to explain what it is. In simpler terms, public relations involves measures designed to improve the image of a service to create a more favourable climate for its advertising and sales support activities. It covers such a wide range of activities and is used for so many different aims that it becomes difficult to define it.

Public Relations is the "art and science of planning and implementing honest, two-way communication and understanding between a company or an organisation and the many different groups with which it is concerned in the course of its operation." It is also defined as "continuous and consistent representation of an Organisation's policies to the public at large and to sections of the public who have a special interest in the Organisation's activities, e.g., to various strata of employees, shareholders, actual and potential customer as well as its local and national governments.

Public Relations News, a weekly newsletter written for the PR profession in United States of America, defines PR as "a management function that evaluates public attitudes, identifies the policies and procedures of an individual or an Organisation as they affect the public interest, and executes a programme of action to earn public understanding and acceptance." The internationally accepted definition of PR however is that it is "the deliberate, planned and sustained effort to establish and maintain mutual understanding between an organisation and its public."

From the above definitions of Public Relations it is evident that its main function is to inform public about the activities of an organisation. In other words, it is a part of an organisation's total communication effort. Its purpose is to create best possible reputation for the organisation by way of presenting facts. Implicit in all the above definitions is the function of the professional public relations expert, which is threefold:

(i) to ascertain and evaluate public opinion;
(ii) to counsel management on ways of dealing with public opinion as it exists; and
(iii) to use communications to influence public opinion

Public Relations is often confused with and used as a handy synonym for some of its functional parts, for instance, press-agency, publicity, institutional advertising, propaganda, product promotion, and lobbying. The field with which PR is most closely identified is advertising. However, advertising pays for the print space, air time or electronic space in order to sell specific product, while on the other hand public relations which may include some forms of advertising as its tools, covers a much wider and broader range. Generally speaking, PR is the overall catchword for all of its functions.

Public relations in tourism

In the field of tourism, the PR assumes special significance because of the peculiar nature of the product. Here the need for making complete information and facts available to both potential and actual tourists assumes special significance. It involves measures designed to create and improve the image for the tourist product, create a more favourable climate for its advertising and sales support activities, especially in regard to travel trade intermediaries and news media. Favourable acceptance of any tourist destination by the public is of utmost importance. In fact, no business is more concerned with human relations than the business of tourism. Public relations in tourism is used to create and maintain a positive image for a country, a tourist destination in the minds of people who are in a position to influence public opinion (journalists, editors, travel writers etc.), or in the minds of sales intermediaries (travel agents, tour operators, etc.). It is oriented towards creating and maintaining an atmosphere whereby travelling public at large is convinced of the advantages of visiting the country concerned.

Public relations is one of the important functions of the official tourist organisation. In fact, tourist organisations primarily are public relations organisations. The objectives of public relations in the field of tourism may be divided into two parts, firstly the dissemination of information, and secondly the creation of a favourable image for the tourist product.

Public relation techniques

Public Relations make use of several communication techniques. These include:

(i) news and feature stories

(ii) press releases

(iii) films and slides

(iv) booklets and brochures

(v) photographs, displays and exhibits

(vi) advertising

(vii) house journals

(viii) radio and TV scripts

(x) newsletters

(x) stockholder reports

Public relations consist of a number of interrelated activities oriented towards creating and maintaining a favourable positive image for the tourist product. The main tools of public relations in tourist promotion are as follows:

(i) Organising familiarisation tours for travel writers, editors, travel agents, photographers and other kev personnel from different parts of the world as guests to visit the country and to get first-hand knowledge about it. These persons then write about the country visited in the well known travel and other general interest magazines.

(ii) Organising radio and television contests featuring the destination country.

(iii) Organising press releases and arranging press conferences with key personnel connected with the tourism field with a view to disseminate information about the destination.

(iv) Arranging seminars and workshops in the place where the tourist promotion office is located.

(v) Organising cultural programmes, musical and folk shows, TV interviews, exhibitions and national friendship weeks in the country where the national tourist office is located.

(vi) Organising various types of contests about the country.

(vii) Encouraging large departmental stores, organisers of fashion shows and manufacturing companies to project the country or a part of the country as a promotion show case in their premises.

Public relations activities in the field of tourism thus range from distributing a newsletter to organising familarisation visits for key personnel in the travel trade and media. To sum up a professional public relations approach of a tourism organisation can:

(a) Develop and maintain a positive image for a country,

(b) Help generate increased visitor numbers;

(c) Encourage investment in tourist plant;

(d) Attract the interest of intermediaries like tour operators and travel agents.

It can best be achieved through:

(a) Professionally prepared publicity material distributed judiciously to main population markets;

(b) Arranging for key influential media representatives to visit the country on familiarisation tours,

(c) Promoting package holidays and transport services;

(d) Creating major events which will draw attention to the country.

Public relations planning and organisation should be an integral part of an organisation's management strategy and must be conducted on a continuing basis. Public relations function of an organisation cannot be considered as an end in itself or something which can be introduced at a short notice to cope with crisis situation. An organisation should have a positive and planned public relations policy. It is no coincidence that most of the national tourist organisations devote considerable effort to their public relations programmes.

Handling the PR functions

The public relations functions may be handled either by internal staff members or by outside agencies. A PR department within a company or organisation may consist of a single person or several persons depending upon the scope and the size. The larger the staff, the more specialised would be the work of each of the staff members.

Public relations agency

Public Relations agencies generally are retained as either an additional arm of an existing PR department or, if there is no PR department as the sole PR wing. The agencies are hired either on a yearly retainer basis or on special projects/assignments.

In the field of tourism a number of national tourist organisations have been taking the services of PR agencies to take advantage of the market. The tourist destinations have recently become increasingly competitive for tourists and visitors from various tourist generating markets. It is a well known fact that all those countries which appear to be attracting the largest number of tourists are succeeding because they market their country's attractions to the right potential audiences professionally and systematically as well as positively. Much of their success can be attributed to a direct result of positive and competent PR efforts.

PR agencies play a significant role in assisting a country getting a larger share of tourist traffic provided they do their job properly. The selection of a proper PR agency, therefore, is very crucial. While advertising and other marketing tools increase the number of visitors to a country, the communications equipped to complement advertising and thus fully realising a country's potential draw can be accomplished through programmed media activity and with well launched public relations support programmes. It is here that PR agencies come into picture.

Public relations properly planned and executed through a public relations agency in a tourist generating market can present a country in a favourable light and help in the country's efforts to attract more tourists. Public relations also go a long way in positioning a country as a nation whose people welcome tourists, whose hotels and resorts, transportation systems are accommodating and efficient and whose history and culture are fascinating. Public relations agencies take up specific areas on behalf of their clients to which public relation efforts are applied by them. These areas are the basics, areas of concentration on which a beginning is made in building an improved image of a country and its tourism environment. Given below in an outline format are specific areas to which public relations efforts are applied by PR agencies in the field of tourism.

a. *Audience*

1. Individual consumer travellers.
2. Special interest travellers.
3. The travel trade industry...travel agents, in particular.
4. Business travellers.
5. Corporate travel managers.
6. Meeting planners... as appropriate.

b. *Media audience*

1. Consumer travel magazines and newsletters.
2. General interest publications (consumer).
3. Consumer newspapers (particularly those which contain travel sections)... both metropolitan dailies and suburban weeklies and dailies.
4. Travel trade publications.
5. Broadcast...both radio and television... when appropriate and on a 'selected' basis.
6. Special interest publications which deal with recreational or sports activities, entertainment, architecture, and the like.

c. *Implementation and general activities*

1. In-depth discussion of the country's current and future plans, its marketing goals, its research findings, and its specific problems.
2. A review of country's consumer and trade media placements over the past two years
3. Establishing specific MM contacts.
4. Coordinating public relations efforts with advertising& sales and marketing personnel.

5. Establishing methods of contact and information-getting from all those entities which participate in the country's programmes of tourism.
6. Exchanging ideas and information with MTO.
7. Obtaining MTO opinion and approval on placement ideas and on all materials for editorial submission.
8. Reporting actions and results to MTO on a periodic basis.
9. Writing with experience, style, clarity and command of the country's many dimensions.
10. Determining media needs... apropos tourism to country.
11. Providing media writers, reporters and editors current data and background information on country.
12. Providing media with story ideas as well as with finished product news releases and feature stories.
13. Knowing consumer and trade media requirements so that information about the country is timely and presented in an understandable manner.
14. Arranging media interviews with MTO personnel and with "personalities" from the country.
15. Coordinating and advising on visits to country by media personnel.
16. Assisting with travel agent familiarisation trips.
17. Participating with MTO in domestic and foreign trade and association shows.. conventions, seminars and the like.
18. Coordinating with tourism officials, tour operators and airline and hotel personnel, as pertinent to related MTO goals and activities.

19. Updating and keeping current a country press/information kit.

d. *Media activities*

1. *Trade Media:* Ensure continued and complete exposure in all travel and tourism industry trade publications in the market.

Among the many opportunities for editorial coverage:

1. Destination stories and reports (features)
2. Personnel announcements
3. Visiting tourism personnel
4. Inclusions in "business activity" stories and general industry round-ups
5. Reception photographs
6. Policy changes
7. Hotel renovations, redecorations, and additions
8. Sales and marketing information
9. General news

2. *Consumer media print:* Work toward the placement of feature stories about the country in a variety of consumer publications with particular emphasis on travel and travel-oriented magazines and newspapers. The story ideas are limitless. Sometimes, such stories are agency-written; often, contributions and help can be given to writers and editors.

3. *Broadcast opportunities:* More and more radio and television time is now devoted to travel subject. With the approaching penetration of cable programming (television), there will be even more opportunity for broadcast media placements concerning travel and tourism topics.

Therefore, and as appropriate, monitor the broadcast situation and work on placements for the country's positioning and for NTO inclusion.

e. *Special events*

1. *Travel Trade Events Participation:* Advise on and assist with all the travel events in which MTO participates. Organise MTO sponsorship of travel writer luncheons.

2. *Tie-in Events and Promotions:* From time to time, opportunities for charity events, fashion shows, athletic competitions and other events of a one-time nature arise. Sometimes such activities are worthwhile, depending on the publicity value and the business and/ or social importance of these varied possibilities.

Press/Information kits

A well informative information package, in the traditional press kit form, is imperative for dealing with the media. Such press/ information kits are very often handy for supplying information about the country and its tourism resources to people and organisations *outside* the media.

Suggested contents

a. A good selection of black and white photographs, suitable for newspaper and trade magazine reproduction.

b. Photographs of top MTO executives.

c. Two or three feature stories about country (in press release format).

d. Hotel and accommodation information (in brochure format or as lists).

e. Airline information.

f. Within country transportation information.

g. Map of the country.

h. Shopping, climate, currency and other pertinent information.

Sales support

Sales support is another important marketing tool. Sales support activities are all those activities and measures which establish personal or indirect contact with customers or trade intermediaries. In the field of tourism, it is considered to be all those promotional activities designed to transmit to the public and to the travel trade specific and detailed information on aspects like transport, accommodation prices, attractions etc. concerning the tourist services to be promoted in the tourist markets. In addition, the sales support is also a process of training employees of an Organisation to be sales-minded. In other words through the process of information dissemination regarding a product the sales team becomes motivated to participate in the product sale.

Sales support has certain distinct closely related functions which neither advertising nor public relations can be expected to fulfil effectively. It is a channel of communications between the manufacturer or the 'producer' of a tourist service and the 'distributor' or the 'seller' of that service. Secondly, it aids and assists the seller to do his job more effectively with the support of different techniques.

The aim of the sales support activities is:

(a) *to inform* the customers or trade intermediaries, travel agents, tour operators, airlines, etc. about the various services available, their price and quality, etc;

(b) *to assist* them in selling these services to the ultimate users;

(c) *to motivate* them to devote a sufficient level of sales activity to the service promoted.

National and regional tourist organisations as well as tourist service enterprise, and tour operators recognise fully well that their sales and profit depend to a very large extent on the support and assistance they provide to travel agents and also the way in which they motivate travel agents. This is done by way of sales support activities. In order to be able to sell a service (a room in a hotel, seat in an airline) or a destination to the prospective tourists, travel agents or other sales intermediaries need to be aware of certain factual information which includes:

(i) The country's tourist facilities such as existing as well as new establishments, accommodation capacities, price schedules for various services.

(ii) Various travel regulations and formalities such as visa regulations including different certificates needed, custom rules, rates of exchange for currency.

(iii) The various transport and communication services available. The 'schedules of airlines, railways, road transport services, shipping services (where available), their rates.

(iv) Weather conditions at different times of the year, and types of clothing required during different seasons.

(v) The utilisation of existing tourist facilities at different times of the year.

(vi) Plans for opening of new destinations, hotels, transport routes (railways, airlines, etc.) and also plans for expansion of existing tourist facilities.

As a result of advertising demand in the form of enquiries *made by* potential tourists, travel agents and other intermediaries will be created. The potential tourists, travel agents and other intermediaries would now require in addition to the type of information mentioned above, materials such as brochures, folders, booklets, guidebooks, directories, maps and illustrations in order to be able to transform demand into definite bookings. Most of the above material is meant for distribution to potential tourists by the travel agents and other sales intermediaries like tour operators, airlines, etc., either directly or through mail. Almost all the tourist organisations and tourist service enterprises produce the material extensively and make use of it by way of distributing it to travel agents, tour operators, etc. Tourist sales intermediaries on their own also produce sales support material for distribution to potential tourists.

Methods of tourist publicity

The methods of tourist publicity in their evolution have lagged behind in comparison with the developments of the publicity methods of other branches of economy which utilise applied psychology and sociology. They are still mainly based on experience, instinct, routine and technique. Publicity still proceeds from the object with a more or less arbitrary combination of rational and emotional appeals and, perhaps, in consideration of the results obtained by research in publicity media, but in utter disregard of the person to whom the publicity is addressed. So it is not yet clear at all how tourism, whose fluctuating character was proverbial, has now grown into a phenomenon or why the tourist need has undergone a reclassification to other needs in order of importance, as also why, despite the fundamental universality of the tourist need, different human groups have different conceptions about its compositions and the urge for experience.

6

International Marketing of Tourism

Promotion strategies demonstrate that there is a fundamental difference in approach between tour operator led marketing, which is highly specific and segmented, and national tourism organization marketing strategy which is more general. Various typical forms of transactions chain My link the tourist with the primary suppliers of goods and services. The tourist product is then defined as all the goods and services for which the tourist transacts and the tourism market as the sum of these transactions. Transactions are classified by their spatial location: origin (the tourist's home), transit and transport, which may be within the origin country or transnational, and destination, which may be local or international. Tourist transactions are here listed as transport, accommodation, entertainment and amenities, and direct spend on (extra) food and accommodation.

The organization of firms in the tourism transactions chain reflects the forces outlined above. In many cases, retail travel agents are able to offer services to tourists superior to those available by direct purchase. The agents' success depends on their superior access to information and specialist knowledge of markets and conditions., This enables agents to offer a service of advice and guidance to the individual tourist. Agents are also able to act on behalf of the principal, be it hotel, airline, tour operator or shipping company, in a personalized manner. The retail travel agent also offers a one-stop facility, allowing choice and enabling the customer to purchase the whole range of tourism products, thereby reducing the tourist's transactional search costs. The tour operator consolidates the transactions that an independent tourist would make separately, and sells a single package to the customer. This not only gives the customer the convenience of purchasing a single composite product in one transaction, it also enables economies to be obtained on the supply side. The tour operator is able to enter into long-term contracts for accommodation and transport (often leading to internalization of this relationship, that is, the two functions are often combined in a single firm). Consequently, this permits high load factors for aircraft (ships and trains) and high occupancy rates for accommodation. Economies of scale and exercise of monopsony power can also reduce the operator's costs. This packaging enables mass marketing and standardization to take place. Branding by the tour operators across destinations results in increased consumer loyalty to the operator (and transference of loyalty from destination to operator). The operator can give explicit or implicit quality guarantees to the tourist and thus reduce the perceived risks of default, poor service and other transactional uncertainties. Tour operators can market their products via brochures, providing an initial screening of the myriad tourist products potentially available. For the tourist, uncertainty is reduced and quality guarantees are provided. M. F. Murphy shows that individual tour operators are perceived very differently with respect to their competition by travel agents.

Implications

The marketing implications of transactions analysis can be derived by reversing the transactions flow and looking back over the transactions chain. It is a peculiarity of the tourism market that final service providers must aim their marketing at quite different targets, as illustrated by the different types of transactions chain. The direct purchase, self-assembly package implied by chain a requires final service providers to reach the individual tourist directly. In the other types of transactions chain, intermediaries occur and marketing needs to be directed at them. These intermediaries may be tour operators and/or travel agencies. Similarly, tour operators must target marketing efforts at potential groups of tourists and travel agencies. In the rest of this chapter we shall examine, first, the marketing of destinations, secondly the marketing of attractions, accommodation and transport, and finally the marketing of tourist packages. The analysis of linkages and the flow of intermediate products has implications not only for the packaging of tourism services but also for the nature of tourism enterprises in general. The above analysis shows that the nature of the transport function is crucial. The transport function is an important point in the exchange of rights in the tourism transaction chain. If this function is subcontracted to an independent operator this delicate and central function can go out of control: hence, the close integration of transport with other facilities in the integrated multinational. There are important cost implications also. Efficient utilization of capacity is crucial in keeping costs down in transport as well as in accommodation. Complete control of a fleet of aircraft or ships (one ship or aircraft for smaller companies) will impose severe cost penalties if these facilities are not fully utilized. Consequently, there is considerable instability arising from the necessity to balance control of transport with cost-efficient utilization. The transport function is also important because it, uniquely, involves the transnational transfer of rights (and tourists). Its management, therefore, requires great skill and sensitivity. Further, it affords opportunities for international arbitrage and utilization of transfer-pricing techniques, which may have a significant impact on profitability. Finally, the theory has important implications for quality management in tourism. Control of the trans-actions flow enables the integrated multinational to monitor and control the quality of services. This is often difficult to achieve through external contracts, because of the intangible nature of services and the difficulties of exercising day-to-day control other than by direct line management.

The analysis of transactions and transaction costs provides a ism framework for the unification of concepts and analysis in tourism research. It provides a core theory that allows the analysis of tourism demand through the transactions chain and the organization of supply by its distinctive view of the forces driving organizational developments. The changing pattern of industry analysis and the scope of firms can be explained and predicted by internalization pressures. The approach has implications for marketing and for the future organization of the tourism industry, which we now examine.

The marketing planning process for a destination

This section concentrates on the marketing strategy of a destination country or region. The formulation of a tourism plan at various levels is essential, especially when the tourist sector has top priority in a country's overall development choices. Further, the overriding aim of a systematic planning process is, as Argenti suggests, to focus attention on the relevant strengths, weaknesses, threats, and opportunities. Consequently, the development of such a 'tourism-marketing planning process' identifies the main variables affecting international marketing operations of a national or regional tourism organization. The marketing of a destination by largely public sector bodies provides a framework within which private sector organizations can work. The focus is on three areas:

1. Where is tourism now?
2. How did we get there?
3. Where do we want tourism to go?

The main emphasis, therefore, is on a dynamic and continuous process with interrelated and interacting variables. It begins with the client (tour operator or tourist) and ends with the client. The overriding aim is to gather, process and utilize data when planning, executing and controlling marketing strategies and tactics in both the short term and the long term.

Visitor survey

Information on the current tourist market is essential. The large-scale survey of the United States pleasure travel market reported by Taylor is a model indication of this key fact. It is important to know:

who the foreign tourist is;
where (s)he comes from;
when (s)he visits
how (s)he travels; and
why (s)he chooses the destination

A random sample of the foreign tourist population can be taken at the place of exit. Even a small sample can give a clear indication of the above vital issues (for the case of Greece, see Buckley and Papadopoulos, 1986). However, the weaknesses of asking about choice of destination after it has been made should be noted. This is sometimes inevitable on cost grounds, but it should be supplemented, where possible, by motivational studies elsewhere than at the place of visit. Reasons for travel to a destination may include: (1) cultural tourism, (2) 'sun and sea' tourism, (3) winter sports, (4) 'lakes and mountains' type tourism and rural tourism. Although cultural tourism is a year-round activity, the other forms of tourism will exhibit seasonality. Luckily, winter sports counterbalance 'sun and sea' tourism to give some destinations all-year-round possibilities. New segments of the market can be investigated including:

1 Health resorts (including spas?)
2 Marine projects
3 Water ski resorts
4 Two-centre packages
5 Short-break holidays (off season?)
6 Conference tourism

Expenditure estimates for different categories of tourism are important. Expenditure varies by type of tourism (e.g. in general, business travellers are by far the biggest spenders) and by nationality. Mode of travel is also important. Air facilities are crucial for international tourism. Good access by road and rail can provide a major boost for tourism . Cruise passengers may provide a further new and expanding segment, as a high proportion on cruise packages go ashore. The marketing challenge here is to increase spend per visit.

Seasonal fluctuations in demand are a considerable problem in planning tourism. Seasonality results in problems of employment, social and developmental difficulties and deterioration in the quality of services offered. These stem from the fact that tourist facilities, in particular in hotels and catering, are used to full capacity (or often overstretched) during the summer, but during the winter they are often under-used. The literature on tourism recommends efficient and effective promotional campaigns as a means to offset an uneven seasonal demand pattern. However, such actions have, on the one hand, to reflect existing and potential winter demand trends in the tourist generating countries and, on the other, to improve standards of winter tourist facilities in the host country. Apart from such promotional campaigns, there are other ways to reduce seasonality including lower fares and accommodation charges during the off-peak season, as well as special package deals for the winter months, conferences, festivals and sporting events. Unfortunately, control of these is not always in the hands of national or regional authorities and seasonality can be mitigated but not eliminated.

Target marketing

Policy makers and developers of tourism in destinations need to pay attention to visitor characteristics when developing a rational tourism marketing strategy. Clear market segments must be identified and an investigation made of the buying decision factors that predominate in that segment. The tourist product must then be aligned with the client profile. The tourist product is a composite product and there is more than one type of client. In particular, a careful distinction must be made between the tourist and the intermediary (tour operator and travel agent) in deciding on the marketing mix, with particular attention being paid to promotional elements and pricing policies. In addition, the products and services offered by the industry must match prevailing market demand.

Although the above tourist profile may suffice when formulating strategies and policies at a general-purpose level for example, planning basic tourist infrastructure and amenities such a tourist profile will do little in terms of developing an advertising campaign policy in a specific country or market segment. Hence, the need exists, for a tourist profile for each market segment (major country of origin), which in turn can be interpreted in terms of an 'advertising brief for individual promotional campaigns. As Kaynak and Yavas suggested in their study 'A profile analysis of visitors to Halifax, Canada', once purpose-oriented segments are identified they can be mapped, and forecasts can be made of their future importance based on projections of trends, thus helping policy makers to target their strategies more precisely.

Tourism-Marketing audit

As far as 'where is tourism now is concerned, the main elements of a tourism-marketing audit consist of the general domestic and international environments and tourism-specific variables. The tourism-marketing audit begins with an examination of data on the general (domestic) economy, and then proceeds to the outlook for the growth of the market segments served by tourism. The international competitive environment is also included as part of the audit of the main tourist-generating markets served by the tourist industry. The main purpose of the 'external environment' audit is to assess the extent to which sociocultural and economic factors affect the likely course of the action the marketing executive might take in promoting tourism in various markets. This is because world tourist-generating countries exhibit considerable variation in industry structure and national income, both of which critically influence the tourist goods and services they are likely to need, and their ability to buy.

When the general domestic and international environment has been examined, the next step is to identify the tourism-specific variables that affect tourism, and study their relative importance when considering international marketing strategies. As regards tourist market data, it is essential to maintain periodic surveys to identify the type of tourist who travels to the destination and to pinpoint the factors that determine his preferences and purchasing behaviour. In considering the stocktaking of resources, the main objective is to develop a comprehensive list of the tourist sector's 'supply elements', such as tourist infrastructure, tourist accommodation and a host of other facilities and services necessary to sustain a growing number of foreign tourists. This is because failure of the tourist sector to meet future tourist demand at the right time, right place and at the right price could lead to social and environmental problems, as well as the loss of much needed foreign tourist receipts. For a marketing audit to be successful, however, it needs to be carried out on a regular basis; audit programmes should be clearly defined and executives should be trained to use them effectively.

Supply of facilities and attractions

Some of the 'supply' aspects of tourism are listed above: cultural sites, sea, climate, winter resorts, mountains and countryside. Tourism based on such attractions is precarious unless the region can provide the various elements of the 'tourist supply', such as accommodation, infrastructure and the host of other services necessary to sustain a growing number of foreign tourists. In many destinations these elements represent a supply side constraint on tourism. There is clearly a need to develop the supply side in parallel with demand (for example, hotels). Segments, such as conference tourism, cannot be exploited until further large investment has taken place.

Implementation of the tourism marketing plan

Once the market study and resource analysis are carried out the planned application of available resources to achieve tourism objectives should begin. The chart identifies objective and comprehensive procedures, which the tourist authorities can take in translating goals into reality. Thus, the overall policy and major functional plans must be linked to, and exercise influence upon, the current operational decision-making process of all parts of the tourist organization. This can be done by bringing longer-term plans together with annual tactical planning activity for compatibility purposes. In this way, the resultant tourism strategy can be; as Glueck said, 'a unified, comprehensive and integrated plan designed to assure that the basic objectives of the enterprise are achieved'. The important distinction to be made between the tourism-marketing planning Process and the tourism-marketing plan is that the former is a continuous function, whereas the latter is an expression of the output of the planning process at a particular moment and for a specified period.

After the analysis of strengths and opportunities, under the Auspices of the marketing audit, setting tourism objectives should be relatively easy. Objectives should be realistic statements (qualitative or quantitative) of what the tourist authorities desire to achieve as a result of market-centred examination of each tourist segment. In addition, these objectives must be reassessed on a regular basis, having received feedback once plans are implemented. The main purpose of step two in the planning process is to identify and coordinate the public and private sectors so that common marketing strategies can be formulated. Related to this is step three, which is to assess opportunities and constraints at the domestic and international levels. The overriding aim of these two steps is to examine the existence and efficiency of the various supply elements (for example, tourist accommodation, infrastructure, labour and other tourist amenities), in order to assess whether the tourist sector can meet future tourist demand.

After the main demand and supply aspects of tourism have been examined, step four proceeds to evaluate and project the potential for each major tourist-generating market by means of specially commissioned market research studies and forecasts. In addition, market intelligence information can be gathered, processed and utilized through a formalized marketing information system. The heart of the marketing plan is step five, where the emphasis is placed upon the manner and extent to which each controllable marketing-mix variable is used and the way such factors are combined into a single strategy for each segment. The construction of individual programmes for product, price, distribution and promotion is a direct consequence of the overall tourism-marketing objectives, which in turn are influenced by internal and external constraints.

After the marketing-mix variables have been decided, the next step is to assign specific responsibility for carrying out individual tasks of the plan to various people, to instruct these people what to do and how to carry out their tasks, and to integrate time schedules so that allocation and sequencing of marketing effort are run efficiently. As soon as specific procedures are agreed upon and implementation begins, a control programme must be established, which should provide the tourist authorities with the necessary information to monitor progress towards predetermined objectives. Once the plan is implemented and performance monitored, implementation and objectives should be re-examined and revised in accordance with newly emerging market facts, and the whole cycle should start again.

The conclusion to be drawn from the above remarks is that the use of such a customer-oriented process has the advantage of being a simple and effective tool for analysis and implementation of strategies. However, it is essential for the tourist authorities to make sure that future prospects of inward tourism are adequately assessed by volume growth, tourism revenue and relative market share in each tourist-generating country before decisions on the desirable target market are taken and the allocation of strategic marketing funds among the various segments is made. The ability of national tourism organizations to have a major impact on the market is limited in many cases because the relative resources available are much less than those of carriers, operators and other actors in the market.

A tourism-marketing planning process has been developed, in which the main variables affecting the international marketing operations of the regional and/or national tourist organization have been identified. The main emphasis is on customer rather than product orientation and on a dynamic and continuous process with interrelated and interacting variables. The importance of a market-driven rather than a product-driven approach cannot be overemphasized. The planning process begins with the client (tour operator/ tourist) and ends with the client. The overriding aim is to gather, process and utilize data when planning, executing and controlling marketing strategies and tactics for both short-term and long-term dimensions.

The purpose of the above process, expressed in its simplest form, is to answer three central questions:

Where is tourism now, that is, what is the current state of the tourist industry?

Where is tourism heading?

How should the regional tourist authorities organize their resources to get there?

This marketing planning process can be used as a marketing tool to identify the problems, in order to avoid treating the wrong symptoms, and to take advantage of opportunities. In short, this is a structured approach to the collection and analysis of information in a complex tourism environment, which is an essential prerequisite to problem-solving. It is a conceptual framework that can be useful to all tourism-marketing planners when formulating target-marketing strategies. Tourism-marketing planning, therefore, is multifaceted and requires an interdisciplinary and integrated approach. In addition, the applicability of the above marketing planning process in a dynamic market place depends on its flexibility and adaptability to market changes.

'The Market for tourist services is not static and it requires constant adjustment on the part of destination marketers. The ability of the destination's organizations to influence other key actors is often limited. One of the key roles that a national tourism organization can play is to increase the bargaining power of domestic actors (such as local hotels) versus tour operators. Cooperative behaviour in the destination country across the public-private sector divide is likely to be important in increasing the local value added from marketing efforts. Studies of marketing destination regions can be found in Goodall and Ashworth, Ashworth and Goodall and Pearce.

The marketing of attractions, accommodation and transport

Classic analyses of marketing examine the four Ps: product, pricing, promotion and 'place' (distribution). These elements are crucial in the analysis of marketing elements of the tourism package. The following section examines the problems of product formulation in tourism. Then pricing is considered, followed by an analysis of promotion and targeting strategies. Distribution systems and their organization follow.

Product formulation

One of the basic difficulties in marketing attractions in particular (historic buildings, parks and gardens, wildlife, museums, art galleries, amusement and leisure parks, natural scenery, monuments, etc.) is product formulation, that is, deciding what the product actually is and how it should be sold. As many aspects as possible should be encapsulated, but the product should not become so diffuse as to be unmanageable. This has a physical aspect delineating and protecting the boundaries of the attraction (and preventing free entry) and a conceptual aspect selling the quintessential elements of the product and appropriating all the returns from this. Consequently, a holistic approach should be taken to packaging, selling, advertising and distributing the attraction: the experience needs to be 'all of one piece' to create distinctiveness. A great danger with high-profile unique attractions is the feeling that the MOW does not need to be marketed. This is a misconception. Benefits to the locality, region and country will be lost if a marketing approach is not taken for instance, excursionists only will be attracted, spending only the admission fee in the locality, or high spending segments (such as business travellers) will be missed altogether.

Similar problems occur with transport facilities and accommodation. Operators are selling a service, and this has to be marketed in a comprehensive fashion. Transport users demand ease of access, promptness, friendly and courteous treatment during the (often harrowing) experience of travel, information, comfort and secure delivery. All too often one aspect is promoted (for example, airline I food) often the most trivial element on the grounds that the operators take for granted more crucial elements, which may lead consumers to discriminate in favour of rival suppliers and substitute means of transport.

Accommodation providers also need to consider the key elements that lead a consumer to choose their product rather than a competitor or substitute. As in all other cases, price will be a factor, but so too will quality, ease of access, location including proximity to other attractions and facilities services provided and promotion.

Pricing policies

Pricing policies in the tourism services industries are dictated by a number of key structural characteristics. These include:

1 Perishability of the product.
2 Volatility and seasonality of demand.
3 Capacity constraints.
4 Competitor strategies and the existence of close substitutes.

The perishability of the product requires that instantaneous decisions are necessary, and continuous reappraisals of strategy and tactics, in the pricing area as elsewhere, are the norm. The volatility and changing nature of demand, both seasonally and secularly (changes of taste), also require attention to information collection, understanding and response. Capacity constraints mean that price can be used to ration scarce capacity or as a weapon to fill spare capacity in order to at least cover fixed costs.

In any discussion of pricing policy it is necessary to say that changes in price are not necessarily the best response to changes in the external environment or to strategy changes. However, price is a flexible tool and one that takes instant effect, given that demand is not completely inelastic. Pricing does not take place in a vacuum. As the customer response or demand side constraint, it will the case that pricing policy will be constrained by the reaction of competition. In markets dominated by a few producers (Oligopolies), it is virtually certain that pricing moves will be matched and possibly anticipated by competitors, leading (in the extreme case) to a price war. The crucial strength of pricing policy is the ability to discriminate on prices. Ideally, different prices should be charged to each group or individual, with a different price elasticity of demand. In an ideal world, this infinite price discrimination would maximize profits. In practice, this can be achieved only imperfectly. To achieve good practice in price discrimination, the operator needs to have a clear view of segmentation possibilities. Price discrimination can be practised spatially, temporally, by price-income elasticity and by, tying in the product to other purchases, including bulk or repeat buying. Success in price discrimination depends on the ability to, prevent arbitrage (or reselling) in the market. Spatial price discrimination can be practised where it is difficult to transport the service (as in most cases of tourism services) or where it is difficult or prohibitively expensive for the consumers to travel to purchase the service in a different location. Temporal price discrimination means selling the same service at different prices at different times. This practice can exist only in the absence of adequate future markets, which is generally the case in tourism markets. Discrimination by income categories depends on a targeting approach. Tied purchases of services are largely involved in package deals and repeat buying in deals offered by chains of hotels. The potential for all these forms of price discrimination exists in tourism services.

We should not, therefore, be surprised by the multiplicity of prices that exist in tourism services or by the complicated price structures that companies offer. In general, the service will have a published price a long-term benchmark price with a number of effective prices, fixed only in the short term. The effective price will vary in space, time, segment and according to what else is purchased.

Pricing, like any other policy weapon, will be used to achieve the goals of the company: profitability, growth, market share, return on investment. The goals will vary according to prevailing demand, competitor reaction and the strategic situation of the company (including the need to cover costs).

Promotion

The marketing of tourism-related services is a complex issue because of the different means needed to reach the end-user. The independent traveller in the unpackaged chain is an end user and, as an individual or family purchaser, he will be difficult to reach other than by mass advertising techniques. The purchase of services through a travel agent requires travel agents to be informed of the services that suppliers can provide, requires point of sale terms to be available to the agent and may require incentives to agents to encourage them to push the services in competition with alternative service providers. The tour operator, who provides an inclusive tour (commonly known as a package tour) will have considerable bargaining power when confronting a single service provider (for example, a hotel) or destination. It will be necessary to present a more subtle type of promotion to the tour operator to gain favourable terms or to achieve a contract! Once an end-service provider is included in an inclusive tour, then the responsibility for promotion rests largely with the tour operator. Having contracted for a given number of beds in a hotel for a season, for example, the tour operator will wish to fill those beds by adequate promotion. In a sense the ultimate supplier of tourist services is even more removed from the end-user by the full transactions chain purchase of an inclusive tour via a travel agent. Independent travel agents will be dealing with a number of competing tour operators, who will be aiming promotional activities at them and through them to the purchaser. Competition for the agent's space and time can lead to a transfer of returns from tour operators to travel agents. This has given a major incentive to direct selling operations by tour operators and to captive travel agencies, related to selling holidays of one operator or to preferential selling of the co-owned operator's holidays. Promotion strategy is thus closely linked to the make up of the market facing the service providers and the institutional setting of the tourism market. Coordination between the efforts of the largely public-sector destination marketing and the more specialized targeted private-sector firms is an essential element in successful marketing and planning.

Distribution

The basic aim of a distribution channel is to bring the product to its market. However, as we have seen, it is difficult to define product and market with exactitude in tourism services. The first part of this chapter illustrated the different distribution chains, and each chain has its own imperatives. For travel agents, like any retailer, the choice of location is vital in order to encourage entrance to, purchasing the goods and services on offer.

The forces making for the internal organization, control and coordination of separate activities within one firm have been the subject of analysis for a considerable time. Indeed the internalization of previously unrelated activities within a single organization determines the scope of the firm. Internal markets, particularly those for labour services, enable coordination and planning of sets of transactions. Such internal arrangements are frequently more satisfactory than long-term contracts. This may be because of increased efficiency, largely through the reduction of transactions costs, or it may enable the entrepreneur to appropriate more of the gains from contracting. The boundary of the firm is governed by the margin where the costs of organizing an extra transaction within the firm are equal to costs involved in carrying out that transaction on the open market. Changes that enable the entrepreneur to carry out direction more effectively (for example, the development of systems of communication, computerization, improved management techniques) will thus tend to increase the size and scope of the firm.

The task of the entrepreneur is thus to carry out the direction of resources at lower cost than the market. He may be aided in this by exogenous factors, such as the tax system. Transfers of intermediate goods and services within the firm are governed by internal transfer prices, largely set at the discretion of management, rather than by market prices. Such transfer prices may be manipulated in order to reduce the firm's tax bill. This benefit of internalization is particularly important in cross-national transactions where transfer prices can be used to move funds and engineer profit increases in low tax regimes.

In markets, like tourism, that are information intensive, there are additional advantages arising from internalization of certain activities. The market for information is subject to uncertainties arising from the possibility that the buyer cannot use or understand the information that he is purchasing. Organizing insurance for buyer uncertainty is costly and difficult. When buyer and seller are the same firm, mutual insurance can be arranged and a satisfactory price can be fixed. Discriminatory pricing of information can also be exercised in an internal market. When resale is possible, price discrimination cannot be practised in an external market. In addition, internalization avoids difficulties arising from bilateral concentration of market power, for example, a hotelier in a favoured location transacting with a tour operator. If the tour operator owns the hotel, uncertainty is reduced, although this, of course, is not insurance against unpredictable externalities such as terrorist activities or political crises. The application of these principles applies in three directions: horizontal integration, vertical integration and conglomerate diversification. Horizontal integration applies to integration Of similar activities. A hotel chain is an example of the integration of similar facilities in order to gain economies of scale and market power. Economies of scale are gained in central booking facilities, staff training, bulk purchasing, etc. Market power is gained in increasing the chain's share of the total market and facilitating practices such as branding (across essentially separate facilities), joint advertising and promotion, and cross-group pricing policies.

Vertical integration occurs where facilities in different positions in the value chain, or marketing channel, are combined under one ownership: for example, the integration of an airline within a tour operator's facilities. The superiority of internalization over contracting out of these facilities is generally that internalization gives complete control and allows quality of service to be carefully monitored. The integration of ownership of travel agents and tour operators is a further illustration. Such vertical integration choices are strategic moves by key actors to secure control over facilities upstream or downstream, in order to improve efficiency (and quality of service) or to deny the facilities to rival operators. Conglomerate diversification is the integration of essentially dissimilar activities within a firm: for example, a book retailer owning a travel agency. Often the motive here is risk-reduction. The firm spreads risk across a number of disparate activities and is able to sustain troughs in business activity is one area while remaining able to siphon off profits during peaks. The naturally cyclical nature of the travel and tourism industry means that many of its constituent parts hotel chains, travel operators and agencies are ultimately owned by large, diversified, conglomerate firms. At a less elevated level, there is often a case for hotels, attractions and leisure facilities to come together on a voluntary basis in order to conduct large-scale activities such as central booking or advertising. This quasi-internalization is an attempt to retain the independence and entrepreneurial flair of the smaller unit while reaping economies of scale in other areas.

Marketing analysis—the SWOT framework

In order to deal with the problems listed above, it is useful to have a fixed framework in which to organize the essential foundations of a marketing exercise. Such a framework is provided by organizing these elements into strengths, weaknesses, opportunities and threats. The best way to illustrate is to give an analysis of one attraction as an example.

The cruciform chart is a means of organizing a considerable amount of information. The upper two quadrants (strengths and weaknesses) are the outcome of an internal appraisal . This is an attempt to identify key competitive competences and significant deficiencies in the operating organization. The lower two quadrants show the outcome of an environmental analysis, focusing on likely changes in the environment, both positive (opportunities) and negative (threats). The SWOT analysis is therefore a distillation of a great amount of (it is hoped) reliable information. The conduct of internal appraisal and external analysis should be a continuous and constantly updated process.

Buyer behaviour

The analysis throughout this chapter has emphasized the necessity to pay attention to demand. Purchasers and their needs are not homogeneous. It is necessary, therefore, to collect and to update information on purchasers and their behaviour. It is dangerous to define buyers and their purchasing behaviour too closely. The alternative purchase for a package holiday may be a new bathroom kitchen or down-payment on a car. 'Do-it-yourself' purchases and leisure expenditure are close substitutes for the disposable income of many families. Factors that reduce disposable income will have, a, prior impact on spending, reducing all forms of consumer expenditure examples are taxation levels, and interest rates, the burden of debt greater. Analyses of consumer behaviour have moved away from reliance on price as the sole indicator of purchasing patterns. There is necessity to investigate and influence wherever possible the motivations underlying the purchase of tourism products by firms hoping to sell them. See, for example, the motivational study on Saudi Arabian travellers by Yavas.

It is essential that tourism firms and operators identify and monitor y variables that determine consumer behaviour. These include income levels, factors that influence disposable income (such as taxation), changes in the distribution of income, patterns in consumer spending.

The understanding and prediction of consumer behaviour is a vital competitive skill for firms in the industry. Social, political and technological change will all affect buyer behaviour. In addition, the Promotion and advertising strategies of tourism companies can affect purchasing patterns. Promotion strategies introduce the product offering, attempt to confirm and reinforce positive attitudes to the product, extend and deepen consumer awareness of the product, and attempt to change attitudes and behaviour toward purchasing the firm's product. Promotion does not end with purchase.

Customer services and aftercare are vital elements of promotion essential to ensuring repeat purchasing.

The key issue in examining marketing in tourism-related industries is marketing by whom, to whom? The crucial operational question for marketing professionals is 'what is the target market(s)?'. It follows from that operational question that product formulation, pricing, promotion and distribution must be predicated on a clear strategy of targeting. This can only be achieved by an extensive and ongoing policy of information-gathering and analysis. An under standing of organizational forces is a key element in a coherent market strategy.

Information is the lifeblood of tourism planning. It is essential for destination marketers to have information on the type of visitor attracted. This also applies to operators of hotels and attractions, whose customer lists are vital sources of excellent marketing information. Marketing efforts must be targeted at those segments most likely to respond and to the desired client profile.

7

Managerial Aspects of Tourism

The importance of planning in the development of tourism related activities is aimed at creating a balance between the tourism related activities and the local environment. This is particularly the case in developing countries. Here the impact is strongest because they must develop an infrastructure that preserves the existing unique cultural characteristics and also promotes all-round socio-economic development. At the same time, they should also preserve and enhance their physical environment in order to promote tourism.

Tourism promotion and infrastructural development for tourism related activities is bound to have a series of socio-cultural, socio-economic, physical and environmental impacts on the habitat which would require a systematic evaluation and analysis, using scientific techniques, before development decisions are taken. These are more conspicuous in environmentally sensitive settings of hill, wild life and beach resorts and other traditional culturally sensitive destinations. Any programme for tourism development should thus have the underlying objective of promoting the positive impacts and mitigating the negative impacts on the social, economic and physical environments of the designation areas. The main thrust areas for development of tourism in the National Five Year Plans having implications on Physical Planning for Tourism in macro and micro contexts are identified as under:

1) Development of selected tourist circuits and centres which are popular with the tourists instead of spreading limited resources over a large number of circuits/centres.

2) Diversification of tourism in Indian from the traditional sight-seeing tour centered (primarily places of cultural tourism interest) towards the more rapidly growing tourism market within the framework of country's milieu with a conscious attention to the aesthetic, environmental and socio-cultural implications of tourism projects.

3) Development of non-traditional areas such as a) trekking b) winter sports c) wild life tourism and d) beach resort tourism to exploit the tourism resource of the Himalayas, the vast coastline with sandy beaches and abundant sunshine and wildlife to attract more tourists and lengthen their period of stay in the country.

4) Restoration and balanced development of national heritage projects of both cultural, historical and tourist importance to exploit advantages if India's unique place as a cultural tourism destination and to utilize tourism as a major force in support of conservation of national heritage.

Planning and development of tourism complexes in their macro, meso and micro dimensions should enable integration of tourism resources and tourists activities to derive the optimum benefits on terms of social m economic and ecological objectives on the one hand and satisfaction of tourists' needs for infrastructure, leisure and recreation on the other. Tourism resources and tourist facilities have their spatial interaction in terms of tourist nodes, areas and networks. Organized development of tourism complexes should be geared to a system of functionalities generated in space, both interdependent and inter-linked to each other, so that in its regional or area-wise context, optimization of benefits from investments accrue.

Tourism Development Plan shall need to cater to the diversified demand for infrastructure of a wide variety of tourism activities projected for different topologies of destination areas, keeping environment all conservation in view. Tourism activity areas embrace a wide variety of destination points:

1) Extensive areas of natural scenic beauty for passive recreation,
2) Recreational and leisure areas like beach resorts,
3) Climatic comfort areas like hill resorts,
4) Cultural tourism areas including historical places, monument complexes, places of fairs and festivals,
5) Religious tourism areas like pilgrimage centres and temple towns,
6) Adventure tourism areas namely are designated for trekking, rock climbing, mountaineering, skiing, etc., and
7) Special interest areas, namely wild life sanctuaries, areas of exotic flora and fauna, bird sanctuaries, etc.

Tourism is a resource based industry and resource evaluation is important to identify areas for resource conservation to promote tourism vis-a-vis other demands. It is also imperative to identify and designate the resource under various competing uses and further to arrive at the capacity which will be matched by the supply location wise and activity wise. The concept of carrying capacity is significant for scientific planning of tourism facilities and infrastructure, particularly in relation to sensitive tourist destination areas like the hill areas. It is the threshold of tourist activity, beyond which facilities are saturated (physical capacity), the environment is degraded (environmental or ecological capacity), or visitor enjoyment is diminished (perceptual or psychological capacity). These concepts are now generally accepted but difficulties in measuring the thresholds (except perhaps physical capacity) have restricted the use of carrying capacity as a planning tool. A blend of factors determining physical and ecological capacity of recreational areas with those that determine the social capacity, makes it possible to determine optimum capacity guidelines. In nature reserve areas and ecologically sensitive areas namely the hilly environment more reliance has reserve areas and ecological capacity guidelines and these would need to be formulated with respect to the environment of which the habitat is an integral part. Very often this is ignored because of immediate profit motives of developers. This is not a healthy trend and needs to be curbed.

Tourist resources: The only sound basis on which any programme of tourism development can be formalized is the complex of natural or man-made attractions that an area can offer to visitors. This resource base is often neglected or taken for granted without organizing a complex systematic inventory or analyzing its special merits, potential and constraints.

Here, two basic questions arise:

a) how to identify the resource base of an area? and

b) how to assess the intrinsic value of such resources to their market?

The first calls for an inventory and the second calls for appropriate evaluating techniques. The resource value in terms of attractions of a tourist resource is a product of demand and supply with minimum social, economic and environmental impact. In this regard, environmental impact studies need to be carried out before undertaking any programme of tourist development.

If tourism is to effectively function as an integral component of the development package for any region, development of tourist related physical infrastructure becomes imperative. Infrastructure should also be conceived on an integrated basic considering the overall needs of the area and the host population. Imparting and adequate measure of attractiveness to a resort is a vital aspect for development of tourist spot. Broadly speaking, the three main components which collectively impart this quality to the tourist centre could be identified as:

i) Assessability; ii) Accommodation Facilities and Services, and iii) Recreation

i) Accessibility

Accessibility in the context of a tourist spot or a tourist destination areas consists of:

a) Local accessibility to the specific place of tourist interest within the town from the nearest transportation inter-change point namely an airport, a railway station or a roadways terminal, or from the entry point to the town as the case may be. It also means connecting roads form one spot to the other to facilitate easy movement of tourists within the town and its vicinity including adequate parking, servicing and garage facilities.

b) Regional accessibility to the tourist centre and tourist destination area by the three conventional modes of transport namely roads, rail and air from the nearest tourist embarkation point in the country, and transport linkages to other important centres of tourist interest within the region.

ii) Accommodation facilities and services

Provision of adequate accommodation at the tourist centres and destination areas satisfying quantitatively as well as qualitatively, the needs of tourists, is an important factor. Accommodation can sometimes provide the incentives to the tourist for a longer stay. In the present context of India, lack of this basic amenity has even been a greater deterrent to tourist influx compared to "lack of accessibility". The quantum and type of accommodation to be provided at individual centres would again depend on an assessment of needs in each case, but by and large, accommodation for tourists should be comfortable, complete with all utilities and services and built-in infrastructure facilities required for residential development as per the location, and varying range and choice from economic as well as physical points of view.

iii) Recreational aspects

If availability of accommodations is largely influential in prolonging a tourist's stay, adequate provision of recreational elements at a tourist centre can lengthen the tourist season as a whole. This aspect of development is vitally important for relaxation and diversion. Recreation, in the context of tourism, has many manifestations, and includes, apart from organized outdoor active and passive recreation, all forms of commercial recreation as well. The problem in the context of metropolitan and major cities is simplified to some extent as the tourist can draw upon such recreational facilities, both indoors and outdoors, which form legitimate requirements of the local population. However, in case of smaller palaces, which may be of even larger tourist interest and attraction, exclusive recreational amenities are to be provided for the tourists. But this has to be done keeping in view the socio-cultural milieu and environment and the destination.

Tourism plan: In all countries of the world where a systematic approach to tourism development has been a part of the national policy, emphasis has been given on formulation of Tourism Master Plan for development of tourist infrastructure. This has been conditioned by several factors: Some of these area as following:

1) Positive and negative factors which have influenced or may influence proper exploitation of the particular tourist resources.

2) Carrying capacity of particular resource for tourism development in relation to environmental and ecological impacts as well as socio-cultural impacts of tourism development programme at macro and micro levels.

3) Problems relating to financing and management of access and infrastructure provision.

In Corsica, designation of favourable zones for tourist infrastructure, identification of important natural and man-made resource areas and their designation for protection, and provision of Access and Land Control Policy for development in and around the designated area, are important components of an overall Tourism Master Plan. Such a policy plan at a macro level shall guide programme at micro levels.

In regard to coastal tourism development in France, the Master Plan lays emphasis on:

a) Tourism development organized generally perpendicular to the coast in the hinterland of existing resorts, and

b) Creation of extended sectors of environmental protection which re designated as protected forests, natural reserves, agriculture and forestry land to provide ecological conservation.

In all these exercises, environmental protection and conservation of tourism resource and natural endowments have been the key factors. In any case, the importance of Physical Development Plans as the key component of the overall Tourism Master Plan at both macro and micro levels can hardly be over-emphasised.

At macro level a comprehensive Master plan for tourism development should consist of:

a) Recommended policies and priorities for tourism and recreation,

b) Programme of infrastructural development,

c) Physical plan detailing location of areas to be developed, conserved and protected and in what manner,

d) Strategy for implementation, coordination and financing,

e) Evaluation of resulting ecological as well as socio-economic impacts and their resolutions,

f) Action programmes, and mechanism of monitoring the changes and their effects.

As a first step towards formulation of a Master Plan, it would be necessary to conduct surveys of the tourist resource characteristics and potential. These should be analysed in relation to physical, social, economic and environmental attributes of the destination area.

The physical component of the Master Plan would establish a framework for spatial organisation of tourist facilities and infrastructure, accessibility and linkages, both internal and external, of various parts of the tourism activity area and zonation of major recreational and open spaces as an integrated open space system.

Measures and programmes for environmental protection, landscaping, site development are important components of such a Master Plan. Besides, linkages of the complex with the surrounding hinterland as well as measures to control development along the periphery of the complex should also be spelt out.

It is also imperative to consider appropriate planning measures to integrate the tourism complex development with the surrounding smaller settlements whose socio-economic development is linked with the tourism activities concentrated in the complex.

These policies and programmes are to be detailed out and concretised through an integrated Physical Development Plan for phased development of the complex and provision for tourism infrastructure.

Physical development issues

Development of tourism is not entirely a matter of economics as it has implications on geography, sociology and ecology of the area and its people. All these need to be thoroughly understood and analysed for optimum socio-economic gains to the host community and the area of tourist activity. It calls for a comprehensive approach to tourism planning, particularly in the areas where products are made up of vulnerable resources with and renewable.

Tourist spots and destination areas are points of high congregation of people and have to be provided with safe and convenient access, parking facilities, pedestrian movement and congregation spaces, tourist infrastructure facilities for boarding and lodging, civic services, tourist shopping, leisure and recreational activities depending on the location, attractiveness and projected tourist infrastructure shall vary from place to place. However, in all cases, all these infrastructure facilities shall have to be spatially organised in relation to the tourist spot proper and functional relationship between them are also needed through proper physical planning and design.

Tourism related activities are by nature land-extensive, whether the tourist spot is part of a town development area or is located in isolation in the form of a complex, or is a township by itself, as tourist resort. Emphasis should be laid on integrated development of the tourist centre as a whole, and each individual development scheme for various tourist spots should be conceived as a part of the larger Town Plan Area Plan. In this context, it should also be emphasised that in the case of metropolitan and major cities, tourist requirements, particularly in the field of infrastructural facilities, could be met substantially from those already available and provided for in the plans for theses cities. But in small towns and isolated locations, infrastructural facilities and services, which have to be provided for tourists, should be so arranged spatially as to enable them to be used by local population as well by appropriate extension and augmentation. As a result, investment in such locations on tourism could largely benefit the all round growth and development of the small towns where the tourist spots are located. Further, the Development Scheme should be implemented in appropriate phases. It should be so conceived as to allow for augmentation and expansion in the future.

Zonation of a tourism activity area is an important first step. In case of tourist spots located within the city, it is necessary to zone such spots alongwith sufficient area around them as Tourism Activity Zone or Special Areas. In a city, which has a number of such tourist spots, (e.g. historical cities and pilgrimage towns) efforts need to be made to identify even larger integrated zones encompassing several spots in one complex to enable integrated approach to physical development. In such cased, tourism infrastructure planning and physical development of individual tourist spots should be conceived within the framework of overall tourism development plan.

The tourism development plan should cover:

(a) accessibility and linkages to various tourists spots as part of the city network,

(b) internal circulation based on limited vehicular accessibility and predominantly pedestrian oriented,

(c) zonation of land around each spot for locating required tourist infrastructure facilities, as well as

(d) ensuring through suitable zonining regulations as far as possible that high intensity development does not come up in the vicinity.

An important underlying concept should be to maintain the identity and sanctity of the tourist spot through zoning of passive uses in its immediate environs.

Within the designated site for tourist infrastructure development, the basic considerations should be that the tourist spot proper should stand out and not get engulfed by infrastructure facilities. To enable this, internal spatial organisation of the designated site should be so conceived that the infrastructure complex is directly accessible from the main access road, leaving sufficiently wide green reservations between tourist spot and the infrastructure complex. It is, therefore, necessary to provide for a low profile development within the designated site. It is also not desirable to spread infrastructure facilities, over a large area but to plan all the facilities as a complex for better servicing in terms of utility and efficiency, leaving majority of the designated site for developing as green spaces.

Conservation through design

Conservation in the context of tourist centres includes preservation of their "tourist character" and this aspect is more vital in the case of small towns which as a whole are tourist attractions on account of their heritage and historical importance. Physical expansion as also economic diversification of such towns should be so planned that their heritage and historical sanctity is maintained physically. This could be done by keeping sufficient green buffer zones around them and the new development, in the larger interests of tourism promotion.

Physical conservation in a tourist spot may be manifested in a general beautification and renovation of the tourist spot to make it look brighter and attractive with well laid out gardens, pavements and tourist equipments, namely tourist literature, guides, curio shops, kiosks, etc. While this is a matter which deserves utmost restraint, design consciousness and sensitivity, emphasis should be more on preservation and conservation rather than resorting to large-scale renovation and beautification.

Conservation of the existing natural features in site development, particularly for tourism related activity zones, is important for maintaining the attraction for tourists. In addition, generous planting of trees according to a properly designated landscape plan should be an integral part of the site development programme. Within the portion of the site designated for the infrastructure facilities, a low rise development should be stipulated alongwith basic design controls for buildings.

Spatial design aspects

The primary objective of a physical development scheme for a tourist spot or a tourist centre is to attract the tourists. For this visual design aspects and aesthetic considerations play an important role in their formulation and implementation. This pertains to laying out and approach road, landscaping, renovation and general beautification, or provision of residential accommodation for tourists.

Physical planning for tourist spots and complexes therefore, should attempt to synthesise basic land and infrastructure planning principles with Urban Form and Landscape Design parameters so that emerging development is functional and environmentally compatible, as well as visually and aesthetically attractive.

For individual spots of tourist interests, or a group of them, a Spatial Design Composition needs to be conceptualised. This should be in relation to physical characteristics of the tourist site and environs. Such an effort enables a rational development of the site as well and optimal exploitation of the Tourist Resource.

The basic principle should be tó arrange and locate all tourist infrastructure facilities off the visual axis to the monument. Similar principle can be adopted in larger complexes, by conceptulaising an overall Spatial Design Composition within individual spots of tourist interest can be treated as part of the overall composition. In exclusive tourism areas of 'Scenic beauty', view-points can be identified for similar design treatment as landmarks and points of maximum attraction, within an overall Planning and Designing Scheme for the designated area.

Community: Tourism as a recreational avenue has immense potential in modern society. In those strenuous days of work culture under the oppressive gaze of the clock, various regional assets of every place are projected prominently to provide evanescent respite. However, the majority of pleasure seekers and tourists take these regional assets to be a means to an end. They are not aware of the circumstances generally, under which the tourist resorts were developed. Human beings should be considered most privileged and fortunate among all species in so much as they utilise nature's bounty to the best of their advantage by the judicious exercise of their thinking capacity. It puts an important responsibility on human begins to conserve and nature earth's resources and various regional habits.

It begins with a discussion on the life style of the village community prior to the arrival of the British in India. In particular, it focuses on the nature of resource sharing by different groups within the community. It, then, talks about how the organisation of the community was transformed by the arrival of the British, who had a very different understanding of the nation of community. Further, it goes on to define and describe various kinds of regional assets. It takes up mountains and cultural environment as two examples of regional assets. This Unit also outline some of the areas of conflict which were introduced in the traditional community with the coming of the colonial rulers. In particular, it takes up the example of the hills of-Uttarakhand where the changes in the traditional economic structure had a far reaching impact on the life and culture of the hill communities. Finally it attempts to explain the concept of sustainable development in the context of tourism and prescribes ways in which sustainable development can be brought about without injuring the interests of the local communities.

In Pre-colonial India, village communities were in many ways self-sufficient and dealt with the machinery of the state as a group. In the plains, taxes were paid in the form of surplus production of grain to the state by the village community as a whole, and not by any individual householder. Village Councils regulated most of their socio-economic affairs themselves. Any recourse to an outside authority was a rare occurrence. Though each member of the community had a piece of land to be cultivated, the peasant did not have the exclusive right to sell or dispose it off. Ownership of the land was collective, more so in the case of common lands. The caste based village society had developed a variety of instructions to regulate the use of resources. The pre-colonial rulers only claimed the taxes on the produce and not the right on the land itself from the village community.

There were various ways in which the traditional communities adapted to their existing habitat. They organised themselves to live in harmony with their surroundings. For instance in pre-British Maharashtra, village community assigned village guards to prevent any unauthorised wood cutting in village common land. In addition, they had to harvest and deliver all the wood needed by village householder. Harvests from village common lands were governed by a variety of regulations, notably quotas on the amount harvested by different families and in different seasons.

Here, it is appropriate to talk of the different ecological stratum of the various caste groups in terms of the habitat they occupied, and the relationship with other caste groups with whom they interacted. We can take the example of Masui Lukheri village situated on an island in the estuary from the river Aghanashine close to the town of Kumta in the state of Karnataka. Spurs of the hill ranges of Western Ghats ran along this region right upto the sea, giving the region a rich mosaic of territorial, repariars and coastal habitats, supporting a great diversity of natural resources. One can find as many as 13 different endogamous groups co-existing in the same region. Resources use was diversified among different castes, fishing community (Ambigas), agriculturists

(Malakkis, Palgars and Naiks), horticulturists (the Haviks), entertainers (Bhandaris and Deshbhandaris), service castes (Kooleyas-barbers and Madwals-washerman), artisans (Slets, Achari and Muhkri) and trades (Gowd Saraswats). These different caste groups had their characteristic modes of subsistence and often occupied their distinct habitat much like the species within a biological community. Within this institutional set up of caste system, different social groups were regularised in harmony with each other and their habitat.

With the advent of Europeans into the largely insular habit, in the mountains or elsewhere, new symbiotic and community based relationship developed between the colonial settlers and the indigenous habitat. Though unified into a single social field, the Europeans tended to form a separate community. This was cohesively strengthened by shared ideas, cultural values, urban tastes and leisure activities. It led to the reorganisation of the community, now comprising European ruling elite and the Indians in a subordinate position, regulated by the local municipal authorities and other kinds of state control. Thus, the diversified grounds, forest dwellers, agriculturists and urban dwellers came into close interaction with each other during the colonial times, which has wide ramifications.

Every place has its regional resources in the form of landscape, ecological settings, historical monuments and other places of interest. World Tourism Report throws light upon the various assets of the different ecosystems:

1) Coastal areas, including beaches, marine areas and wetlands: Well developed beaches have the appeal and the carrying capacity for volume tourism. Marine parks and wetlands with their fragile ecosystem are better suited for adventure and special interest tourism.

2) Mountains and wilderness areas: High mountains, forests, moors, deserts, lakes and rivers are mostly visited by tourists interested in nature or special activities such as climbing, trekking and cross-country skiing.

3) Inland rural areas: Agricultural lands, forests, lake shores and riverbanks can provide appropriate location for country-side retreats and special interest tourism such as farm and village stays.

4) Urban areas: Culture, monuments, special events (sponsored festivals) and special facilities for conventions and exhibitions can attract great number of tourists.

5) Small Islands: Natural resources such as coral reef, mangroves, seagrass beds and forests in addition to the coastal and wilderness aspects of a small area may make islands especially attractive destination areas.

Nature reposes in all its majestic glory in the Himalaya and Nilgiri mountains in India. Most of the hill resorts were developed during the colonial periods mainly as a retreat from the summer heat for the British. Darjeeling, Ooty, Mount Abu, Shimla, Nainital, Mussoorie are a few examples. However, today from the tourists' point of view these hill resorts are being marketed with varied attractions. For example, let us take Darjeeling.

From Darjeeling, the beauty of whose sunrise is famous the world over, one can see Phalut Everest, Mahakalu and Kincherying-the first, third and fourth highest peaks respectively and more than twelve peaks higher than any in the world can be seen. To these natural resources have been added attractions like the Tea Festival during which the cultural heritage of the region is kept alive. A journey on the toy train is another attraction in itself. Mountaineering, trekking, rock climbing sking, river rafting, golf, nature tours, etc. are packaged as tourism products, besides the natural scenic attraction. Efforts are being made by various governmental organizations and the private investors to highlight the natural attributes of the mountain regions to the optimum and maximises their benefits for the tourist industry. Most of the hill stations have been large tourist enterprises, particularly from the colonial period onwards. In many hill regions tourism is the largest business enterprise on which the local economy thrives. Variety of herbs and wild flowers and plants mushrooming in abandon, covering the mountains in thick foliage, add to the natural beauty and richness of the mountains. In order to preserve this rich foliage and plant life, many hill stations have maintained botanical gardens. Llyod's Botanical Garden of Darjeeling far outsurpasses the other public gardens in variety and size. Cryptomaria, introduced from China and Japan (by the British imperial rulers), Briches, alders, maples, oaks, rhododendrons, gloss-leaved pepte, scarlet blossomed Erythrims, dalilias, lilies, and hydrangeous and primrose bloom in abundance. There is another prominent botanical par at Ooty. It was initially laid out by a gardener specially called from Knew, England during the nineteenth century. Emily Eden, sister of the Vicroy Lord Eden during 1830s, expressed these natural aspects the impression it has on the weary travellers. She described the mountain air as "a cool sort of stuff, refreshing, sweet and apparently pleasant to the lungs." She found the Himalayas to be "the sweet pretty like hills, with " red rhododendron trees in bloom in every direction and beautiful walks like English shrubberies cut on all sides of the hills." The colonial rulers likened the Indian mountains to the European hills. Many of the scenic landscapes of the mountain ranges of the Southern Asia (in particular) were compared to the European landscapes. Sir Thomas Munro, Governor of Madras during the nineteenth century, compared the face of Ooty's "numberless green knolls of every shape and size" to the "smooth lawns of an English park".

Mountain's refreshing air also has natural regenerative power to attract the tourists and the invalids. It is not without reason that the mountain places are considered natural sanatoriums. for the tourists, Indian hill places have offered great facilities of restoration to health to those labouring under maladies. Thus, for the aged and the invalids, mountain sites have been ideal environs to recuperate.

For foreign tourists, these hill stations have the climate akin to the temperate climate of Europe. If the heat of the Indian plains becomes unbearable for those from cooler environs, then the hills are the natural choices. It was one major reason why the colonial rulers of Indian set up Summer capitals up in the hills at Shimla, Darjeeling, Nainital, Ooty, Ranchi, etc. A number of educational institutions with boarding facilities at various hill resorts have added to the tourist traffic. The local communities are devising new ways to exploit these natural resources for tourism- the latest being opening of remote hill tribal areas to tourists.

Cultural environment

Cultural environment is composed of people and their culture: folklore, dress, handicrafts, religious handicrafts, work and life-style. It also includes the built environment from individual buildings, historic monuments and archaeological sites.

Indigenous tribes form an important part of the cultural environment. In the context of the hill tribes, their lifestyle and customs form an important part of the habitat. Continuance of the traditional form of customs, rituals and folklore forms an attraction in the world constantly undergoing fast changes. In the records of the travellers to the hills of Darjeeling and other hillstations, there exist numerous references to the customs and practices of the hill tribes. Practices and lifestyle of the tribes are a part of the cultural environment of the hill resorts. They hold an appeal for the travellers from different cultures. It is a cultural encounter of the 'advanced' accident and the traditional, 'exotic Orient" in the most direct manner. Many European writers have written in detail about the tribal settlements, customs, daily life, rituals, festivities and mode of expressing sorrows and joys as peculiarities. Habits and attitudes of various hillmen were broadly generalised by the British writers of the nineteenth century. This general impression has carried forth in more recent times. For example, Edward J. Buck, and early twentieth century author of a book on Shimla, characterised Tibetans as "simple shepherds of Tibet". Wild and unkempt looking fellows with their long hair falling down-a unfavourably compared to the "delicate Aryan features of the Punjab hillmen." However, Buck found Tibetans to be eminently truthful, honest and chaste, easily amused, easily satisfied and very sociable.

The Bhutias include Sikkimese, Sherpas, Dhrukpa and Tibetan Bhutia. These people are a cross-breed between the Tibetans, who settled in Sikkim, and the aborigines of that land, the Lepchas. Lepchas are original inhabitants of the Darjeeling hill tracts. Their number and their customs and lifestyle have been gradually diminishing since the onset of British empire into Darjeeling. Sikkim gazetteer of 1981 describes them as: the 'rongpa" (ravine fold)." They are, above all things, woodmen of the woods, knowing the ways of birds and beasts, and possessing an extensive zoological and botanical nomenclature of their own. They have been rightly considered by scholars as "born naturalists." A characteristic trait of the Lepchas was that they had separate names for nearly every bird, plant, orchid and butterfly to be found in their region. Sir Joseph Hooker, a renowned 19th century naturalist, was full of praises for these naturalists in his Himalayan journal He wrote in 1848:

"A more interesting and attractive companion than the Lepchas I never lived with: cheerful, kind and patient with the master to whom he is attached, rude but not savage, ignorant and yet intelligent; with a simple resource of a plain knife he makes his house and furnishes yours with a speed, alacity and ingenuity that wile away the well known long hour."

Lady Dufferin, during late 1880s, described 'Tendook', A Lepcha chief and the usual costume of the Lepcha men. They dress in "a selves petticoat", wrote Lady Dufferin," red jackets, a hat like flower pot turned upside down, with a peacock feather struck in the front of it. These men all beat big drums." This somewhat amusing description her and the analogies she drew up provide a highly touristic impression of the tribes. A travelogue of the 19th century also observed this distant costume of the Lepchas:

"Their dress is quite unique and graceful. It consists of thick blue and white, or red and white cotton cloth. This is crossed over the breast and back, leaving the arms bare and free, and descends to the calf of the leg, it is then gathered in round the waist by a leather or ornamental girdle,..., the women's dress is a slight modification of the men's but with a loose kind of bed-gown over it. They wear heavy silver ear-rings, a profusion of imitation coral and coloured bead necklaces. They take great pride in their hair plaits."

The fondness of hillmen and in particular hillwomen for jewellery is also drawn out in case of hill tribes around Simla. Edward J. Buck observed the hillwomen to be fond of gay attire and bangles and nose-rings. He also drew up a colourful picture of a Simla hill chieftain" "He is a mountain chieftain, whose home is lonely castle on hillside overlooking a great rich valley which is his own. One cannot help observing how gallantly he is dressed in gay but well matched colours and cloth of richest coloured material." Such descriptions indicate the extent of curiosity that existed among the European visitors vis-a-vis the native hill tribes. Such colourful narratives about their dress, food, habits, fairs and festivals intrigued and enchanted the tourists.

This enhancement for the tourists was further stimulated by the colourful festivities of the hills. Edward Buck vividly described the famous Sipi fair held annually at Tara Hill, Simla. It gives an insight into the traditional form of gaiety of the hill people. He wrote:

"On the one side,... picture dozens of swings and roundabouts crammed with hill people in a blissful state of happiness, on the other a long line of stalls, crammed with glass bead necklaces and cheap finery of every description and surrounded by a merry, excited through of wrangling purchasers. Add to the above the dozens of sweet shops with their overpowering scent of ghi (butter) and frizzling sweet meats, the crash of tom-toms, the chorous of dancing jampanies,'... any you have a fair idea of the fun bustle and noise of Sipi.

Like the Sipi fair of Shimla hills, the Tibetan new year, celebrated in Darjeeling hill tract, has also attracted writers and tourists. 'Devil dance,' in which the participants dance wearing animal masks, is important part of the festivities. Thus it is clear that the culture environment of the traditional hill community is exceedingly light hearted, generous to a fault, fond of pleasure in any form, excitable and aggressive to a degree.

Besides the culture of the hill tribes developed over the centuries, the Raj created its own cultural milieu in the form of the institution of hillstations and its trappings. 'Raj nostalgia' is in evidence in a number of residents of the hills. Many tourists also seek the 'Raj' culture in the country clubs, the English type cottages and hotels with typical English furnishings and tastes. Grand public Buildings erected for the Imperial rulers are the everlasting monument, opened for public viewing. Viceregal lodge at Shimla (now Rahstrapathi Niwas), 'Shrubbery, the Lieutenant Governor's residence at Darjeeling, various clubs and other public buildings, theatres and townhalls are the contribution of the British community to the hill environment along with the mall roads. In fact, cultural environment is a major tourist attraction.

Tourism development and other economic activities, in particular in the hills, such as tea industry affected the lifestyle of the indigenous community. British enthusiasm and assertive display of their technological and bureaucratic superiority, eroded the traditional lifestyle of the local hill habitat.

Local environment of the hills was modified to suit the needs of the European elite. Space was modified for the development of metropolitan forms of amusement for the urbane Europeans. Reserved forests and plantations were encouraged as the imperatives of the colonial state.

In the process, the traditional village community, with its common property rights on the collective holding of the lands and the common pasturage was pushed into background. Easy access of the village community of the Kumoun region, the Lepchas of Sikkim and Darjeeling area of the Todas of Nilgiris was restricted. Large scale feeling of the forests led to the marginalisation of these hill communities. The colonial intrusion disturbed the traditional lifestyle of their hill people centered around their sacred groves and divine herbs. Lepchas, the forest dwellers, and the born medicine men with their extensive knowledge about the Himalayan herbs and flora and fauna were served from their traditional forest habitat by the developmental pressures of the colonial state.

The benefits of these economic enterprises such as tourism and plantations did not reach out to these hillmen in terms of both quality and quantity. These paharies (hillmen), as the British distinguished them from the plains people, were absorbed into these economic enterprises lower down the ladder. They were largely employed as bearers, khidmatgars, peons, pony riders, rickshaw pullers, etc. which did not provide them with the decent source of livelihood.

More direct advantages accruing from these mountain resorts as they emerged as tourist destination, were appropriated by the outsides. Either the British tea planters or the European hoteliers reaped wholesome profits which their club culture contacts enabled them to acquire. These club culture contracts were continued with other Indians from the plains replacing the Europeans.

During the course of the nineteenth century, when the British colonisers ventured into the mountains, one finds the exhaustive description of the mountain landscape. From the scattered references about the main mode of livelihood we find that hillstations were dotted with small hamlets with limited cultivation being carried out, owing to the unevenness of the terrain and limitation of sophisticated technique for leaving the land. Thomas Munro observed in the 19th century about the Ooty region:

A few hamlets inhabited by the Bargaras, an agricultural are scattered on the face of the hills. The cultivated fields, running up the hills to the very top, have a beautiful effect; but the cultivations is thinly spread and probably does not cover one-tenth of th ground.

Agricultural community lived alongside the forest tribes as much in Ooty as in other mountain regions of pre-colonial India. Notwithstanding the spatial separation between the field and forest, these various occupational groups had relationship of interdependence and symbiosis.

In the pre-colonial times, the resource-wise diversification between different castes and social groups had, to an extent, avoided any conflict between these groups. For instance, in the hill range of Western Ghats of Maharashtra the Kunbis had the monopoly of hunting will animals, while the Gavlis maintained livestocks and use of fodder and grazing resources.

Similarly, in the Nilgiris, Todas reputed to be the aborigines of the area, were the pastoralists and nomads. They also practised some amount of shifting cultivation. Badagas were the agriculturists of the area who primarily engaged in tillage and cultivation. Kptars, Kurumbas and Irulas were the menial service class.

In Darjeeling region, Lepchas were the forest dwellers, Bhutias were largely the traders and Nepalese were the agriculturists. This mutual sharing of resources also contributed to a harmonious life.

Aspects of tension and conflict comes into focus, when we place the colonial developments against the cultural ecology of the Himalayas in particular and Indian sub-continent in general. Let us take the example of Uttarakhand (the hill tracts in U.P) to understand this aspect better. Traditionally, the area of Uttarkhand did not witness a sharp class classification, unlike the extremely stratified villages of the Indo-Gangetic plain. This diffused class differentiation prevailed in all the mountainous regions. The absence of sharp class cleavage within the village society, owed its origin to the ecological characteristics of mountain society. The limited extent of the cultivable land restricted the possibility of extensive cultivation. Similarly, the fragility of the soil and poor communications hampered the growth of intensive agriculture for the market.

As a result of these ecological constraints, the agricultural economy of Uttarkhand did not produce much surplus. Also, the small peasant proprietor was the dominant class in Uttarakhand, big land lord and agricultural labourers were very few. Since there was no sustained yield, there was close co-relation between the forests, pastures and the fields. In the permanent hamlets, oak forests provided both fodder and fertilisers. This enabled the hunter gathers and pastoralists to continue their traditional mode of resource use and helped the pre-colonial communities to track a distinctive path on inter modal cooperation and co-existence.

However, the colonial intervention completely transformed the social, ecological and demographic characteristic of Uttarkhand. The traditional structure was destroyed and the new changes only benefited the Europeans. Colonial exploitation was an important part of capitalism as it emerged in Europe. An important feature of capitalism was that it produced an atomised society which was in conflict with the traditional forms of living based on collective activity and consumption by the entire community.

Similarly, colonial state control too meant a negation of the collective appropriation of nature by the community as a whole. Colonial forest laws recognised only individual rights of users and initiated the fragmentation of social bonds. This process was hastened by commercialisation and capitalist penetration. The produce of the forests no longer belonged to the hill villages. Extensive tea and coffee placations were set up by large-scale deforestation and the appropriated produce benefited the colonial elite. In the process, Lepchas of Darjeeling and Todas of Ooty faced extinction as they were deprived of their sustenance from the forests.

In Uttarkhand, negation of community ownership led to a sense of alienation with their habitat. These hill dwellers, who had nurtured the forest growth by preserving sacred groves, etc. now grew indifferent to the forest. Goaded by the loss of their habitat by the 'reserve' forests and scientific management brought about by the colonial rulers, these forest inhabitants quickly exhausted the resources left to them, out of fear that their conservation would lead to state appropriation.

While farming system in the Himalayas continued to be substance oriented, cumulative demographic, social and environmental changes undermined the hill society's capacity to feed itself. Moreover, the rapid developments of the commercial and industrial society degraded the hill ecosystem leading to further reduction in productivity. It led to the fragmentation of the family and community structure. While the diversification of resources use between different castes moderated or removed intercaste competition, the fragmentation of the community structure and lack of livelihood intensified the competition during the colonial times. Once the linkage between the agriculture and forests was broken, there emerged intense competition for the different source of livelihood. All this meant disaster for the traditional economic structure.

Ramchandra Guha thus sums up in his book, The Unquiet Woods:

> "moreover, by exposing their subjects to the seduction of the industrial economy and consumer society, the British ensured that the process of ecological change they initiated would continue, and indeed intensify, after they left Indian shores".

These economic changes have had their political ramifications. The forest communities have often resisted these changes being brought in their region against their will. In Tehri region in Uttarakhand, for example, localised resistance movements against commercial management were organised in 1904, 1906, 1930, 1944-48 to claim a full and exclusive control over forests and pastures.

Characteristics of the host society to be taken into account include population size; demographic composition and vitality; ethnic, social or religious structure. For example, is the population increasing or decreasing, is it composed of more than one ethnic group, what social customs are evident? As White notes, such social/demographic characteristics can have a significant influence on the degree of development and change: 'a strong area can sustain the capitalization and provision of labour from within itself, while a weak area is immediately more susceptible to outside economic influences in the form of external investment and immigration, so that the local socio-cultural structure is quickly changed'.

Economy: The size, diversity and vitality of the economic at various scales—national, regional or local—are further factors which need to be considered. The economy in question may be well developed, developing, depressed or in decline. It may be broadly based or heavily reliant on a single sector, a strong economy or a dependent one.

Tourism may already be a significant sector or totally unimportant. These factors will influence the extent of local participation and degree of external involvement as well as determine the cost and benefits to different sectors of society and the ultimate impact of tourism. Having examined the existing situation and having established contemporary trends, the next step is to predict what would happen/would have happened if tourism does not develop/had not developed. This may involve a projection of demographic and economic trends. What would have happened, for example, to the alpine communities had tourism not been developed?

Tourist development: As has been stressed earlier, it is essential not to think of tourist development as merely the growth of some monolithic phenomenon known simply as 'tourism.' Each particular project or development must be examined in terms of the range of specific elements and the process characteristics. What precisely is being developed, by whom, for whom, how, when, where and why are the fundamental questions which must be asked here. The question of timing, for example, is critical. Where tourism develops gradually over a number of years there will be longer period for social and environmental adjustment and local participation may be increased as needs in terms of labour, supplies and capital will be met more easily by local resources. Where rapid development occurs, there may be apparently greater immediate returns but it will be unlikely that the host community can respond to such demands and provide all that is needed so that, in the medium and long term, 'leakages' from the area may be large, effectively reducing benefits to the community.

What part of the environment, segments of society and sectors of the economy will be affected/have been affected, by what (specially), in what ways and to what extent are the principal questions to be asked next. The impacts of past developments will usually be assessed more readily than future impacts can be predicted, particularly if the conditions existing before the advent of tourism have been satisfactorily established. Comparison with past developments will also be useful in assessing future impacts, keeping in mind, of course, the effect of differing contexts and types of development.

To be able to evaluate fully the impact of tourist development the difference between tourism developing and it not developing must be assessed. This involves measurement of a wide range of parameters in quantitative terms and a more general qualitative assessment of others. What should be examined, and how, are questions which have been subject to a certain amount of debate and answered with varying degrees of success. Two associated problems arise—the techniques to be used and the availability of appropriate data and information. Data deficiencies are very common, particularly in studies of past developments, for as Figuerola points out, there is often a shortage of even the most basic statistics. In general there are few earlier reports to draw upon or with which to compare the present. A further difficulty arises here in comparing the different types of impact. Whereas economic costs and benefits may be presented in purely dollar terms, social and environmental issues cannot usually be expressed so conveniently. Problems may also arise in establishing the causal links between different facets of development and changes in the host society or environment. It might be shown rather readily that new employment opportunities have arisen out of the development of tourist facilities but accompanying changes in the economic aspirations and behaviour of these workers may be due as much to external influences (such as the mass media) as to direct experience of the tourist industry. Various techniques used for examining the different impacts of tourism are described more fully below. Having identified sources of adverse impact, various measures might be suggested to reduce these. Spatialy, for example, two broad strategies might be adopted—concentration or dispersal of tourist activity. The seasonal concentration of tourism is a further problem and a staggering of holidays may alleviate social and environmental pressures and lead to a more balanced economy. More specific suggestions might be to relocate facilities, increase the capacity of sewage treatment plants or to limit the activities of visitors through zoning.

Where alternatives exist, the merits of each case should be assessed and their impacts compared. Basically, two sets of alternatives may be identified. Firstly, there may be alternative sites available for a specific project, for example, the development of a new ski-field. Is site A more environmentally stable than site B? Second, in a particular context, a range of development possibilities may exist. Overall, is project X more desirable than project Y? In addition, it may also be necessary to compare the impact of tourism with other development strategies if a range of choices exists. What will be/would have been the impact of developing forestry or expanding agriculture instead of tourism? In practice, many studies, particularly of past developments, have ignored several of these steps. Attention has commonly focused on step, what resulted when development occurred with only cursory discussion of the context and project and little or no consideration of what would have happened had there been no tourist development. Moreover, few impact studies are at all comprehensive, with most concentrating on a single domain be it economic, environmental or social/cultural. Factors accounting for the incompleteness of past studies include: data deficient, inadequate methodologies, lack of resource, a failure to appreciate the different processes of development, the belated recognition of issues other than economic ones, the scale of analysis and the lack of an interdisciplinary approach to the problem—most impact studies have been written by one or two researchers is more often undertaken on a broader basis. There has also been a tendency for research on the impact of tourist development to concentrate solely on the destination areas. This is in part an outcome of the lack of emphasis given to the processes of development and a failure to recognize the linkages between origins and destinations or demand and supply, both geographically and structurally. Thurot adopts a more holistic approach in his review of carrying capacity and presents a model in which he distinguishes between internal (contextual) factors in the destination region associated with the host society and economy and the local environment, and external ones, whose origins lie elsewhere, either in the generating region or the transit region. In particular, conditions in the generating region will not only affect total demand, but factors such as institutionalized hodidaymaking and national habits and attitudes may give rise to a marked seasonability in demand and to distinct preferences for certain types of holidays and destinations. These conditions can accentuate the impact felt in the destination region by concentrating demand spatially and at certain times of the year, week or day. The nature, capacity and organization of he transport network in the transit region may accentuate further this spatial and temporal concentration. Conditions in the transit region, notably those which influence the cost and ease of travel, may also significantly affect the volume of traffic generated and thus the pressure which develops at the destination. This region will also be affected by demand emanating from the generating region. Severe bottlenecks may be experienced at the interfaces of the different regions; that is, the outskirts of cities and the approaches to resorts, at the beginning and end of the main holiday season and at the start and finish of the weekend. Moreover, feedback loops might be built into the system. If the destination region becomes saturated, this will limit the propensity to travel from the generating region, reduce the amount of choice available to potential holidaymakers or lower the quality of their experience such that the original need to escape may not be satisfied. However, the impacts felt in the generating region need not necessarily be all negative, particularly if economic considerations are taken into account.

While some of these relationships have already been identified and explored to some extent elsewhere, the approach has not yet been generally adopted in the tourist impact literature. One of the few impact studies incorporating processes of spatial interaction is that by an interdisciplinary team concerned with assessing environmental stress arising out of the growth of ski tourism in Switzerland. A central feature of their study was a model of ski tourism and the natural landscape comprised of three sub-systems: A—the outward and return trip, B—accommoda-tion and stay in the resort, C—skiing and associated facilities. Each of these sub-systems was then examined in more detail in terms of the specific problems which arose and possible solutions which might be implemented. Problems in sub-system A, for instance, essentially result from the traffic generated by skiers and give rise to such impacts as an overloading of arterial routes, congestion in villages *en route* to the forth. Solutions to these problems include extending existing roads or building new ones, creating a more efficient public transport system or building new ones, creating a more efficient public transport system or developing alternative ski-fields and redirecting traffic to them. Each of these choices may ease the pressure in one area but generate new skiers elsewhere.

The regional development of tourism continued to grow in importance being integrated with the planned development of other economic resources and environmental protection. Government financial assistance to tourism, now available in most countries, became increasingly available for tourism infrastructure as well as accommodation. Public vocational training facilities for tourism grew rapidly and more efforts are being made to balance future supply and demand. Co-operation between tourism and environmental authorities increased and a more vigorous application of planning law to protect the environment made it imperative for tourism authorities to be consulted in physical planning matters likely to affect the future development of tourism. Tourism marketing was characterized by a growing body of research and forecasts mainly conceived for marketing-strategy. Certain countries took action to improve their marketing management. As in past years. significant amount of publicity were centered on special promotional themes. An increasing amount of investment and promotional expenditure was devoted to extending the tourist season. Certain countries participating in a special OECD Working Group on this to each other, agreed to explore the possibility of solving their own peak problems at the regional level.

Technical assistance in the field of tourism continued to grow in size and scope and now covers the most significant aspects of tourism. Such assistance ranges from group training courses to direct financial participation in tourism investments. Facilitation of tourist travel abroad showed little change as a high degree of liberalization is already enjoyed by Member countries.

Today most of the hill stations are over crowded and all types of scarcities have emerged because of the unplanned growth of tourism. It is time to realise that tourism can play a positive role in the socio-economic development of the hill areas and hill towns of the Himalayan and Sub-Himalayan region. However, this possible provided resource planning and management is done on scientific lines. Tourism planners must recognise that the models applicable to the plains would not fit the Himalayan terrain, nor would the experience of European and American mountain resorts be necessarily ideal in the Indian context. Accelerated pace of development since the 1950s, gradual socialisation and broad basing of tourism, education awareness, and improved transport and infrastructure facilities, have all contributed to enormous proliferation as well as concentration of tourism related infrastructure in the popular hill-stations like Simla, Nainital, Mussoorie and Darjeeling, to name a few. In the absence of advance planning in a systematic manner, relentless influx of the tourists to such centres has disturbed the demand and supply equilibrium. This has given rise to: acute problem of landuse; environmental pollution and degradation; stress condition on infrastructure, transport and services, and creating conflicting conditions.

A scientific approach to tourism planning in the hill regions and the habitat, would require analytical studies relating to:

i. likely impacts of development on the local environment and the hill habitat,

ii. evaluating the tourist resources and infrastructure needs,

iii. establishing certain developmental thresholds consistent with the carrying capacity of the area and similar aspects.

The focus in all development programmes,

particularly tourism related development, should be primarily on:

i the upgradation of the quality of life,

ii. safeguarding and maintaining their socio-cultural identity, and

iii. a general improvement in the town's economy.

In fact tourism should be arrive at a consensus on the policy of resource use in the Himalayas. Equally important is to identify and conserve the sensitive eco-systems in the higher Himalayas. This could be done by designating them as biosphere reserves with buffer and core zones. Tourism activity should thus be pursued with care and sensitivity in such zones. Hill districts and regions are characterised by a dispersed settlement pattern. Here individual settlements and settlement clusters exhibit a low structural profile. The built form is characterised by tradition hill architectural styles and motifs, intimate social spaces, interplay of levels and gradients, and never-changing street scape. The design of the tourist complex, and facility clusters should be sensitively dealt with and should not result in a loud imposition of an alien, cosmopolitan massive looking built mass in a low profile traditional setting. Maintaining a design continuity according to the architectural heritage in tourism complex development should be a prime concern. A dispersed locational pattern of tourist amenities and facilities in a hill-tourism region, linked to select nodes will enable development of a hierarchy of tourist village complexes. This can also be catered to, by non-conventional sources of energy, and thus economise on conventional energy consumption. Moreover, such a spatial pattern of tourist complexes will help diffuse tourism related activities and its concommitant benefits over a wider area, rather than concentrating at one or two spots in hill districts. This will avoid causing conditions of conflict and the threat to the hill environment. Tourist village concept on a reduce scale, should also be incorporated while planning for addition tourist infrastructure in an existing resort. This shall enable planned dispersal of tourist related infrastructure wherever necessary.

The major coastal settlements, like port cities tend to attract not only the location-specific port and maritime activities, but also allied activities and uses. These include industry, trade and commerce, as well as institutional uses, which have a tendency to proliferate, through a suction phenomenon, rendering other off-coast settlements impoverished. As a result of this the coastal tourist resources like beach, etc. get depleted owing to urban and industrial expansion or pushed out to more outlying locations. An integrated policy approach, therefore, becomes for overall development of a coastal settlement to cater to both tourism and non-tourism functions effectively. Development of a coastal settlement as a tourist resort requires a scientific approach to planning interventions. The planning interventions have been identified as follows:

a) Sea resorts and beach tourism complex should be ideally conceived as separate entities. They should be physically separated from the main urban node to avoid functional conflicts in tourism and non-tourism activities.

b) Tourism infrastructure should also be planned in dispersed manner along vantage stretches of the coast-line appropriate for tourism activities. It should not be unduly concentrated at one or two locations only. This would extend benefits from the tourism activity over a wider area, particularly to the smaller rural settlements of the coastal hinterland.

c) A comprehensive scheme for extensive water-front development incorporating various recreational elements should be formulated for optimal utilisation as also protection of the tourist-resource.

d) It is also imperative to discourage proliferation of tourist infrastructure along the coast, by organising its development perpendicular to the coast, generally in the hinterland of existing resorts. At an area level, the main network should be planned to run along but a distance away from the coast, connecting various urban centres in the hinterland region and having link roads leading down to select points of tourist infrastructure on the coast. This concept widely advocated in coastal resorts development in several European countries like France, Yugoslavia, Cyprus, Corsica, Turkey, Greece and others, is directed at regulating, reducing and restricting the development pressure on a resource of finite capacity like a coastal zone, exposed to incompatible uses. Its salient points are restricting access, limiting facilities, zoning the various activities, scheduling the activities and developing alternative destinations.

Tourism can be major stimulus for conservation of important elements of the cultural heritage of an area because their conservation can be justified, in part or whole, by tourism as tourist attractions. In other words, the conservation of the cultural heritage acquires a certain economic incentive through the instrumentality of tourism. These are as follows:

1) Tourism provides the incentive and helps pay for the conservation of archaeological and historic sites and as attractions for tourist that might otherwise be allowed to deteriorate or disappear, thus resulting in the loss of the cultural heritage of an area. In South and South-East Asia, most of the archaeological and

historic preservation taking place can be economically justified in such lower income countries because they provided attractions for tourists. In some cases such a Sri Lanka, admission fees paid by tourists is used directly for archaeological research and conservation.

2) Conservation and revitalisation of traditional arts, handicrafts, dance, music, drama, customs and ceremonies and certain aspects of traditional life styles directly feed into tourism.

3) Conservation of important natural areas also acquires an impetus. Without tourism, those natural areas might be developed for other uses or allowed to ecologically deteriorate, with consequent loss of environmental heritage. This factor can be of especially important benefits in countries with limited resources for nature conservation. For example, marine conservation especially of reef areas, is receiving much attention in some places because these are important attractions for tourism.

4) Financial assistance for the maintenance of museums, theatres and other cultural facilities and activities and for supporting the organisation of special cultural festivals and events because they are important attractions for tourists as well as for residents. Admission fees paid by tourists at some major museums in the world, for example, provide substantial revenues to maintain those institutions. Similarly, tickets purchased by tourists at important urban theatres help support their maintenance and other facilities.

8

Travel Agency in Tourism

The role of private sector in the organisation of tourism is very crucial. In most countries which are in any manner concerned with the tourist industry, the private sector plays a very important role. The private sector's role is not limited merely in selling the tourism product but often also in producing it as many individuals, companies and corporations are involved in promoting, developing and financing tourism. Travel agency is one such organisation in the private sector which plays a key and crucial role in the entire process of developing and promoting tourism. It is the travel agent who packages and processes all the various attractions of the country and presents them to the tourists.

The organisation and sale of travel as it is known worldwide today, really began in July, 1841. A book salesman, Baptist preacher of Derbyshire was on his way to a temperance meeting in Leicester when he was inspired with "the idea of engaging a special train to carry the friends of temperance from Leicester to Loughborough in England and back to attend a quarterly delegate meeting". He thought that it was a sounder proposition to persuade a railway company, then in its infancy, to carry a train load of passengers at a very cheap fare than to run the train at 'Standard' fares, but possibly only a quarter full. The man was Thomas Cook and his idea was put into operation with characteristic speed and efficiency. A few weeks later 570 travellers made the journey by the Midland Counties Railway at a specially reduced fare. This venture was soon followed by excursions to various other places, and in 1843, 3,000 school children were taken on a trip from Leicester to Derby in England. However, Cook's real beginning as a 'mass excursionist' was the Liverpool-Caernaryon trip of 1845. The tourists travelled by rail to Liverpool, from where they took a Steamer to Caernaryon. The advertisements for the trip caused a sensation and the response was so overwhelming that a second trip had to be arranged. Cook thought of every detail.

The grand circular tour

By the mid-nineteenth century 'holidays away from home' had become customary for a larger social group than ever before. Cook's initiative and organising genius provided the final impetus. In the winter of 1850-51 Cook was already negotiating for a tour of America, but his attention was diverted when he was offered the opportunity of conducting excursion trains to the Great Exhibition of 1851. Altogether, Cook conducted 1,65,000 people to and from the Crystal Palace. In 1856 Cook succeeded in organising his first 'grand circular tour of the continent'. The tour was so successful that it had to be repeated six weeks later.

Thomas Cook's conquest of Europe began in 1862 when he made arrangements with Brighton and South Coast Railway for passenger traffic to the continent. Cook's Paris excursions are the first true 'package tours'; all the details of transport and accommodation were prearranged. In 1863 Cook Visited Switzerland where his ideas were greeted with enthusiasm by hoteliers and railway proprietors. His next stop was Italy. Cook first made a personal survey of Turin, Milan, Florence and Genoa, to familiarise himself with their touristic attractions and facilities. In 1864 the first guided tour of

Italy left England with applications far in excess of the available tickets.

The 1860s also saw the introduction of Cook's railway and hotel coupons. Cook personally examined the system by travelling through Italy to Vienna, down the Danube into Hungary and from there into Switzerland. By the 1890s, 1,200 hotels throughout the world accepted his coupons. Starting in 1868 Cook arranged regular circular tours of Switzerland and Northern Italy. 'Thomas Cook and Son' had established their first official London office in 1865. John Mason Cook now joined his father as a permanent partner and took charge of the London office. From that year on, the history of Thomas Cook and Son was one of continuous expansion. In the year 1880 John Mason Cook left for India and established offices in Bombay and Calcutta and formed the 'Eastern Princes' Department. In 1887 this department arranged the visits of Indian princes to Queen Victoria's Jubilee Celebrations.

By the end of the, century, by taking advantage of nineteenth century advances in transport technology, Thomas Cook and Son had effected a revolution in tourism No longer the preserve of the rich and he aristocrats, tourism was now an industry. Armed with Cook's hotel and rail coupons, the tourist could demand uniform prices and standards of service and accommodation. This new standardisation had distinct advantages. It meant comfort and convenience and less need for decision making on the part of the individual tourist. The tourist was less likely to experience discomfort or embarrassment.

The management of the Company passed on to John Mason Cook's three sons in the year 1898. At the time of John Mason Cook's death, the Cooks business included three main aspects of travel--selling tours, banking and shipping. Soon after the Second World War, the British government acquired the principal interest in the Company. In 1972, the British government sold the company to Midland Bank Consortium. Much has happened since that date. The business of the Company is now one which, together with its associates, has over 700 offices and 13,000 employees covering the world from the Antipodes to the North American Pacific Coast and from the North Cape to Cape Town and South America.

The American express company

By an interesting coincidence, the two largest worldwide travel agents, Thomas Cook and Son and the American Express Company, may be said to have had their origins in the same year 1841. While Thomas Cook persuaded a railway company to carry a train load of passengers at very cheap fares in that year, Henry Wells started his freight business in the USA at the same time. Henry Wells commenced his business initially as a shipper who later began the well-known company of America known as Wells Fargo.

The American Express Company popularly known as AMEXO is the world's second largest travel agency after Thomas Cook and Son. It was an offshoot of Wells Fargo Company. Besides selling tours, the company deals in travellers cheques. The American Express Company is a major participant in international currency transactions, buying and selling huge amount in foreign currency on each working day. The company has also introduced American Express Credit Cards. These cards are very popular all over the world and the holder can pay his hotel bills, buy an international air ticket and many more things from places where these are accepted. The company also provides service for life insurance and property insurance.

Introduction of air travel

Much has changed since the year 1841, when Thomas Cook chartered a train to carry 570 travellers at a specialty reduced fare from Leicester to Loughborough in England. Thomas Cook who bought railway tickets in bulk and resold them to members of his group can be credited with being the first bona fide travel agent to work as a full-time professional. However, neither Thomas Cook and Son nor American Express Company was then a retail agent as the modern complex distribution chain had not yet evolved in any trade including tourism. The scope of the roles of these two companies was also limited in the beginning as the mass tourism as we know it now had not yet begun. It was however the introduction of the air travel which gave boost to the travel agency business. The introduction of an 'economy class' on aeroplanes crossing the North Atlantic heralded the era of travel agency and was responsible for their growth. This introduction or an 'economy class' in effect, was nothing more than a projection of Thomas Cook's original idea of adjusting prices to encourage full capacity use of every means of transport.

Continuing development of transport system especially the jet travel, improved living standards combined with reduction in working hours is the root cause of today's upward surge in travel. Side by side with the rapid improvements in industry and technology, practically all aspects of life have become more and more complex, particularly during the past half century. This is certainly the case in the travel industry in which, only a century ago, the job consisted almost entirely of arranging a simple reservation for the travellers in some means of transport. Today the functions and the duties of a person at the travel agency counter are vastly different and more interesting. He is now called upon to perform a variety of duties rather than just to issue tickets and reserve seats in a train, aeroplane or accommodation in the hotel. Travel today is no longer the privilege of the few, but is sought by millions. No longer does the travel agency exist for the sole purpose of selling tickets from one point to another. With the worldwide demands on its services, the travel industry developed along certain well-defined lines. The urge to travel became so intense over the years resulting in widespread growth of travel agencies in the world. Most of the travellers wished to have their travel arrangements made in advance and to be relieved of the difficulties of coping with various pre-travel arrangements of which they had only a very limited knowledge.

Profile of modern travel agency

The scope of the functions of a modern travel agency has widened greatly over the years and especially after the introduction of the jet air travel. The scope of the activities of the travel agent in the context of modern tourism can be described as follows: "to give advice to the potential tourist on the merits of alternative destination and to make necessary arrangement for a chosen holiday which may involve the booking of accommodation, transport or other relevant services." As the travel agent has accumulated knowledge, expertise and contacts with providers of services, he is a useful and sometimes invaluable intermediary. The retail travel agent provide: a direct link between the consumer (traveller) and the supplier of tourist services, i.e. airlines, transport companies, hotels, auto-rental companies, etc. The retail travel agent is one who acts on behalf of a principal, i.e. the original provider of tourist services such as an hotel company, an airline, a shipping company, railways or a tour operator. The retail travel agent sells the principal's services and is rewarded by a commission.

Functions

To deal with the subject of travel agency, the best method of approach is, perhaps, to consider the functions of a travel agency. The function of the travel agency will again depend upon the scope of activities it is involved in and also the size and the location. It is, no doubt, true that if the organization is large, the range of activities will be more wide. In this case the agency will have specialized departments each having to perform different functions. Some of the major functions of a travel agency may be classified as follows.

Provision of travel information

One of the primary functions of a retail travel agent from the point of view of the tourist, the general public is to provide necessary information about travel. This information is provided at a convenient location where the intending tourist may ask certain questions and seek clarifications about his proposed travel. This is a very specialized job and the person behind the counter should be a specialist having excellent knowledge of various travel alternate plans. He should be in a position to give up-to-date and accurate information regarding various services and general information about travel, etc. The presentation to the potential customer must be forceful, and exciting variations must continually be devised to help sell wares. A good travel agent is something of a personal counsellor who knows all the details about the travel and also the needs and interests of the intending traveller. Communication plays a key role in dissemination of any type of information. This is equally true in case of dissemination of travel information. The person behind the travel counter should be able to communicate with the customer in his language. The knowledge of foreign languages is an essential prerequisite for personnel working in a travel agency.

Preparation of itineraries

Tourist itinerary is a composition of a series of operations that are a result of the study of the market. A tourist journey is characterised by an itinerary using various means of transport to link one locality with another. Preparation of different types of itineraries is another important function of a travel agency. A travel agent gives advice to intending travellers on the type of programmes which they may choose for their holiday or business travel. The study and the realization of the itineraries calls for a perfect organisation (technical and administrative) as also knowledge of the desires of the public for a holiday and the propensity to receive tourists by the receiving localities.

Liaison with providers of services

Before any form of travel can be sold over the counter to a customer, contracts have to be entered into with the providers of various services. These include transportation companies, hotel proprietors, the providers of surface transport like motorcars of coaches for transfers to and from hotels and for sight-seeing, etc., and also for general servicing requirements. The work carried out under these headings is usually that of the owners or senior employees of agencies concerned. In the case of a large agency with worldwide ramifications, the liaison work involves a great deal of coordination with the principals.

Planning and costing tours

The contracts and arrangements having been entered into, there comes the task of planning and costing tours, both for inclusive programmes and to meet individual requirements. This job is intensely interesting and at the same time challenging. This job calls for a great deal of initiative and drive. The job calls for travel to those places which are to be included in the itineraries.

Paradoxically, many of those who do this type of work visit comparatively few of the places included in the itineraries they prepare. This is essentially a job for a meticulously minded person and calls for considerable training and ability. Many agencies with the cooperation of airlines and other transportation companies take the opportunity of arranging educational tours for such staff to countries with which they deal. Many large agencies have people who are authorities on particular countries and, in addition to a general programme, many will issue separate programmes dealing with specific territories. Separate programmes dealing with holiday offers based on specific forms of transportation, e.g., air, rail, road or sea may also be prepared. Programmes also have to be issued to cover different seasons of the year.

Publicity is an important part of the programme. Having spent considerable time and money on preparing all that goes into the issue of a programme, publicity must feature considerably in the activities of a travel agency and more so if the agency happens to be a large one. The majority of large travel agencies have their own publicity departments under the management of an expert in publicity.

Ticketing

Selling tickets to clients using different modes of transport like air, rail and sea is yet another important function of a travel agency. This calls for a thorough knowledge of schedules of various modes of transport. Air carriers, railways and steamship companies have hundreds of schedules and the man behind the counter should be conversant with all these. Ticketing is however not an easy job as the range and diversity of international airfares is very complex and varied. There are nearly 50 different types of fare combinations alone on the North Atlantic route. Changes in international as also in the local air schedules and additions of new flights from time to time makes the job of the travel agent one of constant challenge. An up-to-date knowledge about various schedules of air companies, steamship companies and railways is very essential. Computerised reservation system has in the recent years rather revolutionised the reservation system both for air and rail seats and also a room in a hotel. Many large travel agencies are using this system. This system comprises a computer network that can be used by the travel agent to reserve an air or rail accommodation as also accommodation in a hotel. Through a wide network confirmations of reservations are available in a matter of seconds.

Linked with the function of ticketing and reservation of accommodation in a hotel is the settlement of accounts of the clients. Accountancy plays a great part and is one of the important duties to be performed by the travel agency. Dealing with the settlement of accounts in all parts of the world calls for a thorough knowledge of foreign currencies, their cross-values and, above all, the intricacies of exchange control regulations, which vary from country to country.

Provision of foreign currencies

Provision of foreign currencies to intending travellers is another specialized activity of a travel agency. Some of the larger travel agencies deal exclusively in the provision of foreign currencies, travellers' cheques, etc. This is an important facility to intending travellers as it saves them a lot of time and energy in avoiding to visit regular banking channels.

Insurance

Insurance, both for personal accident risks and of baggage, is yet another important activity of travel agency. Some of the larger travel agents maintain sizable shipping and forwarding departments, aimed at assisting the traveller to transport personal effects and baggage to any part of the world with a minimum of inconvenience. Looking at the various activities mentioned in the above paragraphs, it is clear that the travel agent's range of services in modem times has expanded a great deal. His field of expertise is quite large and is constantly growing with the fast changing travel needs of the people. The job description of a modem travel agent was summed up in an American magazine in the following words:

(i) Preparation of individual pre-planned itineraries personally escorted tours and group tours and sale of prepared package tours.

(ii) Making arrangements for hotels, motels, resort accommodation, meals, car rentals, sight-seeing, transfer of passengers and luggage between terminals and hotels, and special features such as music festivals and theatre tickets.

(iii) Handling of and advising on the many details involved in modem day travel e.g., travel and baggage insurance,. language study material, travellers cheques, foreign currency exchange, documentary requirements (visas and passport) and health requirements (immunisation and inoculations).

(iv) Possession of professional knowledge and experience, as for instance, schedules of train connections, rates of hotels, their quality, whether rooms have baths, etc. All of this is the information on which the traveller but for the travel agent will spend days or weeks of endless phone calls, letters and personal visits.

(v) Arrangement of reservations for special interest activities such as religious pilgrimages, conventions and business meetings and sports events.

Source of income

The travel agency's source of income is the commission which it receives from various sources. He is also remunerated from certain other sources. Following are the sources: (i) Commission on the sales he makes of his principal's services. The main principals include an airline, a hotel company, a shipping company and a tour operator. (ii) Commission earned from ancillary services such as travel insurance and charges made for such services as traveller's cheques. (iii) Income earned from 'he short-term investment of money received from his customers, and deposits and advance payments. *(iv) Profit from the sale* of his own, tours if he operates as a tour operator.

Setting up of a travel agency

Opening a travel agency is not an easy job as it involves lot of planning and organisation. Running a travel agency requires a high degree of specialization and organisational ability. A travel agency may have a very large setup or a limited scope of activities. This will depend on the extent of people's participation in travel activities. In industrially advanced countries of the world, where a large number of people engage in travel, a large percentage of them utilize the services of a travel agency. In these countries, the travel agencies tend to be large having many specialized departments. On the other hand the services of travel agencies in developing countries are limited making them smaller in size.

The main divisions or sections which a travel agency or a tour operator would have to include are Sales, Research and Planning, Finance and Accounts.. Destination and Service and Publicity and Public Relations. All of these departments play an important role in the work of the travel agency, especially the large travel agency. These departments must be staffed with efficient personnel. There is also a need for greater coordination among various departments in order to achieve the best results. Approval by International Air Transport Association (IATA) is also necessary before starting a travel agency. In addition to approval by IATA, travel agencies also need to have certain other approvals/recognitions. These however differ from country to country.

Organisation of travel

How does a travel agency organise a travel? We have seen that there are various activities which a travel agency has to perform in order that an intending traveller undertakes his proposed journey and enjoys a holiday of his choice. There are various steps involved from the time a traveller visits a travel agent to buy a ticket until he returns back home after visiting a place of his choice. The various Steps involved in organising a travel are discussed in the following paragraphs.

Organised travel by a travel agency can be of two types, i.e. (i) *single client and (ii) group client.* In order to effect the journey, the following main elements (in both types of travel) need to be considered: study of the journey, estimate of expenditure, execution of the journey, and presentation of accounts.

Individual or ordinary trips

The following steps are involved in organising individual or ordinary trips.

(i) The client turns to the travel agent to organise for him a particular journey (cultural, natural, religious, etc.).

(ii) The agency from this angle will examine as to what will be involved e.g. scope of journey, when the journey is to take place, various services needed and the accessories required.

(iii) Based on the above evaluation and other elements in his possession, the travel agent will suggest itinerary and will then communicate to the client the estimated maximum cost for the client's approval.

(iv) Travel agent will then compile the definite estimates, a total of a series of various costs added up e.g. transport, accommodation, the services such as those of guides, operative costs (postage, telegrams, telephones, etc.).

(v) Travel agent then will present a document in duplicate to the customer of the amount of money to be paid. The client should return one of the debit copies signed for acceptance accompanied with a deposit (in anticipation). The deposit normally is about 25 per cent of the total cost.

(vi) Once the client's approval has been obtained, the travel agent's `operation' department can now execute the journey.

(vii) The 'operation' department's task now is to book for the established dates the transport and various other services. After booking confirmations have been received, the travel agent issues the vouchers.

(viii) The travel agent will now prepare the tourist itinerary' that will accompany the client through the entire journey. It will indicate the tickets to be used, the hotels and other services booked and will include vouchers, etc. Normally the itinerary is made in triplicate: one for the client, another for the agency and the third for the hotelier or those who will provide the required services paid by means of vouchers.

(ix) The last formality is the delivery to the client of the vouchers, confirmed tickets, the technical itinerary and of all the papers and the necessary guidance about the journey.

(x) On receiving the documents, the client will pay to the agency the remaining amount of money.

Group or organised trips. The following steps are involved in organising group or organised trips.

(i) This type of travel is customarily arranged by the travel agent after establishing the estimated number of participants.

(ii) Group travel can be a request from an enterprise (company) or a community and in this case the travel agent should be able to determine in advance, the number of participants,

(iii) Even in a group travel, the implementation phases can be identified as (a) study of itinerary, (b) compiling or estimates, (c) execution of the journey, (d) documentation of accounts.

(iv) For the preparation of the itinerary it is necessary tc know the type of locality to be visited, means of transport and type of hotel, etc., to be used. An important element regarding group travel is the itinerary planning.

(v) Group travel can also be arranged for certain events e.g., Olympic etc., and in this case, there will be a need for launching a certain type of publicity campaign.

(vi) While compiling of estimates, travel agent needs to evaluate various services to be offered (accommodation, entertainments, cost of messages, etc.).

(vii)For hotel bookings, the travel agent uses various means. During `low season', he uses the allotment system: the hotelier pledges to hold at the disposition of the travel agent a certain number of beds that he will utilize and for which he need not pay a penalty if he is unable to fill them.

(viii)Once the consent has been received, the travel agent will send to the hotel or hotels a tentative rooming list with indication of names and various types of arrangements needed. Only at the time of group departure, the travel agent will transmit a confirmed rooming list to the hotel with last minute variations, if any.

(ix) When the group is particularly large, e.g., for sports, etc., the travel agent needs to take extra care by way of informing public authorities for the purposes of security, etc.

The activities and the range of services described above are very wide and comprehensive and are covered by the travel agents in a highly developed market. The role and the activities of the travel agents in any country depend on the extent of the economic development of that country. In advanced countries of the world people due to higher standards of living and increased leisure time engage more in travel as compared to in developing countries. The services of travel agents are increasingly utilized in developed countries. In some of the advanced countries like USA, Canada and Germany, a very large percentage of tourists use the services of a travel agent.

Need for legislation

The role of travel agencies was discussed at length by the United Nations Conference on International Travel and Tourism held in Rome in 1963. The Conference noted that in many cases the responsibilities of the travel agent, both towards his principals--carriers, hotel operators, etc.--and towards the general travelling public are not fully recognised within the community. These responsibilities were of great importance, and travel agents should therefore be regarded as having professional status. Some delegates attending the conference were of the view that this could best be brought out by introducing appropriate legislation. The view was also expressed that legislation should be internationally uniform. Some representatives felt that each country should decide on the measures it should take in the light of its own particular problem.

A further view regarding legislation expressed was that the travel agents should be "self-regulating" in the sense, for example, of establishing their own code of ethics, should set up special training schools, should take such other measures as are likely to enhance their status and provide the travelling public with service and protection. It was suggested that it would be a great advantage if the major national and international associations of travel agents were to cooperate in drawing up an international code of ethics. It was also felt that an effort should be made to prepare a draft statute governing agency regulations.

In the conference the point was also strongly made that the rights of principals as well as of agents should be protected if legislation were introduced. In particular, the right of principals to appoint the agents of their choice must be preserved. It was mentioned that in some countries satisfactory. bonding arrangements had been made by agreement between principals and travel agents, thus providing some assurance that travel agents were financially sound and efficient and affording principals and the public added protection.

The tour operator

The dramatic growth of tourist traffic to the Mediterranean countries of Europe is a principal feature of the history of mass tourism in the last twenty years. A major contributing factor in this growth of air travel holiday tourism has been the development of the 'inclusive tour', a method of packaging a holiday. The idea of buying a package of travel, accommodation and perhaps some ancillary services such as entertainment etc., became established in Western Europe in the 1960s. Essentially an 'inclusive tour' is a package of transport and accommodation and perhaps some other services, which is sold as a single holiday for an all inclusive price. This inclusive price is usually significantly lower than could be obtained by conventional methods of booking transport and accommodation separately from individual hotel and transport tariffs.

Unlike the travel agent who is the retailer of the tourism product, the tour operator is a manufacturer of a tourism product. He plans, organises and sells tours. Tour operator makes all the necessary arrangements transport, accommodation, sight-seeing, insurance, entertainment and other matters and sells this 'package' for an all inclusive price. A package tour is designed to fit a particular group of travellers. These may be special interest tours i.e., mountain tours etc., and can be escorted. Escorted tour normally includes transportation, meals, sight-seeing, accommodation, guide services, etc. It is the escort or the group leader who is responsible for maintaining the, schedule of the tour and for looking after all the arrangements.

'Group inclusive tour' (GIT)

This is the most popular form of tour in this category where people travel in groups of 15 or more persons. These tours are available for any destination. The terms and conditions for group inclusive tours are laid down by IATA. The escort for such groups normally travels free as the airline provides him with free passage and accommodation. *Foreign Inclusive Tours'* (FIT) on the other hand are unescorted package tours. These tours are comparatively more flexible The traveller can buy a predetermined package with arrangements for sightseeing, hotels and certain meals, where necessary. He does not tour with a group. He can make his own arrangements and programmes according to his liking. The inclusive tour is one of the several devices which enable tourists to enjoy the lower price.

Lower unit costs

How does the tour operator manage to sell the package to the traveller at such a low price? The low price of the package holiday or inclusive tour is made possible by reason of the lower unit costs obtainable both for the air travel and for the hotel accommodation. The tour operator enters into long-term contracts for aircraft and making similar contracts with hotels. By mass-producing holidays in the form of package tours, the tour operators are able to procure substantial discounts from carriers, hoteliers, etc., and offer their package deals at much lower rates. The profits of the tour operator and the success of his operations however, depend on the achieving of very high load factors for the aircraft and very high occupancy rates for the hotel. In this way unit costs can be maintained sufficiently low to enable the tour operator to offer his package at a price which is often less than the cheapest available fare alone. A breakthrough in the business of tour operation came when airlines recognised that tour operation could fill the empty seats and introduced special fares for use exclusively by tour operators for combining into an inclusive tour.

The tour operator has thus emerged as the true manufacturer of the tourist product. The product is the inclusive tour, packaged, standardized and mass produced. The tour operator may sell this product directly to the public or through the channels of the retail travel agencies. It can be marketed successfully in the tourist generating countries to a mass market just because it is standardized, packaged and quality controlled. The product is therefore susceptible to the similar marketing techniques that are applied to the marketing of consumer goods.

Travel organisations

The American society of travel agents, Inc. (ASTA)

ASTA is the leading professional society of travel agents in, the industry. The world's largest professional travel trade association, ASTA was established in New York in 1931. Originally named the American Steamship and Tourist Agent's Association, its present name was adopted in the year 1944. The Society was established to foster programmes for the advancement of the travel agency industry, promote ethical practices and provide a public forum for travel agents. It has now over 16,000 members and is the only organisation representing all segments of the travel industry. The membership consists of travel agents, carriers, hotels, etc.

Purpose. The purpose of ASTA is the promotion and advancement of the interests of the travel agency industry and the safeguarding of the travelling public against fraud, misrepresentation and other unethical practices. The Society maintains legal representation and also a Government Affairs office in Washington, D.C. to provide direct contact with the Federal Government and the regulatory agencies in the travel and transportation field, and to protect the legitimate interests of travel agents.

ASTA's services to travel agents often also benefit the general public. Such activities include sponsorship of frequent conferences on travel matters, involving airlines, steamship companies, agents, municipal and government officials, and other interested parties; discussions with airlines or fare structures\ and travel destinations; research studies into traveller preferences; close cooperation with various city, state and government agencies across the country in travel-oriented matters; assistance to all agencies across the country in travel-oriented matters; assistance to all levels of government consumerism departments in upgrading standards of service to travellers.

Membership. While ASTA is still primarily the trade association of the travel agency industry, there are more than 16,000 members in the Society covering all segments of the travel industry. Out of the total membership of 16,000, over 8,500 are travel agents in the United States of America and Canada. In addition to travel agents, there are allied members representing airlines, railway, roads, hotels, government tourist offices, etc. The Society has a membership in over 120 countries all over the world. In order to qualify for the membership of the Society, an applicant must be in the business of travel under its present ownership or control for a minimum period of three years.

There are two basic classifications of membership, active and allied. Active members are year-round travel agents or tour operators; allied members include airlines and steamship companies, railroads, bus lines, car rental firms, hotels, resorts, government tourist offices and other organizations regularly engaged with the travel industry or associated industries. Membership has recently been increasing at the rate of 1,000 members annually.

ASTA has over 2,000 travel agency members outside the USA and Canada. All are engaged in travel agency operations on a year-round basis and have been in business for at least three consecutive years. The international roster has its own elected governors and actively participates in all phases of Society meeting.

International members come from Algeria, Bolivia. Sri-Lanka, Denmark, Ethiopia, Fiji Islands, Ghana, India, Iran, Japan, the Netherlands, Portugal, South Africa,

Sweden, Turkey, Yugoslavia and 120 other countries and territories.

Membership advantages include education and training in ASTA's comprehensive travel courses and seminars, guidance from ASTA headquarters in resolving many business and trade problems, and a weekly newsletter and monthly magazine containing important reports and articles from the travel front and related information of value to agents, tour operators and other members.

World Travel Congress. The year's foremost meeting place is the ASTA World Travel Congress. The Congress is the single most important meeting held annually in the travel industry and the programme includes workshops, seminars, business meetings, film presentations, and social events. Members from throughout the world travel industry participate, give talks, lead discussion groups and conduct sessions. Recent ASTA meetings have been held in Madrid, New Orleans, Rio de Janeiro, Montreal, Acapulco, Las Vegas, Amsterdam, Sydney and Munich, Germany.

The ASTA World Travel Congress has been the platform for launching many important and beneficial education programmes for agents. The Madrid Congress granted four more Travel Hall of Fame awards, an honour given to those whose careers have made longstanding impacts on the development and expansion of the travel industry and tourism.

The Society consists of the following departments: policy implementation and administration, industry relations, memberships relations, and communications. The members of the Society derive various advantages which include education and training. ASTA has a comprehenisive list of travel courses and seminars which are attended by its members. The Society also offers professional training courses to senior travel agency personnel. Various research papers and newsletters are brought out from Society's headquarters for use of its members. The Society also brings out a monthly magazine--ASTA Travel *News*.

Structure. The Society has 28 Chapters in the United States of America and Canada and another 28 Chapters overseas. Each Chapter has elected officers and appointed committees. There is a National Board of Directors which establishes policies of the Society. Every two years a new President and Chairman of the Board are elected by Active Members. Day-to-day activities of the Society are looked after by a professional staff which works under the guidance of an Executive Vice-President who, infact, is the Chief Operating officer of the Society. He makes recommendations on policy matters to the Board and Executive Board. He directs the headquarters staff in providing a broad programme of services and facilities to ASTA's membership and carrying on the day-to-day business of the Society. ASTA world headquarters are located at 711 Fifth Avenue in New York City, USA.

Universal Federation of Travel Agents Association (UFTAA)

Universal Federation of Travel Agents Association is an important organisation of the travel agents on a worldwide basis. The Federation was founded in Rome in November, 1966.

The aims of the Federation are as follows:

(i) To act as the negotiating body with the various branches of tourism and travel industries on behalf of travel agents and in the interest of the public.

(ii) To ensure for all travel agents through their national associations, the maximum degree of cohesion and understanding, prestige and public recognition, advancement of member's interest and protection from legislation and from other legal points of view.

(iii) To offer its members all the necessary material, professional and technical advice and assistance to enable them to take their proper place in the economy of world tourism.

Over the years, the Federation has been responsible in improving the professional status and business standing of travel agents. It has a series of achievements to its credit. Prominent among its achievements is its collaboration with the International Rail Union. This collaboration resulted in obtaining increased commission from 7.5 to 8 per cent on several railway networks, creation of professional training courses and introduction of Rail inclusive Tours. With regard to air transport, the cooperation between the Federation and IATA over a number of years has resulted in raising of commission to 8 per cent, introduction of an overriding commission of 4 per cent, 50 per cent reduction for the spouses of travel agents and creation of international correspondence courses for the training of agency sales staff. Regarding hotel industry, the Federation following negotiations with the International Hotel Association has created an international convention setting down regulations for bookings, cancellations and cancellation fees. A court of arbitration to settle disputes between hotels and travel agents located in different countries has also been created.

The Federation consists of the national travel agency association of over 74 countries which in turn represents more than 18,000 travel agencies from all over the world. The membership of the Federation is split into nine regions each covering a group of countries. UFTAA headquarters are located in Brussels, Belgium.

Travel agents in India

As long back as in the year 1954, the Government was aware of the important role which the travel agents were to play in the development of tourism. It was recognised by the Government that tourists who visit a foreign country often prefer to secure the services of travel agents who assist them in I order to make best use of time and money at their disposal. The Government felt that many a time unauthorised persons offer themselves as agents and in return fail to render satisfactory services, and even exploit the ignorance of the tourists for their personal benefit. With a view to curb this, the Government evolved a system of granting recognition to travel agents. The rules for recognition were as follows:

(i) No firm shall be granted recognition unless it has been engaged actively in handling tourist traffic for at least one year before the date of the application.

(ii) Firms granted recognition shall be entitled to such rights and privileges as may be granted by Government from time to time and shall abide by several terms and conditions of recognition.

(iii) Firms granted recognition shall undertake to maintain an office under the charge of full time members of their staff, who should, apart from issuing rail tickets, be in a position to give up-to-date and accurate information regarding transport and accommodation facilities, currency and customs regulations and general information about travel, etc.

(iv) The recognition may be extended for the whole of the country or be limited to a particular region.

(v) Firms granted recognition shall undertake to employ only guides approved by the Department of Tourism.

(vi) All recognised firms shall furnish yearly statement of their activities and such other information in regard to the volume of tourist traffic actually handled and other relevant matters.

(vii) The decision of the Government in the matter of recognition shall be final and it reserves the right 'to cancel or withdraw it at any time.

Subsequently, following clauses were also added:

(i) The recognition to be granted by the Department of Tourism shall not automatically entitle the firm to be appointed agents for the sale of rail tickets by the Ministry of Railways (Railway Board). The Agencies thus recognised shall apply separately to the Railway Board.

(ii) Firms seeking recognition as travel agents should have a minimum paid up capital of Rupees one hundred thousand.

(iii) Applications for grant of recognition by the Department of Tourism will be considered only if the firm:

  (*a*) *is* approved by the IATA;

  (b) has licence to book foreign passages issued by the Reserve Bank of India;

  (c) has the approval of the Ministry of External Affairs to handle travel documents and to deal with passport offices;

  (d) is registered under the local Shops and Establishment Act.

The recognition is now granted by the Central Department of Tourism in the Central Ministry of Tourism and Civil Aviation. The application for grant of recognition is to be made in the prescribed form and is to be addressed to the Director General, Department of Tourism, Ministry of Tourism and Civil Aviation, who is the authority empowered to grant such recognition.

Travel Agents Association of India (TAAI)

The travel agents decided to form an association on all-India basis as long back as in the year 1952, when an All-India Travel Agents Association was established. The main objective of the Association is to safeguard and protect the interests of its members by way of having a constant dialogue with the concerned government agencies. From a small beginning in the year 1952, the Travel Agents Association of India (TAAI) today has over 300 members. However, only 75 are on the approved list of the Department of Tourism. The activities of the Association are very wide. The annual convention of the Association is attended by a large number of representatives from travel trade both government as well as non-government. Important matters related with the promotion of tourist product are discussed in these conventions. The Travel Agents Association of India has its registered office in Bombay and regional offices in Calcutta, Delhi and Madras. The Association publishes a monthly magazine Travel News for the benefit of its members.

The vital role played by the travel agents in the growth and development of tourism in the country and its promotion is recognised by all segments of the travel industry. The Government works in close collaboration with them not only in India but abroad as well, encouraging them to plan and organise package tours for various destinations in India. In suitable cases, the Department of Tourism recommends the release of foreign exchange to travel agents to enable them to open their branch offices abroad. The Department has also instituted a special Tourism Award which is given every year to a travel agency earning maximum amount of foreign exchange.

9

Cultural Tourism

It is important to identify what particular groups or segments of society are experiencing what specific effects of tourist development. The social impact of tourism will vary according to the difference between the visitors and the visited, whether in terms of numbers, race, culture or social outlook. Lundgren, observes that in general: 'the force of tourist-generated local impact seems to increase with distance from the generating country'. Several specific characteristics of tourism must also be kept in mind. Firstly, the transitory nature of the relationships between hosts and guests, often coupled with language barriers, allows little opportunity for understanding to develop between the two groups. Secondly, the fact that the tourist is on holiday while the host is at work may heighten differences between the two, especially as holiday behaviour is generally much less restrained than usual. Thirdly, the seasonal nature of much tourism tends to be more disruptive than year-round activities, often creating the need for seasonal workers and exacerbating any tensions which might exist between the different groups. Finally, the outword signs of tourism may be more manifest than other types of development; for example, agricultural reform or the introduction of television. As a result, effects which have their origins elsewhere may be attributed to tourism. At worst, the industry may become the general scapegoat for any every social *malaise*. In modern times the drama tradition emerged in a new form. New theatre auditoria came into being. The exposure with the west brought in the influence of the Greek tradition and the modern western theatre tradition. Modern Indian theatre has benefited from both, the popular folk tradition and the western drama tradition. Simultaneously the modern play wrights have also made new experiments. A knowledge about these aspects would enable you to put in perspective the development of Indian theatre. Such knowledge is crucial to those involved in the field of tourism, as they would be able to appreciate the specificities of Indian theatre in the overall context of Indian Culture.

Many scholars believe that a folk theatre existed in Ancient India along with a rich classical Sanskrit theatre. With the passage of time the Sanskrit tradition faded but the folk tradition continued unhampered. As many as 20 different forms still exist and flourish in different parts of India. These include Ramlila and Raslila in North India, Jatra in Bengal, Akiya Nat, Kittania and Bidesia in Bihar and Assam, Khyal and Kathputli in Rajasthan, Tamasha in Maharashtra, Swang and Nautanki in Punjab, Bhandjashan in Kashmir, Kariala in Himachal Pradesh, Bhawai in Gujarat, Manch in Madhya Pradesh, Kudiattam and Chabitta in Kerala, Bhawatmel in Tamilnadu, Yakshagan in Karnataka and Kuchipudi in Andhra Pradesh.

The forms of folk plays are said to have originated from sangitaka referred to in the old Sanskrit plays. Sangitaka contains five elements-song, musical instruments, dance, auditorium and the Nat-Nati (compare or the story telling couple). These elements were shared by both the classical and the folk plays although the nature of the auditorium varied. Some of the folk plays did not need the stage at all. For instance Raslila could be performed on the stage as well as on the floor in the midst of the audiences.

The thematic content in the folk plays was generally of two kinds-worldly and religious. Ramlila and Raslila were primarily religious plays. Kirtania and Ankia Nat were also portrayals of religious stories. Nautanki, swang, Bhand, Tamasha and Khyal were based on worldly tales. Certain folk plays like Jatra combined both. As has been said earlier, the modern Indian theatre draws itself from three different traditional i.e. the Sanskrit theatre tradition, folk theatre tradition and the tradition of western theatres. It is actually the third which can be said to form the basis of the modern Indian theatre. The Sanskrit tradition had evaporated in the medieval times and there was no significant trend of plays being performed for the ruling classes. This view is now being contested and some researchers feel that the Sanskrit tradition did not decline in the medieval times. Among the common people, however, the folk tradition continued as we have discussed in the Sub-sec.

Modern Indian theatre started after the advent of the British in India. The British developed Calcutta in the east, Bombay and Surat in the west and Madras in the south as important centres of trade and administration. They also set up theatres in these cities for their entertainment. Levdef, a gentleman of Russian origin, established a theatre by the name of Bengali Theatre. Abridged versions of plays like Disguise and Love is the Best Doctor were enacted on 21 November 1765, well over 200 years ago. Many rich drama lovers followed the example of Levdef and started conducting shows in their houses, laws and gardens. This set in motion a process in which many theatres were established and plays enacted. Once general interest developed in the plays, their commercial viewing became inevitable. This led to the formation of theatrical companies among which the Parsi theatrical companies became most popular. These companies toured various provinces and made money.

But, more significantly, they contributed to the popularization of the plays by writing them in Indian languages. Since money making was their main aim, these companies did not either promote excellence or bring about any experiments in the methods of presentation. Nonetheless, they helped in providing a popular platform to plays. The modern India drama was greatly influenced by the west. It, therefore, contained all the features of the western theatres. The Ancient India tradition rested on a happy ending of the plays whereas in the western tradition the tragic ending was generally in vogue even though comedy was not completely absent there. Although influenced, modern Indian theatre was not merely an imitation of the west. On the contrary, it was a product of certain Indian social developments. The processes of modernisation and Renaissance in the Indian society, brought about socio-cultural changes and these changes were reflected in the field of art and literature. All this influenced the Indian theatre as well. The initial thematic content of the modern Indian plays rested on the historical and the mythological themes. Later the social and political themes were also given a place. Along with this, Indian theatre soon began incorporating elements from the classical Sanskrit theatres and folk theatres. This combination brought about many changes in the Indian theatre. For example, plays in the Parsi theatres gave tremendous importance to music, song and dances which was the influence of the traditional folk plays. The postindependence theatre also incorporated much of the folk and the Sanskrit traditions but, in essence, retained the realist western tradition.

Firstly, tourism may affect the demographic structure of their population as studies have shown in such diverse contexts as the coast of Spain, the French Alps, the Highlands of Scotland and Nepal. Development of the industry will usually affect the size of the resident population, as the creation of new jobs slow out-migration of attracts new workers or residents to the area. Ultimately there may even be a significant change in the degree of regional urbanization as development and migration tend not to be a spatial. These processes also tend to be age-and sex-selective, thereby altering the composition of the population as well as its size. The age-sex pyramid of Queenstown, New Zealand, and shows that compared to the national average, the demographic structure of this major resort is characterized by an excess of residents aged from twenty to thirty, by a shortfall of under-fifteen-year-olds and by a larger proportion of females. Greater occupational and geographical mobility may also modify personalities and family structures. In any given area, particular processes of development and local factors will combine to produce a set of population changes and impacts. Figures shows tourism-related growth in the Badenoch-Strathspey district of Scotland has mainly been in Aviemore and other large villages, with smaller rural settlements continuing to experience population decline. Different structural changes and related social impacts have also occurred in the two sets of areas. Occupational changes may also stem from tourist development. Language can be a critical factor in determining which sectors of the population will profit from tourism. Many native spectacles, for example, are presented by expatriate entrepreneurs or organized by the better-educated indigenous, the so-called 'culture brokers.' White has shown a more general decline in Romansch speaking in a multilingual area of Switzerland as tourism has developed there. The prospect of good jobs in the tourist industry may increase the desire for educational attainment. However, if initially the demand for qualified staff exceeds local capabilities or if control is in the hands of external promoters, then the better positions will be filled from outside, leaving the local residents the more menial tasks. Continuation of this policy will lead to frustration and perhaps hostility towards tourism. Employment opportunities in tourism may draw workers from other sector of the economy - for example, agriculture—with consequent effects on class or social structure. Preau's detailed longitudinal study of the impact of Courchevel highlights the occupational changes which have occurred from one generation to the next. In his sample the percentage engaged in agriculture declined from 85 per cent in 1948 to 6 per cent in 1973, with nine jobs out of ten at this later date being tourism-related. New occupational structures have also brought about attitudinal changes with further changes being anticipated amongst the third generation. Elsewhere, jobs which previously had not. cash return in many societies, such as cooling and cleaning, may now become income-earning if performed in hotels, thus altering the status of these workers, particularly of women. Resorts dependent on significant influxes of seasonal workers may suffer from a lack of social stability, the constant turnover in the population allowing little time for lasting relationships or community spirit to develop. Added to this are the work patterns of the tourist industry, often characterized by long hours and split shifts. On the other hand, some, particularly the younger seasonal workers, may be attracted by the excitement and interest of continually meeting new people or welcome the freedom which leaving their more traditional settlements has brought.

Values may be transformed through the brining together of different groups of people, even if at times only very briefly. This .is commonly known as the 'demonstration effect'. On the Greek island of Myconos, for example, the sociologist Lambiri-Dimaki notes the: 'democratization and modernization of attitudes' amongst the young, arising out of contact with youthful Western tourists. In this case it was the observed behaviour of the visitors, especially the equality of the females, which was an important as direct contact between the local residents and the tourists.

Increased prostitution is commonly associated with an expansion of tourism, with vacations providing an opportunity for the inversion of sexual and other restrictions. Sex tours to Korea, Thailand, the Philippines and other Asian countries have drawn strong criticism from religious, feminist and other writers. Joes, in his brief study of prostitution in Bali, concluded that it is usually changed, not caused, by tourist demand. Cohen, in a more comprehensive study of tourism-related prostitution in Bangkok, highlights the broader social and economic conditions which lead Thai women into prostitution, notes that 'the majority of prostitutes still serve a local Thai and Chinese clientele' and 'that the women working with *farangs* are in many respects the "elite" among the prostitutes'. Cohen emphasizes the complexity of the different relationships which may exist and concludes: 'While it enables the girls to resolve some of the pressing problems caused by the precariousness of their life-situation, it does not usually resolve the problem of precariousness itself, but often exacerbates it.' Elsewhere, sex roles may be reversed, as with the 'beach-boy-Canadian secretary' syndrome of the Caribbean or the liaisons between young males and Scandinavian tourists in the Gambia.

In some cases it is the tourist who is influenced the most. This is especially the case with those seeking to reinforce or expand their political, ideological or religious beliefs by visits to such places as Israel, India, Cuba, Mecca and Lourdes. The oft-cited increase in worldwide understanding resulting from international tourism is perhaps exaggerated, given the nature and duration of tourist-host contact, but what information there is available suggests tourism has a positive effect in this domain. Survey research in the European Community, for instance, indicates attitudes towards the unification of Europe are stronger amongst those who have travelled, especially those visiting several countries, but the nature of this relationship requires further elaboration. Mings examined the attitudes towards and knowledge of the United States and American visitors were expressed by the hotel employees and control groups of students in Barbados. Strongly positive attitudes towards American visitors were expressed by the hotel employees but the analysis of differences in levels of knowledge between then and the control groups proved inconclusive, in part due to the effect of information obtained through sources other than tourism. Mings concluded: The fundamental question remains: Does tourism help set the stage for improving international understanding? The results of this research suggest a qualified yes. However, perhaps the strongest statement possible at this junctures that very little evidence was discovered to indicate that international tourism is obstructing intonational understanding in Barbados. Fears that "ugly American" tourists may be spreading ill will and generating international misunderstanding everywhere are not consistent with the findings of this study.

The impact of tourism on traditional life-styles is especially important where those traditions form the basis for the development of tourism. Ethnic tourism is particularly a feature of the Third World but the arts in general have been, and still are, a very significant part of Europe's appeal to the traveller. Basically who differing schools of thought and bodies of evidence exist. Tourism is held by some observers to have a corrupting influence, brought about by the cheapening of artistic values or the commercialization of local traditions and customs; for example, the performance of religious or historical ceremonies on demand, out of context and for monetary reward. Other writers suggest tourists can have a strengthening and stimulating effect, either by reawakening interest in a society's own culture or simply by supporting the ballet, theatre or museums by their presence and entrance fees. Overseas tourists are estimated to have bought a third of all theatre tickets in London in 1977. More generally, seasonal tourist demand and other business generated from .ourism-related workers may support shops and services which might otherwise disappear from some rural and other communities. Tourism may also impose other more banal but no less significant pressures on host populations, as when visitors are served ahead of local residents in shops and the latter are jostled in the streets during the height of the season, or restricted from the use of certain beaches.

The demonstration effect noted earlier also encompasses daily patterns of consumption. Emulating the visitors, the residents may adopt new clothing styles, begin eating and drinking the imported food beverages favoured by the tourist, or aspire to obtain the transistor radios, cameras and other material goods so causally displayed by him. Inability by the local to emulate the visitor, if so desired, may lead to a greater awareness of poverty, envy, frustration and consequent ill-will towards the visitor or to his compatriots who have been more successful. At the same time, fulfillment of the desire for more imported goods may have significant adverse economic effects. This is not a one-way process, however, for on their return home, tourists may, for example, retain a taste for food and drink experienced abroad and sweet out ethnic restaurants or food stores. McElroy and de Albuquerque argue, however, with respect to the Caribbean that the nature and extent of the demonstration effect, together with the processes by which it operates, have yet to be soundly documented by researchers.

Other impacts may be felt in the generating regions. Although vacations are spent at the destination, from the tourist's point of view many of the benefits may be felt most at home where a phase of eager anticipation precedes, and a period of fond recollection follows, the holiday itself. If tourism is seen as a means of meeting personal needs and resolving interpersonal problems, then the fulfillment of these needs and any resolution of these problems through a successful holiday should be beneficial not only to the individuals concerned but also to the communities from which they are drawn.

Within destinations, attitudinal surveys have been the common method of addressing a range of social/cultural impacts, with some surveys also encompassing economic and environmental issues. In this approach, responds are asked to indicate their attitudes and feelings towards the impact of tourism, sometimes through the use of unprompted open-ended questions, more frequently with a set of closed questions or statements. Such surveys can yield useful information on types of impact but it must be remembered that what is being recorded is the respondent's perception of those impacts and these may or may not accord with reality. Pearce and Cant foundation Queenstown resident's views of increased employment opportunities generally reflected the trends revealed by labour force surveys. In Gwynedd, Wales, tourism's economic contribution was underestimated when compared to revenue generated by other sectors. Such cross-checks, however, are often not undertaken and for many social/cultural issues there may be few objective controls. Attitudinal surveys can be especially useful in distinguishing the impacts felt by different groups within the community, provided the sample is large enough to be disaggregate. Comparison of results is limited by different approaches and means of analysis but some common patterns do emerge. There are also signs of considerable variation from one case to another and much evidence of the complexity of the impacts which tourism may generate. Studies in coastal resort communities in North America, in three Scandinavin resort towns, in Sri Lanka and in Rotorua, New Zealand indicate that attitudes vary with the degree of involvement in tourism - more positive and fewer negative impacts are expressed by those economically dependent on the tourist industry. However, Liu and Var's research on attitudes in Hawaii revealed few differences between those working in tourism and in other sectors; this they attributed to the maturity of Hawaii as a destination. Analysis of the attitudes of three community groups—tourism entrepreneurs, public providers/administrators and residents—has been undertaken in Corpus Christi, Texas and in three different types of tourist centres in England. The reaction of the three groups in each case was reasonably favourable, with the business sector again generally being the most positive and the residents having more reservations. In the American case the administrators felt winter visitors placed strain on community services while in the British centres they were encouraged that the differences between the groups communities he studied were sufficiently close that they could be overcome.

Socio-economic status was reported to have little effect on attitudes to tourism amongst residents of Santa Marta, Colombia, nor on acceptance of foreign visitors in West Virginia. However, in a survey of three New Zealand resort towns, Garland and West found: 'Younger residents, Maori residents, women and lower-class residents were less enthusiastic about the role of tourism in the community'. There was also less support from those without overseas travel experience. Some of these findings contrast with those reported by Keogh in Shediac, New Brunswick where the young generally had a favourable attitude as the result of the prospect of summer jobs and greater social contact with tourists.

Despite uncertainty in economic conditions generally during 1971, international tourism in OECD Member countries continued to grow fast, thus demonstrating its ability to withstand perturbations in the economic climate. 1971 was, therefore, yet another good year with Member countries' foreign currency earnings from tourism increasing by 17% to $16.8 billion in 1971 and frontier arrivals increasing by 6% to 133 million while nights spent in thirteen European Member countries and Yugoslavia rose by 6% to 596 million.

The 1971 situation was characterized by an increase of about one fifth in the international tourist receipts of European Member countries for the second successive year, and buoyant tourist travel from Germany, the United Kingdom, Italy and Japan offsetting the much lower level of foreign travel from the United States and France. In *European Member countries earnings* from international tourism totalled $12.9 billion (+21%). In *Canada* a 7% increase brought earnings up to $1.3 billion and in the *United States* earnings rose by 6% to $2.5 billion. *Australia's* receipts from foreign tourism grew 10% to $168 million in 1971 while the decrease in *Japan*, following on the peak in 1970, the year of the Osaka Expo, was 26% with receipts falling to $172 million.

In the transport field, the private car remained the dominant form of tourist transport during 1971. Considerable public and private expenditure in such facilities as car-ferries, motels and motorways is planned in order to cater for the further growth expected in motor tourism. As regards air travel, charter traffic continued to show faster growth than scheduled passenger traffic while in the maritime transport sector scheduled passenger traffic contained to fall and cruise traffic to boom. In European Member countries the fall in rail traffic noted in recent years levelled off in 1970-71 while there was official action in the United States to re-organise rail passenger services.

Available data suggests that during early 1972 international tourism in most Member countries grew faster than in the corresponding period of 1971. Tourist travel from the four main generating countries, namely, the United States, German, the United Kingdom and France, was buoyant. Departures of United States citizens to Europe during the January-July period of 1972 are estimated to have grown much faster than in 1971 (+24% against +8%) while there was also a considerable recovery in scheduled two-way North Atlantic air passenger traffic during the first four months of 1972 (+1% against +3%) with the greater increase taking place in the North America-Europe direction (+33% against +4% in 1970). Available data on *frontier arrivals of tourists in European Member countries* cover, in general, the first three to six months of 1972 and large increase were recorded by certain Member countries for whom this data is available: Portugal +32% (5 months) Greece +29% (5 months), France +20% (4 months; classified hotels), Italy +17% (2 months), Spain and the United Kingdom +15% (6 and 5 months), Turkey +14% (2 months), Denmark +9% (5 months), the Scandinavian Passport Control Area +8% (5 months) and Switzerland +5% (5 months; hotels). *Nights* spent in hotels or registered tourist accommodation showed the following increases; Portugal +15% (4 months), France +14% (4 months), Austria and Germany +15% (5 months), Italy +8% (2 months), Denmark +7% (4 months), Belgium +6% (3 months) and Switzerland +3% (5 months). In *Japan* foreign tourist arrivals increased by 15% (5 months).

The phenomenon of movement of people from one place to another for varying periods of time is usually analyzed in terms of pull and push factors. Pull factors refer to the various reasons which attract people to come to one place from another. Push factors are those factors which provide an incentive to leave or go out form a particular place. The strength of pull factors is extremely significant in determining the tourist inflow and consequently the commercial viability and popularity of a hill resort. These pull factors may be classified into the following five categories;

i) Geographical location

ii) Accessibility

iii) Availability of services

iv) Adequate information, and finally

v) A congenial political and social atmosphere.

Geography

One of the most important factors which determines the popularity of a hill resort is its geography and topography. Altitude, the presence of natural features such as rivers, lakes, alpine meadows and proximity or atleast a good view of high snow clad peaks considerably add to the charm and the pull of a hill resort. In a country like India the elevation or the altitude of a mountain resort is of crucial significance as it has direct bearing on the climate of the place. A large number of Indian tourists visit the hills in the summer months to escape the enervating heat of the plains. The high elevation of the hill resorts makes them cooler and offers a pleasant change. However, resorts located at high altitudes in the Himalayas tend to be seasonal ones because they become snow bound and very inaccessible in the winter months for the ordinary tourists. Most of the Himalayan hill resorts are thus located within an altitude range of 1900 to 3000 meters above sea level.

The presence of natural features such as lakes, rivers, rapids, rock formations, closeness to high altitude peaks and trekking routes also increase the popularity of a hill resort. For example tourists love to view the snowclad Nanddevi from Ranikhet or at practically every hill station climb up the highest point to have a view of snowclad mountains. Apart from adding to the esthetic beauty of the resort these features also provide opportunities for the setting up the specialised sports such as river rafting, rock climbing, mountaineering and trekking. The availability of good snow clad slopes, for instance, permit the organisation of winter sports such as skiing. Hill resorts of the country located outside the Himalayas may not be able to offer the pleasures of snow, ice, and coniferous forests to the visitor from the plains, but they do beckon them with cooler climates.

Accessibility

A large number of places in the hills posses the natural potential for attracting tourists but are frequented rarely by outside visitors because of their remoteness. The most popular hill resorts of the country are located relatively close to major urban centres in the plains, This is so because the major catchment area of potential tourists are to be found in large urban centres. However, with the growth of faster and more efficient transport services and the willingness of entrepreneurs to develop far flung centres as hill resorts this problem is gradually becoming less important. However, it must be noted that air travel and long train or bus journeys mean a drain on the pocket and a less affluent tourist continues to prefer resorts which re within close reach.

This explains why many of the hill resorts located in the lesser Himalayas, in spite of being crowded continue to attract the bulk of the tourist traffic from the major cities of northern and eastern India. The availability of convenient rail or road links greatly stimulate tourist inflow. Air links also facilitate in boosting the number of visitors, but this category is generally limited to the more affluent section of visitors. Similarly, we and Mount Abu are also located very close to large cities.

Services

Most tourists will venture to a hill resort only if they are assured of the availability of adequate services apart from communication such as boarding, lodging, medical aid and recreational facilities. An adequate number of hotels and lodges which cater to tourists from a wide income spectrum is an absolute necessity for attracting large numbers of visitors. The basic requirement for hotels, lodges and eating places, as well as for the resort as a whole is cleanliness. All tourists will look for these attributes. Once the basic requirements are met, the tourism industry can provide different classes of hotels tc cater to its specific clientele. Medical aid, adequate policing to ensure law and order and the efficient supply of information and help are vital prerequisites for the growth of any hill resort.

Linkage effects of hill tourism

Like other industries, tourism has the capability of exerting strong backward and forward linkage effects with a number of other related areas of the economy.

Backward linkages pertain to the demand exerted by tourism on input sectors namely transport, the demand for specialised equipment, services of tour agents and travel companies.

Forward linkages, have a more immediate and direct impact on the local economy of the tourist resort. These include the growth of local hotels, local sight seeing-services, the demand for services such as that for tourist guides, porters, entertainment facilities. Further, local handicraft industries of the region also receive a tremendous demand stimulus for their products with the growth of a brisk tourist traffic.

Now that we have sketched a general picture of the prerequisites for the growth of a tourist resort and some of its possible positive effects on the economy, let us briefly state a few precautions that have to be kept in mind in the course of the development of hill tourism.

One crucial factor which motivates the tourist to visit a hill resort is the desire to experience the clean environment of the hills which stands in marked contrast to the pollution and crowding of the city from where he comes. These days one finds that driven by the highly lucrative nature of him tourism, this industry is developing in many areas at a very rapid rate in the totally haphazard and unplanned manner. Resorts, such as Manali, which once used to be perfectly quite and picturesque retreats have in the recent past been transformed into highly commercialized and crowded settlements replete with smoke and noise pollution. The burgeoning expansion of this industry in other hill resorts such as Mussoorie, have led to serve deforestation, and ecological harm. Rapid , unplanned tourist resort expansion might earn the smart investor a fast buck in the short-term, but this leads to a serious decline of the area's tourist potential in the long run. The tourists must be made aware of the serious harm that are capable of inflicting on the environment. They should be constantly remained and educated about the need, for instance, of not littering the countryside with waste or denuding natural flora and fauna. The tourist should realize that though on a short vacation at a hill resort, he or she should not offend the sensibilities of the local population. For example, many hill folk do not like being photographed by strangers. The camera toting visitor in his eagerness to take back home photographic memories of his short holiday should not go around clicking madly and earn the displeasure of the locals. The attempt of the tourist, as an outsider should be to understand the customs of the area and try not to force himself on the local people.

Hill resorts

We shall now study some representative hill resorts form various parts of India to illustrate concretely the points discussed above. The hill resorts selected for such study are located in the Himalayas, the Aravallis and the Western Ghats.

The Himalayas, in an are shaped formation, extend 2500 kilometers from west to east and over 250 kilometers from north to south. They are divided into the Main, Middle and Outer or Lesser Himalayas in terms of the altitude of the mountain ranges. It is within the Outer Himalayas that the Sivaliks (in the west) and the Doars (in the east) are located. The Himalayas, vary greatly in their climate from region to region. Tropical climate characterizes the foothills, whereas moderate climate marks the foothills of the outer Himalayas. As one travel further north, the alpine climatic conditions are found in Central Ranges and a dry continental climate in the valleys and plateaus north of the Main ranges.

The important and popular tourist hill resorts lie within an altitude range of 1600 to 2000 metres in the moderate climatic zone in the Sivaliks, the valleys south of the Central Range and in the eastern Doars. In India, these include the Kashmir Valley, Kulu, Kanghra, Manali, Simla, the middle part of Sikkim and Darjeeling.

i) Manali: Manali which is connected by road to major North Indian cities such as Delhi and Candigarh, has developed into a most popular hill resort in the past few decades. Located in the upper reaches of the

Kulu valley at an elevation of 1220 metres, it permits a spectacular view of snow capped mountain peaks both to the north and south.

The view of high awe inspiring peaks, freshness of its cedar forests, the gurgling of the river Beas which flows through the town, and its use as a base station for mountaineering expeditions attract both the adventurous as well as the most sedate visitor. The geography and topography of Manali have contributed significantly in making the town a major tourist attraction. Manali is the major take off point for a large number of trekking trails, including those in Lahaul and Spiti. Treks to the Rohtang Pass, Beas Kund, Chandertal and many other places can be accomplished within two to four days of easy walking. Mountaineering expeditions to the Shitidhar Ridge in the north and peaks to the north east such as Deo Tibba and Aliratni Tibba also have to use Manali as their logistics centre. The Mountaineering Institute at Manali organizes courses on rock climbing, high altitude trekking, mountaineering and skiing.

Manali had in the last few decades also developed a s centre for winter sports. Solang, located just 12 kilometers to the north of the town has excellent slopes suited to both the beginner and the expert. Apart from trekking and mountaineering, the Beas is famous for trout fishing. A license for this can be obtained from the Tourist Office. For the less adventurous, the hot sulphur bath at Vashist, located only 3 kilometers from the town, the medieval temple of Hidamba Devi, a Tibetan monastery and the market would be of interest.

Manali is well connected by long distance buses to Delhi. Chandigarh and Simla. The tourist can choose between the more plebeian ordinary bus or the deluxe coaches run both by the Government as well as private operators. Taxi cabs can also be hired from Delhi,

Candigarh and other places to Manali. The resort is also accessibly by air. Indian Airlines and private air taxis ferry passengers from Delhi to Bhuntar, which is located in Kulu.

Manali caters very well to all the needs of a wide variety of tourists with different interests and budgets. The Government runs hotels and restaurants which range form the relatively cheap but comfortable to the extremely luxurious up market ones. In addition to State run tourism services private entrepreneurs are increasingly setting up similar establishments. The Tourism Office provides a wealth of information to the new visitor ranging from the names of tariffs of hotels to detailed trekking maps of the region. With the marked increase in the popularity of trekking and mountaineering a good number of companies have been set up in Manali which hire camping gear and make arrangements for porters, pack animals and high altitude guides. The Manali Mountaineering Institute provides trained mountaineers to help in rescue work in emergencies. The rapid growth of Manali as a hill resort has led to a proliferation of tour operators and travel companies who undertake to make arrangements for tourists from big metropolitan cities like Delhi. Communications with this resort have also been upgraded in response to incre^sed tourist demand.

The resort's marked growth has greatly stimulated local building industry in the region and has provided a large number of local youth an opportunity to get employment in the local hospitality industry.

However, while Manali's exponential growth graph augurs well for short-term profitability, it is vital to safeguard the town the dangers of ecological degradation and the forcing out the genuine people by profit hungry entrepreneurs.

ii) Darjeeling: Darjeeling, nestling among in the Kanchenjunga ranges, is the major hill resort of eastern India. Like Shimla and Mussoorie in the north west, Darjeeling too owes its origins as a hill resort to the colonial government. During British rule it was the summer capital of the Bengal Government. The town was planned and established by Lord Napier of the Royal Engineers and separated from Sikkim in 1835. Its cool and fresh climate, combined with its connection to the plains by rail and the development of tea plantations in the area, stimulate its growth as a hill resort.

After Tenzing and Hillary scaled the Everest, the Himalayan Mountaineering Institute was set up in Darjeeling. This Institute, while being a premier training institution is also a place of tourist interest. Compared to the hill resort of North India, Darjeeling is still much less crowded. One area of tourism which has tremendous potential but is as yet relatively untapped in this region is that of trekking. While nearby Nepal is synonymous with hiking and trekking, this activity is still to be exploited fully in Darjeeling. The area's rich flora and fauna makes trekking a most rewarding experience. The toy train is a great attraction for the tourists.

Non-Himalayan hill resorts

It must be kept in mind that hill resorts are not always located nestling in the lap of high snow clad mountains. Apart from the Himalayan hill resorts, the other hill 'nations' of the country are found in the Aravallis of western India, the Western Ghats and the hill ranges of central India. These resorts, such s Mount Abu, Matheran, Ootacamund, Kodaikanal, Ponmudi and Pachmarhi, have the advantage of a cooler climate and lower population density compared to the major urban settlements in the vicinity, as they are located at relatively high elevations.

Amongst the more popular and well known hill resorts which lie outside the Himalayas are Mount Abu in Rajasthan, Pachmarhi in Madhya Pradesh and Ootacamund or Ooty in Tamilnadu.

i) *Mount Abu*: Mount Abu is the only hill resort of Rajasthan. It caters mainly to Indian tourists. The cooler climate of this 1220 metre granite plateau in the Aravallis attracted the attention of the British. In 1845 it was leased for the British Resident of Rajputana as a summer resort from its native ruler. The history of Mount Abu, however, goes back by about a thousand years, not as a hill resort but as a Jain temple town. The bulk to tourists visiting Mount Abu come form the cities of Rajasthan and Gujarat. Some visitors from Delhi can also be found frequenting this resort, which is open the year round. Mount Abu is located just 27 kilometers away from the Abu Road which serves as the rail head and 185 kilometers from the nearest airport, which is at Udaipur. Long distance buses also connect the resort to the major cities of northern and western India. Its cooler climate, its picturesque craggy outcrops, the central Nakki Lake and the plethora of marvelous Hindu and Jain marble temples are the major tourist attractions. The steep granite rock formations which surround Mt. Abu make excellent rock pitches. These range from slopes for scrambling to climbs of great heights. This potential of the resort has been recognized by the State government which has established a training establishment for rock climbers. However, with adventure sports fast becoming very popular, adequate publicity and necessary infrastructural facilities such as accident relief units, maps and supply of equipment will go a long way in attracting many more rock climbers to Mt. Abu.

A relative advantage which Mt. Abu has, in spite of not possessing many of the climatic and geographical features of the Himalayan hill resorts, is its ability to attract those tourists form the neighbourıng states, who prefer not to venture too far to enjoy the comforts of the hills. Many such, hill resorts are to be found in a number of non-Himalayan Indian states which include Madhya Pradesh, Maharashtra, Rajasthan, Tamilnadu and Kerala. In terms of tourists inflow many of these may not match the Himalayan hill resorts, but are locally significant nevertheless.

ii) *Ootacamund:* Ootacamund or Ooty as it more popularly referred to is another major non Himalayan hill resort. Once again we see that it was developed as a hill station by the colonical rulers. Discovered by accident by some British Officers, Sullivan, the Collector of Coimbatore immediately set about establishing a new station here. What drew the immediate attention of the British was the areas similarly with the landscape and the climate of their homeland. Stephen Lushington, the governor of Madras took a great deal of interest in developing Ooty as a hill station. One British official remarked, "I will be the glory of Mr. Lushington's government without any extravagant hyperbole that he has introduced Europe into Asia or such are his improvements in the Neilghirries." Located at 2240 meters Ooty offers a pleasant climate, with temperature ranging from 25°C to nearly 0°C in winter. Apart from its coniferous flora and comfortable weather, this hiss resort is in many ways a living monument of a British colonial summer resort. Imported names, architectural forms and even some of the idosyncrasies of the English have been carefully preserved hire. The Weslyan Church, the Collectorate, the Ootacamud Club, the fox Hunt and Snookers all bear testimony to this. The Ooty is in more than one way a good example of a typical Raj period summer retreat. Ooty is well connected by road, rail and air to the major cities of South India.

Other than the above discussed few major hill resorts most of the northern States of India as well as the peninsular states can boast of a number of hill resorts. These may not be as well known and lucrative in terms of tourists turnover, but they do met the minimum requirements of a hill resort. These include Ponmudi and Munnar in Kerala, Madikeri in Karnataka, Pacmarhi in Madhya Pradesh, Kailmpong and Gangtok in the north east, and a large number of relatively unknown mountain resorts in Garhwal, Kumaon land Kashmir.

Need for new hill resorts

In the interest of equitable development of the tourism industry and to prevent irreversible environmental degradation it is crucial that the tourism industry makes a concerted effort to develop new hill resorts. Most of India's hill resorts were developed as summer retreats and senatoria for colonial bureaucrats and soldiers. These hill stations were thus not planned for accommodating highly seasonal and heavy tourist inflows. The increase in vehicular traffic has led to atmospheric pollution. Similarly, the cutting down of forests to construct potentially lucrative hotels have resulted in considerable deforestation. Deforestation in the hill areas poses a great threat to the fragile ecosystem of the hills. In many places such as Mussoorie and the Donn Valley excessive quarrying to supply the increasing demands for building materials in the expanding hill resorts have led to deforestation and consequent landslips and landslides. Unplanned municipal expansion of hiss resorts located on rivers and lades have led to the possibility of these water bodies getting polluted. The case of the Dal lake in Srinagar is a case to point

While regulating the flow of tourist traffic to hill resorts which seem to be on the brink of environmental collapse by administrative fiat may not be received well, it would be a good idea to develop newer hill resorts. These will provide the visitor with the welcome features that he or she is in search of like uncrowded environs, a sense of distance from the bustle and din of the cities, in short, a refreshing change. While allowing the visitor to be closer to nature and the hills, the developing of a number of hill resorts will ease the mounting pressure on the existing high profile hill stations.

The development of the lucrative tourist industry is increasingly becoming more capital intensive. The emphasis is to attract the upmarket end of the tourist clientele and provide them with the most up to date and expensive facilities. These, in turn have meant that the hospitality industry has become more and more capital intensive. An increase in capital intensity consequently emasculates the potential of small local entrepreneurs in entering this field. One impact of the increasing flow of tourists into a concentrated geographical zone is to widen the economic gulf between the visitors and the local population. While tourists must be told how not to insult local customary practices, it is also important that the local population should look on the tourist as a beneficial visitor and the tourism industry as not antithetical to their daily welfare and interests. For such an attitude to develop in the long run it is necessary that the local people have substantial stake in the industry and are empowered to take long-term policy decisions.

Tourism, as we have mentioned earlier, is an activity that is serviced by an increasing number of personnel through various types of services. Besides providing direct employment it also stimulates the need for a number of services that are subsidiary in nature. This, in turn, provides indirect employment and also has an impact on the local economy. However, the type of subsidiary services required depend on the form of tourism promoted. For example:

— luxury foreign tourists demand services that are vastly different from the demand of low budget tourists or domestic tourists, and

— services required at adventure tourism destinations would be different from those required at pilgrim destinations, etc.

We had discussed the importance of informal services. Now, takes into account the services like tourist police, link transport, performing arts, communications, etc. Certain other categories like photography, publishing tourism related literature, etc. have also been discussed.

The information provided in this Unit is of help for tourism professionals in many ways. For example, while marketing a destination some of these services can be offered in the package; a tourist can be advised on what is available and cautioned as to what will not be there. Similarly those who want to start small-scale enterprises can look into these services and choose as per the requirements in their areas etc.

Subsidiary services develop naturally ;in the process of urbanisation. It is a curious feature of tourism that as it opens up remote places (which are often attractive because they are underdeveloped), it creates the demand for services which are generally not required by local residents. For example an air-conditioned taxi will not be the demand of locals. Certain subsidiary services are common to practically all destinations. Of course, in some cases their nature may change or vary depending on the type of destinations.

Link transport needs

Tourist movements at the destination and nearby attractions give demand to local transport needs. This demand first emerges from the very point where the tourist disembarks from the main transport i.e. Railway station, Airport or Bus stand. Different agencies cater to this demand. For example, take the case from an airport:

— Government transport corporations ply their buses to different routes, to a specific point in the city or connecting the airport with Bus stand and Railway station.

— Airlines ply their coaches up to certain points in the city.

However, besides these there are other popular modes to cater to this service. For example: taxis on hire are available for local transportation as well as long routes. There are separate counters for local prepaid taxis and long route taxis; auto rickshaws are also available, and at the Railway stations and Bus stops one finds other services also like, rickshaws and tongas. Taxi operators get a special chance with the growth of tourism in a region-particularly when the tourists visiting the area are high-budget luxury tourists. They need private transport to complete their travel as speedily as possible during their brief holiday.

To cite an example from Goa, some local unemployed youth often with the help of loans from nationalised banks, run 'motorcycle taxi' services. For a fee-which is naturally lower than four-wheeler taxi rates-the commuter is transported to some destinations, whether in the state's small towns, or to villages beyond.

Such motorcycle 'pilots' as they are locally called used to ply on state roads even before the current tourism boom. But, the influx of tourists to some parts of the state has given a fillip to their 'business'. These motorcycle taxis are treated as legal 'taxis' and the idea seems to be catching on in a few other pockets of the country. In some areas two wheelers are also given on hire to tourists. Some luxury hotels prefer to run their own luxury-bus or transport service. This is turn cuts down on the employment potential available to taxi-operators. The Taxidrivers; must know the city well; should be polite; have correct metres; follow traffic rules, try to learn more languages, etc.

Entertainment is an essential component in tourism. On an average foreign tourists in India spend about 10 per cent of their total expenditure on entertainment. Mostly it is during the evening or night that tourists look for or are provided entertainment through various means. This may include dance, theatre, movie, theme dinner, musical evening etc. At many destinations this has provided employment to local artists and performers. For example the Goa Tourism Development Corporation provides evening and night cruise on river Mandovi. Local dances, music and songs form a part of the cruise. Similarly many hotels organise musical nights or dance performances during the tourist season.

Another recent development is the organising of short duration entertainment festivals by some State Tourism Departments like the Qutab festival in Delhi or Taj festival at Agra. However, sincere efforts are needed to attract tourists to these performances and they should not just be for the entertainment of bureaucrats or politicians. Certain countries offer gambling, casinos and night clubs as entertainment but this is not the case with India. This is perhaps one reason that those who demand such services find entertainment very dull in India. At many destinations the poor, with the help of family labour or child labour attempt to provide entertainment to tourists for the sake of money. Children doing acrobatics, snake charmers, tribal dances, puppet shows, etc. are some examples.

As a tourism professional you may face queries from the tourists regarding where to shop or what to shop.

Similarly if you are a small entrepreneur you may have to decide what to sell and how to sell. In fact shopping is an important agenda for a tourist and some time is always allotted for this in any itinerary. In India we have a rich tradition of various handicrafts, handlooms and other art works produced by artisans. These not only represent our heritage and culture but at the same time are great shopping attractions for tourists.

Most of the foreign tourists coming to a country want to learn about its culture. This is equally true in the case of domestic tourists visiting another region of their country. Culture is best absorbed by acquainting oneself with language, food, dress, and traditional arts and crafts. The arts are presented through periodic programmes of music, dance, theatre, temporary exhibitions of paintings and photography, etc. At the same time it is the acquisition of crafts and textiles as souvenirs that have the most lasting impression of a nation's/region's skills, artistic sensibilities and items that form part of the daring lives of its people. It is for this reason that shops and emporia play an important part as show windows. These tend to be centered in large cities, competing with high technology, mass produced and aggressively advertised consumer products.

From small towns and villages crafts or locally made rural products are fast disappearing. Where do we find them? How do we preserve them? How do we create new shops to serve rural craftspeople? How do the craftspersons serve society and how does it serves them? These are important questions for the small entrepreneur and also for those involved in the promotion of tourism.

This Unit starts with a discussion on the traditional marketing outlets of handicrafts like the haat. Certain seasonal festivals and melas have also become tourist attractions where various craft products are on sale. This is another selling outlet taken care of in the Unit. Further the role of the emporia and private shops has also been discussed. The Unit also takes into account the marketing organisations at the grassroot levels. An important aspect dealt with is the life of artisans and certain efforts that are being initiated to improve conditions for them, like the setting up the Delhi haat.

The concept of marketing evolved as an offshoot of the advent of technology. In early times the potter, both man and woman, but mostly the latter, moulded mud pots by hand for domestic use. Once the potters wheel was invented and production increased, the excess quantity produced became items for distribution to others through the exchange of goods. If goods and services between two needy parties matched, the barter system came into play. When the purchaser of the commodity had nothing worthy of exchange the monetary system was introduced when goods were exchanged for money.

In self-sufficient village economies land owners would sell their agricultural produce while village artisans sold their goods such as ropes, baskets, iron ware, cloth, metal vessels and agricultural implements. These would be exchanged or bought by the very same society that brought goods to the village haat, mela or bazar.. All sorts of activity takes place in such a bazar, where apart from exchange and trade of goods ear cleaning, medicinal remedies, tatooing, astrological predictions and entertainment through song, dance and music were also conducted as part of the interwoven human relationships that extend beyond "market" and economics" and become a cultural entity in itself. A typical village or small town marketplace is therefore the most indigenous, flexible; and at the same time multi-layered and infinitely complex structure which accommodates economic activities of various nature.

In many parts of India there are informal marketplaces called haats. These are generally seen in village clusters, small towns and even capital cities. They operate either one day a week twice a week, for a few hours a day or even every day. They may be stationery or mobile, as in the case of Delhi where a pavement or bazar spreads out along the pavements of different designated areas each day of the week, ending behind Red Fort on Sundays. In cities it is mostly second hand machine produced goods which are sold. They range from books, garments, fused bulbs, knives and tools, old newspapers, furniture, plastic toys, crockery and glassware etc. The rural market place called a haat, chanda or athwada bazar depending on which part of the country it is almost a mirror image of village society and its life. The items put for sale vary region to region. For example, they may sell exclusively handwoven mats, handloom cotton cloth or earthenware pots. The weekly market at Mapusa in Goa sells almost ten thousand screwpine leaf floor mats in one hour. Haats in Rajasthan sell leather shoes, hand printed, tie dyed or embroidered head clothes, skirts, camal decorations, woollen blankets and edible commodities. Similarly, the number of haats also vary. For example, there are as many as sixty haats in one single district of Bihar.

Thus each haat is a display of the products, skills and culture of that particular area. The marketplace in any rural area best conveys the vitality and dynamics of village life and is the basic arena for local trading. These are the characteristics that attract many tourists to haat who also know that what they are going to buy is the genuine local product of the artisan.

Government incentives for the development of tourism

In view of the increasing demands, for government financial aid, the Tourism Committee draws the attention of tourism authorities to the desirability of directing such incentives on a selective basis towards the attainment of governmental objectives. This would enable them to present a more convincing case when requesting public funds for tourism as such requests have to compete with an increasing number of similar requests from other sectors of the national economy.

Although the number and variety of training courses on tourism offered by publicly-owned educational establishments is increasing, the Tourism Committee considers that more emphasis might be also given to training staff for some of the newer tourism profession. Member countries could moreover, publicize as much as possible existing educational facilities and career opportunities in tourism. The Committee also feels it to be of importance to increase the facilities for tourism studies in universities, both for first and higher degrees. However, in the Committee's view priority ought first be given to detailed assessments of present and future manpower needs of the tourism sector so as to draw up national policies for the training of tourism personnel. This is essential for the effective planning of the future expansion of tourism in all OECD Member countries.

The Tourism Committee draws attention to the increasing government involvement with environmental questions which is leading to the creation of more specialized official departments and agencies in this field. In particular, the Committee points to the growing tendency for governments to adapt existing physical planning legislation to deal with the problems of environment and pollution. The Committee, therefore, considers it advisable for tourism authorities of Member countries to co-operate with the physical planning departments in their respective countries so as to ensure that tourism interests are taken into consideration when physical plans are being drawn up. This need has already been recognized by several Member countries who have set up, or are setting up, the appropriate administrative machinery. The Committee also draws the attention of tourism authorities in Member countries to the need for actively supporting those aspects of environmental policy that also help to improve the quality of tourism supply, e.g., the creation and upkeep of national parks and nature reserves.

In spite of the increasing amounts of public funds being spent on special infrastructure for all-year-round use or on specific off peak promotions the Tourism Committee does not feel that any large measure of success has so far been attained in reducing the economic impact of the peak period on the tourist industries of different OECD Member countries. The Committee considers, therefore, that Member countries might experiment with a wider variety of methods, e.g. pricing and diversification of supply, so as to assess their relative effectiveness in smoothing the summer peak.

The Tourism Committee notes with satisfaction that, during 1971, bilateral technical assistance in the field of tourism by individual Member countries continued to grow in size and scope. Such assistance, which now covers most of the important aspects of tourism, ranges from group training schemes to direct financial participation in tourism investments. Moreover, OECD is currently administering a programme of technical assistance which includes tourism.

10

Tourism Research

'It seems reasonable to assume that by the end of the century tourism will be one of the largest industries in the world, if not the largest' Kahn. This prediction by Herman Kahn appears to be in the process of vindication as, indeed, both international tourism receipts and arrivals in 1992 reached the highest levels ever. In 1992, over 476 million tourists traveled internationally and spent over $279 billion. Expenditure on tourism services worldwide (including both domestic and international travel) reached over $2 trillion in 1992, representing approximately 12.5% of the world's consumer spending.

Statistics such as these clearly indicate the global volume and extent of tourism. However, to what extent is tourism research state-of-the-art in comparison to this global expansion? In keeping with the focus of the conference, this article analyzes reported research to help determine possible answers to the above question. In assessing tourism research as state-of-the-art it is necessary, like the god Janus, to look back as well as forward. The citation analysis reported in this research provides a backward view as well as possible indications for the future of tourism research.

History of tourism research

Despite the global volume and economic aspects of tourism, the research literature relating to this field of study presents a relatively brief and disjointed history.

Before the 1970s, there was little cohesive presentation of tourism research. Tourism studies were reported in a wide variety of sources, from government documents to books. The only tourism journal in existence was *The Tourist Review*. Consequently, scholarly articles on tourism appeared in a multitude of journals (e.g., from anthropology to transportation journals) and by authors from a multitude of academic and institutional backgrounds. Many governmental bodies, consulting companies and academic disciplines contributed to the 'hodgepodge' of reported tourism research.

In recent years there has been discussion regarding the possible maturity of tourism as an academic discipline. A focal point of such discussion concerns the extent and development of tourism research literature. Sheldon refers to tourism as a 'maturing field of study' and cites research as important for 'extending knowledge of the tourism phenomenon, and by contributing to the field's academic stature—an important consideration for a maturing field'.

In assessing the possible maturity of tourism, as with any growing discipline, it is crucial to periodically 'take stock' and analyze the extent and direction of its evolving research literature. This can lead to a better understanding of likely continued development (or possible lack thereof). Sheldon quotes Van Over and Nelson who summarize this viewpoint: 'In a relatively new field... it is periodically necessary to identify and evaluate major research contributions. Such an exercise serves not only to document the historical evolution of a discipline, but to give it a sense of its future as well'.

There are many routes to evaluating major research contributions to a growing area of study. These include analysis of conference presentations, proceedings, books, dissertations and academic journals. However, with tourism, as with most academic areas of study, the research journals are considered to be the major showcase of research in the field. Alternatively, as succinctly stated by Van Doren and Heit, 'academic journals mirror the direction of a discipline's research'. The literature in the journals reflects, among other items, the authorship, institutional productivity and topical areas of study. Usually included is discussion of the methodology and statistical techniques employed in the research. Also, the use of citations provides valuable information as to who and what is being quoted. Journals typically represent state-of-the-art research, as the time lag for article publication is generally much shorter than is necessary for book publication or conference planning. Thus, in this citation analysis, journals were chosen for analysis as the best indicators depicting the evolution of tourism research.

The rationale of conducting a content analysis of journal articles to assess the growth of a discipline's research is not new. This methodology has been used in other fields of study, for example: by Vellenga et al. and Allen and Vellenga in transportation; and by Stahl, Leap and Wei in management. Other authors have analyzed academic journals by focusing on specific sections of reported research, for example: an analysis of the statistical techniques commonly used in the marketing journals; an evaluation of business journals; and an identification of the subject areas and research techniques used in hospitality-related journals. Several studies have been conducted in the recreation/leisure arena. A content analysis and appraisal of the Journal of Leisure Research was conducted to assess the match between stated goals of the journal and reported research. A citation analysis of the primary leisure journals was undertaken to provide insight into the structure and boundaries of leisure research.

Within the tourism literature itself, several authors have broached the question of identifying the state-of-the-art extent of tourism research and hence, hopefully of the field itself. Dann et al. consider the question from the interplay between theoretical awareness and methodological sophistication within tourism research. A meta-analysis was conducted for two journals (Journal of Travel Research and Annals of Tourism Research) over a 10-year period. Findings indicated a gradual increase in the reporting of scientific research (as opposed to descriptive feature articles) as well as a steady growth in the use of more sophisticated analytical and statistical tools. While showing promising growth, 'maturity' of field is not indicated as the authors claim that tourism researchers must continue to develop the balance between theory and method.

Some researchers have examined the titles of published doctoral dissertations in tourism while others have concentrated in analyzing the choice of statistical methods. The authors conclude that prior to 1984 journals tended to lack diversity and show an overwhelming dependence on the use of descriptive statistical techniques. Since 1984 there has been a definite trend to the usage of more sophisticated methods and analysis, Reid and Andereck.

More recently, the work of Pauline Sheldon has contributed much to using journal analysis to provide vital statistics regarding the growth of the development of tourism literature. Her first study considered the perceptions of publishing faculty in both tourism and hospitality journals. The first portion of the study involved a ranking of the tourism and hospitality journals according to quality, frequency of referencing and frequency of publication. The second segment concerned the respondent's use of journals in allied fields which publish tourism research articles.

Sheldon's second study examined selected issues of three journals over a 10-year period (Annals of Tourism Research, Journal of Travel Research and Tourism Management). She presented the results in four segments: percentage of authors affiliated with academic and nonacademic institutions, the geographic contributions of authors, the research contributions of different universities and the degree to which repeat authorship exists'. She concludes by stating that substantial progress' has been made towards developing tourism research and that this trend can be expected to continue: 'the 1990s can be expected to produce even greater gains' Sheldon. The citation analysis conducted in this article may provide more insight regarding the progress that has been made in the evolution and development of tourism research.

Methodology

The citation analysis reported in this study is a portion of a larger unpublished research undertaking which involves a content analysis of tourism journals. It is a systematic, empirical analysis of six refereed journals (published in English) from 1971 to 1 ' 990. The journals have been selected to represent the four continents publishing tourism journal research (i.e., N. America, Europe, Asia and Australasia). The refereed journals analyzed in the study are: *Annals of Tourism Research* (ATR) and *Journal of Travel Research* (JTR) both published in N. America, the *Journal of Tourism Management* (JTM) and *The Tourist Review* (TTR) from Europe, *Tourism Recreation Research* (TRR) from Asia and the *Journal of Tourism Studies* (JTS) representing Australasia. All journal issues within the 20-year period were examined, including research notes which reported scientific research. When the first publication of the journal was later than 1971, the citation analysis was conducted from the first issue onwards. The journals in this category are as follows: the ATR, the TTR, the JTM and the JTS. Due to unavailability of earlier issues of the TRR, only issues from 1984 onwards have been incorporated into this citation analysis.

For each journal article a complete content analysis was conducted. First the subject and authorship of the article was identified. All articles were then classified as either research (based on the principles of scientific enquiry) or feature (a narrative approach). For research articles the methodology and statistical techniques employed were also identified. A comprehensive citation analysis was conducted for all articles (both research and feature) reported in the above six journals over the 20-year period.

The citation analysis resulted in a total of 19 576 citations over the twenty years. The actual unit of analysis utilized, the 'citation' was considered to be any source listed by an author. Each reference was coded as a single entry, irrespective of the number of times it was cited in the article. This approach was adopted because the objective was to identify the diversity of sources which contributed to the literature over time, rather than to identify which citations were most heavily relied upon by any single author. This method of citation analysis has an extensive pedigree within the social sciences, e.g. Garfield et al., Blume, and Goldman.

Six indicators were utilized to assess the citations reported in the six tourism journals. The first indicator involved an overall comparison of tourism and nontourism citations. The second considered the extent to which citations originated from tourism journals, including two non-refereed journals: The International Tourism Quarterly (ITQ) and the Travel and Tourism Analyst (TTA). The third indicator analyzed contributions from nontourism academic journals in related social science disciplines or professional studies. The contribution from nontourism journals is then further analyzed by reviewing each of the six refereed tourism journals to determine the academic subfields utilized. The fifth indicator relates to the use of non-refereed publications in tourism research. Finally, a comparison across time is provided, in increments of five years. This examines the evolution of tourism research by assessing the developmental growth patterns of the following: tourism journals, general tourism publications, nontourism journals, non-English citations and other citations. All of the results of this study are presented in descriptive form.

Frequently a new field of study, discipline or profession is measured by the degree to which it draws upon its own literature in scholarly writing. The six refereed travel and tourism journals draw approximately 15% of their citations from eight tourism journals. In addition to the six refereed journals, two non-refereed journals are also included—the International Tourism Quarterly (ITQ) and the Travel and Tourism Analyst (TTA). If the number of citations from tourism books is added to that of tourism journals, then almost one-quarter (23.5%) of all citations originate directly from tourism books and journals. When the remaining four tourism categories shown in Table 3 1. 1 are included, the total contribution from the tourism literature rises to 39.95%. This indicates a substantial degree of quoting from within the field and is one of the indicators of maturity of a field (Van Doren et al., 1984). The interdisciplinary/professional base of travel and tourism is demonstrated by the 38% of citations that are from nontourism journals (30.55%) and nontourism books (7.730/o). The category of 'Tourism government documents/reports' includes national and state/provincial government reports as well as items such as technical reports published by planning agencies. Trade publications refer to the variety of magazines and newspapers printed for the tourism industry. Tourism conferences are those sponsored by recognized tourism institutions (academic and industry). The remaining category, WTO/IOUTO reports, was included to determine the extent to which international reports and statistics are commonly cited in tourism journals. This category provided the smallest contribution from the tourism literature and may be an indication of the time lag necessary to collect and assimilate international statistics regarding tourism.

The 'Nontourism literature' section of Table 31.1 includes general sources of citations, e.g. magazines and newspapers. The section entitled 'Other' includes unpublished theses/dissertations, citations resulting from personal interviews and any other citations that could not be classified under the other stated categories.

A good indicator of the development of tourism research is the fact that a substantial portion of tourism citations originate from refereed journals (both tourism and nontourism).

A comparison of tourism journal citations in the six refereed journals reveals that the four journals with the largest number of citations all have the highest number of citations from their own pages. The remaining two journals, TRR and JTS both cite the ATR most frequently. However, due to the tender age of the JTS, it was not possible for the JTS or any other journal To cite the JTS in the journal issues incorporated in this study. Clearly, the Annals of Tourism Research (ATR) is the premier journal referenced by scholars. It is both the most cited journal (1171 citations) and uses the most citations (1233 citations). Also, it is one of the top two cited journals for all journals except the JTM where the ATR is a close third

(127 citations) behind the JTR (133 citations). The JTR, like the ATR, is widely cited (941 citations) while the newer JTM is cited less (381 citations). However, on its own pages, the authors in the JTM use almost as many references from other journals (502 citations) as do the authors in the JTR (667 citations). These three journals (the ATR, JTR and JTM) together constitute 2493 citations, or an overwhelming 89.04% of all refereed journal citations. According to Goldman domination of an academic discipline by a small number of journals can be construed as evidence of a maturing academic field. Thus the increasing compactness of tourism research may indicate a burgeoning state of maturity. Another positive indicator of the evolution of tourism research is the fact that 96.25% of tourism journal citations were reported from refereed tourism journals. The two non-refereed tourism journals (ITQ and TTA) only accounted for 109 citations, or 3.75% of citations.

Authors of tourism research often declare that the study of tourism is supported by a multidisciplinary contribution from a variety of other fields of academic study. This is substantiated in this research. Nontourism journals account for 1982 citations or 30.55% of all citations. A closer analysis of the contribution from other fields which provides a more detailed overview of the sources of nontourism journal citations and solidifies our knowledge that the subject draws its strength from other disciplines and professions. To assess the contribution of other subjects, nineteen academic categories and one miscellaneous/other category are identified in the population of nontourism journals.

In the attempt to more closely identify links with other disciplines, the closest relative (that of business) was further subdivided into four categories: economics, marketing, management and general business. The total number of citations from these four categories is 1865 citations representing a substantial contribution of 31.18% to all citations in the refereed tourism journals.

Marketing was the clear leader in terms of contribution to tourism research (744 citations, 12.44%). Much of this contribution resulted from the reliance of business citations in the JTR and the JTM. Marketing is closely followed by three other disciplines, sociology (694 citations, 11.60%), recreation/leisure (621 citations, 10.38%) and economics (610 citations, 10.20%). When geography, the fifth-ranking discipline is added (481 citations, 8.04%), the top five contributors to tourism research account for over half of all nontourism journal citations (3150 citations, 52.66%). Thus these five academic disciplines represent the most dominant subfields supporting tourism research. This clear identification of subfields may prove useful information to tourism authors in terms of possible joint partnerships for research and funding. Within the top five disciplines, the social sciences contributed the most—sociology, recreation/leisure and geography resulted in 1796 citations (57.02%) while marketing and economics resulted in 1354 citations (42.98%). Thus, it is clearly indicated that the tourism journals are based in the social sciences with a prominent secondary base in business management.

The five prominent citation sources from nontourism journals are listed and in every case the top five categories account for the majority of nontourism citations. The range is from 54.85% with the TTR to 70.05% with the JTS. The academic structural strength of each of the journals is clearly reflected in the top five categories of citations represented in each journal. In all cases the structural underpinning of the journal is congruent with its stated objectives. For example, the Statement of Purpose contained in the ATR declares the journal to be a social sciences journal focusing upon the academic perspectives of tourism [and]... is structured by the research efforts of a multidisciplinary community of scholars'. This mission is reflected in the fact that the two highest sources of nontourism journal citations are sociology and anthropology, followed by economics, recreation/leisure and geography. Similarly, the JTR, published by the Travel and Tourism Research Association, clearly demonstrates its marketing/ promotional flavor with 30% of its citations directly from marketing, In addition, a further 100% of citations originate from management journals and another 8% from psychology. The JTM likewise is based in the management sciences with 37% of its citations originating from management, hospitality and marketing, subjects that reflect its purpose and contribution to this field of study.

The remaining three journals would seem to mirror strong social science orientations although The Tourist Review (TTR) does include hospitality and marketing citations that are not as evident in TRR and ITS. The Asian journal, TRR, appears to have a strong base in the social sciences rather than management sciences. This journal, and the ITS are the two tourism journals to feature environment/natural rescurces in the top five categories. It would appear that North America and Europe each have a social science and management science-based journal—the ATR and JTR for North America and TTR and the JTM for Europe, respectively. While all these four journals have an international purview, the researchers and journal editors in the two traditionally wealthy regions of the world have proceeded along two distinct paths of inquiry--academic and practical. Both paths are necessary and essential to tourism and travel knowledge. The appearance of two new refereed tourism journals in the 1990s, indicates that further frontiers and opportunities to fill needed research niches are essential. The largest growth pattern is that of tourism general literature. This attests to the growing availability of tourism and travel publications. The increasing storehouse of tourism sources (from books to trade magazines) is being amply utilized by tourism researchers. Thirty-one per cent of the citations in the three journals of the first half decade are from the tourism literature. By the 1986-1990 period, this had increased to 40% from tourism within the TTR and the newest journal (M) which contained more than 50% from tourism citations. The overall use of tourism citations over the 20 years has grown to 39.93% of all citations. Included in this figure is the use of tourism journals which increased steadily in each five-year block to a total of 14.86% of all citations.

One measure of the maturity of a discipline is the proportion of citations from its own journals relative to journals outside the discipline. Previous studies have stated that physics draws almost all of its citations from its own literature, economics 70% and marketing and sociology 45% and 40% respectively.

11

Tourism Education

Rapidly increasing demand has led to the advancement and sophistication of all areas of Australia's tourism and hospitality industries since the mid-1970s. This has been fortuitous, not only for the Australian economy but also for those seeking employment. However, such rapid changes have led to increasing demands for more highly qualified, sophisticated and entrepreneurial employees. Along with the changing demands upon the tourism and hospitality industry have come changes in the educational requirements of employees serving in these industries. As a consequence educational institutions are being asked to provide employees with the necessary qualifications to meet the needs of a rapidly changing industry.

Questions remain as to whether our educational institutions are meeting these requirements. As is, the question remains as to whether our educational institutions should be providing for all the changing requirements of the industry or whether some of the responsibility should fall upon the industry associations and employers to provide appropriate employee training.

While such debates have been progressing other external forces have had considerable impact on the training and educational environments in not only the tourism and hospitality industry but in industry as a whole. The Australian system of higher education has been restructured from a three-level system of Colleges of Technical and Further Education (TAFE), Colleges of Advanced Education (CAE) and Universities, to a two-level system, which has evolved from the combining of Colleges of Advanced Education and Universities. The second major influence has been the introduction of the training guarantee levy. This levy was introduced by the government to encourage employers to invest money in the training and development of employees. Employers are required to invest 11/2% of gross salaries into the training and development of employees. Another area of influence was the Charmichael Report which urges new entry-level training and presses for competency-based training in Australia.

Educational institutions must now meet not only the changing demands of a rapidly evolving tourism industry, but also the demand for additional short courses which have increased since the introduction of the training guarantee levy. All this must be done within the confines of a rapidly transforming educational environment and short courses must meet competency standards.

Workplace demands on the tourism environment

Australian tourism and hospitality employers have, in the past, tended to rely on short-term casual employees who had no desire to develop careers within their particular industry. Edgell suggests that as the environment changes we must recognise the need for a highly educated and trained professional workforce that is well-motivated and well-paid. This has not necessarily been the case, as the Australian taxation system, in the early 1970s, supported people holding more than one job. This meant that employees within the tourism and hospitality industry tended to be employees with no long-term commitment to the industry. The lack of clearly defined career paths for employees in the tourism and hospitality industry has contributed to the disproportionate number of semiskilled jobs. Department of Employment, Education and Training (DEET) statistics, show that 59% of jobs within the tourism and hospitality industry fall into the category of either semiskilled or trade skills jobs. The statistics point out that almost half, or 42%, of all workers in the tourism and hospitality industry are employed in the semiskilled sector, for example, waiting, housekeeping, bar and clerical workers, while 17% were employed in trade areas such as silver service or chef positions.

Of the education that has been provided for these semiskilled employees much has been on-the-job training and very few, if any, of the employees that fall into this category would have had post-secondary education. Vocationally skilled employees have normally received some post-secondary education through Colleges of Technical and Further Education (TAFE). Government pressure for investment in further education evolving from the Finn Committee suggests a more general education in TAFE training and development of employees. This leaves the way open for employers to fink with education providers to supply the tourism and hospitality industry with a more highly skilled workforce. The benefits of investing in higher levels of education are twofold: individuals who are more highly educated can be more easily trained to meet the needs of their employer, and employees are enabled to meet their own intrinsic needs through increased career opportunity.

The TAFE sector has been the traditional provider of training for employees within the tourism and hospitality industry. Employees have been provided with traditional vocational training such as apprentice-chef and barattendant skills, while a more recent trend within Australian TAFE Colleges has been to skill employees for more sophisticated levels such as silver service training. Andrew Smith suggests that such TAFE courses now be linked to Competency Based Training (CBT) based on the Australian Standards Framework (ASF) and form a focus for career development. Stone suggests that through this form of career development various benefits emerge for employees: they are more promotable; it reduces turnover of employees; it taps employee potential; it satisfies employees' needs; it assists affirmative action plans and reduces managers' hoarding of key subordinates.

The College of Advanced Education (CAE) sector of the Australian education system, which has now been combined into the Australian University system has traditionally provided a niche for potential management employees in the tourism and hospitality industry. Traditionally a small number of these institutions provided their tourism and hospitality students with block release thus enabling trainees to gain some hands-on experience within the particular industry. Block-release required that the student be placed as an employee for one semester in specific tourism or hospitality areas to facilitate the transfer of the students' learning of theory to the workplace. However this system appears to expose a real weakness. No clearly defined links have been made between the needs of the individual and that of the organisation within which the work practice is being gained, other than that of the student gaining 'a bit of practical experience' while the links to the organisational needs are even more imprecise.

The opportunities gained through such work-experience programmes do contribute to the learning process, especially for those students who come straight from high school. These programmes expose often under-age-student/employees to work experience in areas such as alcohol and gambling within the constraints of an academically based course.

The ability to confirm that learning has actually taken place and that transfer of knowledge has occurred through hands-on work experience and that this knowledge and experience is meeting the needs of both individual and employer alike is imperative. What processes can be put in place to facilitate the transfer of learning and the utilisation of classroom skills in the workplace and the reverse?

Transfer of educational training to the workplace

The Australian government has placed a new and increasing emphasis upon the training and development of employees. Employers must spend 1.5% of gross wages and salaries on training. For many larger employers that is much less than they had traditionally spent on training. In the area of tourism and hospitality this has frequently been the case, as employers, owing to the low levels of education of their semiskilled employees, have traditionally had to spend an inordinate amount of money on the training of lower-skilled employees, thus enabling them to meet the organisation's established work skills requirements. Notwithstanding this point, it is critical that any monies invested in education and training is transferred with learning to increased workplace activities and gains.

Learning by doing, or on-the-job training (sometimes known as 'sitting with Nelly') methods of training transfer have been adequate in meeting the training needs of the tourism and hospitality industry in times gone by. Notwithstanding this, employees not only need the traditional theory of educational institutional training, but they also need something that makes their particular competencies stand out from others graduating with similar qualifications. The hands-on practical experience that is provided by traditional 'sitting with Nelly' work experience programmes does have its benefits, but the student or new graduate needs to be seen to have more. Wexley and Latham confirm this when they suggest that on-the-job training should be conducted in conjunction with other training.

Academic programmes and those integrating block work release are of benefit to students and organisations alike. However, in order to ensure that the benefits of both traditional academic programmes and work experience support the transfer of theory into work practices, formal mentoring is recommended. This has been confirmed by Austin in concluding that students that are involved in their own educational processes are more likely to have increased levels of growth and achievement.

Evolving from this is the question which forms the focus for this paper. Should a formal mentoring programme be introduced to integrate and facilitate the transfer of traditional theory-based learning to the workplace? How car mentoring assist students and new graduates to combine study and work experience to achieve increasing levels of growth and satisfaction?

The increasing demand for more highly qualified employees within the tourism and hospitality industry often means that employees graduate with tertiary qualifications and enter the industry without any practical experience prior to employment. The rapid growth of fast-food chains such as McDonald's and KFC have been extremely beneficial in the hands-on educational experiences of many secondary and tertiary students. Students who are studying at tertiary institutions and have had the benefit of having worked for one of the international food chains have had the opportunity of obtaining additional experience to offer to any potential employer. The benefits of having worked part-time in this or similar type organisations prior to or in conjunction with academic study can only continue to contribute to a more effective and efficient workforce.

Hands-on work experience cannot be surpassed as a means to a more rapid transfer of knowledge as well as contributing to the student's own investment in the learning process. It is in this area that the answer to the question asked in the title of the paper begins to emerge. Is formal mentoring the 'state-of-the-art' method through which employees can gain the competitive edge educationally by more effectively combining traditional processes with work experience under the guidance of a mentor and, in doing so, transferring their theoretical knowledge into workplace productivity?

What is mentoring? Is it 'state-of-the-art'?

The art of informal mentoring is certainly not 'state-of-the-art', in terms of educational processes. Informal mentoring has been utilised as a teaching tool for centuries. Mentor was identified as a teacher, trusted adviser and friend by Homer in his poem *The Odyssey*. Homer identified through Greek myth the story of Telemachus, son of Odysseus, who was left in Mentor's care, while his father went to the Trojan War. This relationship was that of a caring person who offered more than just friendship and support for a young person's future. The relationship between Mentor and Telemachus was an, informal relationship in which Mentor provided an affiliation similar to that of a father and guardian identified such informal mentors as primary mentors. That is, the mentor is an individual who is selfish, caring and altruistic and extends a one-on-one relationship beyond that of a normal caring work relationship. While the informal mentoring relationships discussed above are not 'state-of-the-art', formal mentoring, which has been utilised as a staff development tool since the middle of the 1970s, can be identified as being 'state-of-the-art'. Mentoring can not only assist in developing employees but also contribute to the students' ability to actively participate in their own education as the mentor assists in the transfer of knowledge from educational institution to workplace. Mentors in formal relationships established for the purpose of facilitating training transfer from educational institution to workplace are known as secondary mentors. Kram suggests that secondary mentors are much more formal. These mentors offer their proteges an exchange of ideas on a businesslike basis, and encourage and challenge the students to engage in their own educational development. This role has been equated to that of the master in an apprenticeship.

Mentoring is much more than a relationship similar to an apprenticeship. Kram defined it as 'a relationship between a young adult and an older, more experienced adult that helps the younger individual learn to navigate in the adult work and the work world' while Bowen defined mentoring as 'the process which occurs when a senior person in terms of age and experience (the mentor) undertakes to provide information, advice and support to a junior person (the protege) in a relationship lasting over an extended period of time, and marked by substantial emotional commitment on the part of both parties'. For the purpose of this paper, mentoring is a means by which a senior and more experienced individual acts as a facilitator of self-education and learning to a more junior member of staff. The paper takes this definition one step further and suggests that senior members of staff in the tourism and hospitality industries should be appointed as formal mentors to students perusing tertiary studies in the area to encourage their participation in their own education and development. This 'state-of-the-art' process of formal mentoring is recommended in situations where students obtain the benefits of hands-on work experience at the same time as they are pursuing their tertiary studies. The mentoring process establishes a support system in which the student (protege) is matched with and supported by a senior employee (mentor) who has extensive organisational knowledge and a high level of aptitude and work-related skills, as well as the personality and motivation to assist the trainee not only to attain the greatest possible benefit from their university or college study but also to utilise this in their own desire to learn through work experience.

Since the mid-1970s, trainers and educators in the United States of America, Canada and the United Kingdom have been translating the benefits gained from informal mentoring to meet the educational and training needs of both students and employees. Mentoring has been used as a staff development tool in nursing, in business management development, and in multicultural and multinational work environments, as well as being used in education at primary, secondary and tertiary levels and to facilitate corporate mergers. However, Rutherford and Wiegenstein found little evidence of formal mentoring in the hospitality industry in the USA, and our research has confirmed this is the case in Australia as well. Educational requirements and staff skills required to meet the needs of the tourism and hospitality industry frequently overlap many of the areas identified as being assisted by traditional formal mentoring programmes. Frequently staff in the tourism and hospitality industry 'have to work in multicultural environments as well as in countries which are not their countries of birth. Both these situations create difficulties that can be overcome through effective mentoring situations. Mentoring has been used in numerous areas of education: Wenn demonstrated the benefits of mentoring for preschool children; Silrum and Pullen utilised mentoring in high school teaching and their programme is suggestive of the recommendations put forward in this paper. Monash University's Centre for Retail Management is integrating mentoring programmes to support distance education students who are studying for the Bachelor of Business (Retail Management). Students, while working in the retail sector and studying their bachelor's degree by distance education are appointed to a mentor within their work environment. The mentor ensures that the student has the opportunity to put what they are learning in theory into practice in the work environment. The APM Training Institute which is training marketing diploma students in Sydney has a similar process where students are linked to a mentor in an organisation where they obtain work experience one day each week under the guidance and support of their workplace mentor.

Workplace mentors are appointed to encourage and motivate students to take control of their own educational and developmental outcomes while they are still participating in their high school or tertiary study. Mentoring can also be utilised for short developmental courses or in transitional situations where it is necessary for the transfer of theoretical knowledge in moving from student and tertiary institution to employee and workplace utilisation. Formal mentoring programmes at this stage can facilitate development and reduce the potential of becoming student or workplace dropouts. Cosgrove confirms the contribution of mentoring by suggesting that students who participate in mentoring programmes are more satisfied with their university environment and show greater developmental gains than those not involved in mentoring programmes. Similarly this process can be adopted for tertiary students in either the university or college of TAFE system participating in tourism and hospitality study. Formal mentoring is also recommended for facilitating learning where courses already include block-release work experience—thus integrating more senior management into the teaching process and exposing them to the problems and difficulties experienced in the transition process from university to tourism and hospitality workplace.

Formal mentoring has many benefits that can be utilised, not only by the mentor and protege but also by the organisation as a whole. Mentoring is in fact the product of high achievement. However, high achievement cannot be attained without the dedication of the person wishing to learn, grow and develop (the protege) and the person that is willing to contribute unselfishly to the development (the mentor). Of this person Hurley suggests that the 'mentor [is] to success what feathers are to flying'.

Without such a relationship the organisation would not continue to benefit from the outcomes of the affiliation. Benefits to the organisation come in tile form of reduced turnover of staff, an area in which the tourism and hospitality industry have an extreme record. Mentoring can also provide the organisation with a pool of 'upwardly mobile' young employees from which to develop their strategic human resource needs. The mentoring process also adds to the organisation's stability as mentors impart the norms of the organisation to new individuals, thus promoting a cooperative rather than competitive relationship. Although research has not yet been able to offer definite balance-sheet gains to the organisation, socialisation and cultural gains are significant even if it is difficult to put a price on socially desirable outcomes.

Kram suggests the mentoring relationship consists of two specific functions. The first career function group consists of sponsorship, exposure-and-visibility, coaching, protection and challenging assignments. The second area she identified as contributing to protege development is that of psychosocial functions and these consist of role modelling, acceptance and confirmation, counselling and friendship. Both career and psychosocial functions can be present in the mentoring support process established to encourage students and new graduates to take control of their own growth and achievement through their educational experiences. Students participating in tourism and hospitality education courses which integrate mentoring into their work experience activities would be more inclined to initially experience Kram's psychosocial functions; however, as their contribution to their own learning experience increases, the career functions will expand. The mentoring process and the individual's contribution to their own desire for a satisfying educational experience will not continue if the match between mentor and protege characteristics are not complementary and if the protege does not possess internal 'locus of control', that is does not have control of their personal situation and career outcomes.

Mentor and protege must have certain characteristics in order that the mentoring relationship contributes to outcomes which encourage the protege to contribute to their own achievement and growth. It is imperative that mentor and protege characteristics are compatibly matched in order to receive successful mentoring outcomes that encourage proteges to invest in their own development as well as the opportunity to transfer skills learned and utilise them effectively. Cameron and Jesser, basing their study on work done by Hunt and Michael, examined some of the factors that mentoring offers as a contributory factor in the transfer of training to the workplace. Figure 61.2 identifies the fact that the mentor and the protege must be matched effectively in order not only to attain successful mentoring outcomes for the organisation but also to encourage the individuals to seek their own satisfaction, growth and development.

Without the correct match between mentor and protege characteristics the mentoring relationship will not promote the protege to achieve his or her own educational outcomes within the confines of the protege's locus of control. This will reduce the mentor's ability to act as a facilitator by assisting the protege to transfer theoretical skills learned in academic courses, such as, tourism and hospitality courses to workplace environments. Formal mentoring programmes ensure that money spent on training is put to the best possible benefit of the individual and the organisation. But, as with any form of training, support must also come from top-level management. Mentoring programmes that integrate senior-level management staff into the mentoring of junior employees or undergraduate students, assist in developing the level of support contributed by management. Clutterbuck suggests that mentoring provides the opportunity for senior management to take some responsibility for staff development.

Research by Buonocore suggests that employees in the tourism and hospitality industry often experience feelings of abandonment, confusion, fear and helplessness. Pavesic and Brymer confirm these findings when identifying stress, demanding supervisors, routine jobs, lack of career paths for advancement, company politics and low motivation as significant contributors to poor worker attitudes and lack of fulfilment.

Our research makes a contribution to a better understanding of how employees feel about their mentor's or proteges characteristics and how appropriate orientation training of mentors and proteges if matched correctly can give rise to a desire for exceptional educational growth and achievement and the successful transfer of theoretical skills to the workplace.

This chapter is informed by the examination of three different mentoring systems that have been established to support new graduates entering the workplace. The three organisational cases have evolved from research into employee development, with the core of the research aimed at improving the transfer of theoretical training to meet the needs of the Australian workplace. The three diverse industry areas examined were communications, petroleum and the tourism and hospitality industry. The examination is of developmental tools utilised by Telecom Australia, Esso Petroleum and the tourism and hospitality industry based on an analysis of five-star hotels in Australia.

The research instruments varied and took the form of either telephone or mail surveys, observation, or structured interviews based on preestablished questionnaires. Opinions were sought riot only from the training and development managers the human resource managers but also from the mentors and proteges themselves. Various areas in relation to employee investment in learning, self-development and mentoring were examined; however, for the purpose of this paper only selected areas of our research will be discussed.

The three organisational areas of our research were clear in identifying that mentoring is not a stand-alone developmental tool. Notwithstanding this, formal mentoring programmes will provide support to the proteges desire for self-development, the mentor's desire for intrinsic rewards and positive organisational outcomes alike when integrated with other forms of tertiary training an d education. This chapter examines only two areas of our research which we feel can offer an immediate contribution. to tourism and hospitality industry educators wishing to implement this new 'state-of-the-art' method of development with other more traditional forms of education and training, The first area to be covered are the methods we have identified which may facilitate the introduction of formal mentoring in encouraging undergraduate students and new employees to participate in their own educational process and assist the transfer of their formal training to the organisation. Both Merrill and Reid and Byrd and Moore suggest methods that demonstrate appropriate workplace behaviours and provide confirmation that learning transfer has taken place. The chapter will go on to show how formal mentoring processes, as outlined in the decriptive models, can be introduced to best support those tourism and hospitality organisations aiming for state-of-the-art developmental processes in the education of new graduates and students and in encouraging them to participate in developing their own ability to transfer theoretical skills to the workplace. While these are minuscule in terms of the mentoring process, they are offered as a means of introducing a new 'state-of-the-art' model of learning transfer to an area that seems certain to benefit from it.

The first of the areas are the characteristics that mentors must possess in order to make a positive contribution to the career development of their proteges It is evident that the characteristics of mentor and protege must be matched in order to obtain successful mentoring outcomes. These characteristics fall into four specific areas. It is suggested therefore that organisations within the tourism and hospitality industry should be aware of these characteristics if they wish to introduce mentoring programmes to assist in the development of employees that are willing to take control, or at least contribute to, their own growth and achievement by the transfer of training from educational institution to workplace environment.

Characteristics that contribute to learning and development

Our research into the three respective organisational areas revealed strong ideas held by both mentor and protege as to how they felt formal mentoring could contribute to an individual's desire to learn, succeed and transfer knowledge. Characteristics such as age and gender have been identified previously by other authors such as Hurley, who suggests that a successful mentoring relationship normally has a mentor who is 8 to 15 years older than their protege, and Levinson *et al.* who recommend that same-gender mentoring leads to more successful mentoring relationships.

Firstly, the characteristics governed by the organisation need to be addressed. The mentor should be allowed to volunteer and in doing so this person must be made aware of the time commitment that is to be made to facilitating the learning processes of the new protege. This is the case whether the protege is an undergraduate student undertaking a work experience programme or a new graduate going through a workplace orientation programme. The mentor must also encourage the protege to take responsibility for their own mentoring outcomes. Tourism and hospitality industries wishing to develop mentoring programmes or support educational institutions introducing mentoring can do so in this area by ensuring roster systems facilitate mentor availability.

Secondly, not only must mentors be selected on their aptitude to perform their respective work requirements but their selection must also be based on knowledge developed over years of experience. Such aptitude and knowledge skills fall in line with Kram's career functions of formal mentoring in which she suggests the mentor provides sponsorship, exposure and visibility, coaching and protection, and challenging assignments for their protege. It is through the industry or through educators identifying mentors with skills similar to those in Figure 61.3 that the career functions can be integrated into the transfer of learning and students or new graduates challenged by their mentor-driven assignments to seek their own growth and achievements.

Thirdly, the mentor's personality and ethical standards will have enormous influence upon the behaviour of the junior protege in the transfer of learning. The mentor must possess a people-oriented leadership style. This should expose the psychosocial functions identified by Kram and outlined in Figure 61.1. A people-orientated mentor will provide the protege with a role model of people-orientated behaviour that encourages the undergraduate or new employee to grow and develop in the image of their mentor. It is imperative that the organisation or educator introduce role models that develop proteges who are keen to invest time and effort in their own development with the support of their mentor.

Finally, the mentor's motivation toward their work organisation, toward their job and especially toward their protege must be high. The proteges should also be motivated toward their job, their workplace and their own educational outcomes if their mentor exhibits high levels of motivation.

It is evident from Figure 61.3 that there are many contributory factors to the successful matching of mentor and protege characteristics. It is imperative, however, that these factors be taken into account when encouraging new employees and students to take control of their own career outcomes with the help of mentoring, this 'state-of-the-art' learning tool. The disabilities suggest that the characteristics of successful mentoring fall into four specific categories. First there are those things governed by the organisation and over which the mentor has little or no control, but without which the transfer of learning from theory to workplace would not take place. However, from the proteges perspective, the mentor can assist the protege to understand the organisational factors governed by the organisation. Secondly there are those characteristics related to the mentor's aptitude and knowledge of the organisation and his or her job. It is imperative that the mentor has not only sound knowledge of the organisation's norms and protocol but also sound technical competencies in order to ensure that the protege has the opportunity to utilise their theoretical skills within the workplace under the guidance of the mentor.

However, the protege should be equally intelligent in order that these mentoring characteristics are matched. Thirdly there are those characteristics related to the mentor's personality and upbringing; they would be present in the mentor's attitude to any protege and they should conversely be present in the protege; such matching will facilitate the process of self control of learning in any organisational environment. A mentor who demonstrates people-oriented leadership skills will provide a learning environment that encourages their protege to utilise their theoretical skills and encourages them toward growth and achievement. Finally there are those characteristics that are directly related to the mentor's personal motivation. When the mentor's motivation is matched by the enthusiasm and ambition of their protege the opportunity for successful transfer of learning is expedited.

The protege is normally the major benefactor in the mentoring process. Mentors must be senior personnel who have personal maturity, who possess sound knowledge of the company and who also have a high level of technical skill and aptitude in performing their particular job. The mentor must also have people-oriented rather than task-oriented leadership skills, as leadership and role modelling are key factors in successful mentoring outcomes. It is imperative that proteges secure a mentor who can control but not dominate each of the four areas identified in order to expedite the protege's abilities to take partial control of their own learning process. As the protege is introduced to new work experiences they can utilise the mentor's characteristics identified in each of the mentoring roles.

Proteges must also be selected to suit their particular mentor's characteristics. Protege who were either interviewed (in structured interviews) or whose opinions were sought through survey questionnaires expressed opinions along similar lines to those of their mentor in relation to what skills they felt that they should possess in order to fully utilise their mentoring experience.

A major mentoring difficulty that was exposed in our examination of formal mentoring cases was the fact that, even though formal mentoring programmes can be described as 'state-of-the-art' in the transfer of theoretical learning from educational institution to workplace, at least one of the three mentoring programmes examined appeared to receive inadequate basic orientation training. Some of the processes in the relationship that were recommended by training and development managers, by human resource managers and by mentors and proteges. Such processes not only encourage proteges to take responsibility for their own educational development and growth under the guidance of their mentor, but also encourage the transfer of academic theory learned into workplace training by utilising the mentoring function.

Orientation to mentoring as a facilitator of learning transfer

In our research into the use of formal mentoring programmes in Australia it became evident that one of the major problems that had occurred was that the mentors and proteges had received induction into the organisations but had not received adequate orientation to the mentoring processes. These difficulties were expressed by both mentor and protege alike, and such failure to understand the basic principles of the mentoring process can discourage proteges from taking control of their own desire for education and growth as well as slowing the training transfer process.

Ten training tools to facilitate orientation to formal mentoring programmes

1. Discussions to clearly define mentoring
2. Discussions to clearly define roles of mentor and protege
3. Training to identify the benefits of mentoring
4. Training in communication skills
5. Training in counselling skills
6. Training in leadership skills
7. Training in time-management skills
8. Training must identify company structure, salary and promotion systems
9. Training must combine mentors, proteges and mentoring programme coordinators
10. Follow-up training must ensure the process is occurring

The training programmes recommended as part of mentor orientation form the core of training necessary to ensure the rapid introduction of both mentor and protege to the process. Training sessions can be introduced either at the same time as the matching process or following on from the mentor pairs being selected. One of the difficulties experienced by mentor and protege participants in our research was that training sessions for mentors and proteges were not conducted concurrently. In order that the relationship between mentor and protege is given every opportunity to grow and develop, training programmes should be introduced as joint training., so as to enable each party to develop similar interpretations and understanding of the processes involved. In this way proteges are encouraged to take responsibility for their own learning while at the same time mentors are encouraged to enable the protege to support but not dominate the proteges development within the guidelines identified. Training which assists participants to define the process, roles and benefits of mentoring should be participated in together. Details of company structure, salary and promotional prospects should be covered in the organisation's orientation training; however, because of the time differences between orientation of mentor and protege it is possible that this can be reinforced in a mentoring training session.

Counselling and leadership training should be orientated toward mentors, but can also benefit both parties, as can training in time management.

A deficiency that appeared in the training of individuals participating in the programmes that were covered by our research was that no follow-up occurred to ensure that any weaknesses that may have appeared could be corrected through further training or in the redesign of new mentor orientation programmes.

12

Coping with Tourism

According to Krippendorf, the social effects of tourism are so significant that they 'should have been studied before everything else'. It has also been suggested that 'investigations of the consequences of tourism in tourist areas ought to begin from an analysis of the individual and collective adaptations made by a host people... such adaptations may be considered the primary consequences of tourism'. Despite these pronouncements, the academic literature includes very few studies which have focused on host adaptations to tourism. This chapter will discuss the type of modifications to their daily life-style made by members of a host community in response to the social impact of tourism. Craik has suggested that in contrast to the dissipation of economic impacts and imbalances across a whole economy or region, social and cultural impacts have immediate consequences... on the everyday lives of residents'. These consequences are unlikely to be evenly distributed throughout the year; they will be most pronounced during the peak tourist season. As Dogan has noted, 'local inhabitants who appear to change their behaviour in the presence of tourists are observed to return to their customary life-style after the tourists have left'.

The chapter will include the results of an exploratory study which was based on the proposition that residents develop ways of coping during peak periods of tourism activity. Coping strategies would entail temporary changes in behaviour, when residents do things differently to how they would be done in 'normal', non-peak periods. They could be categorised, using McConnell's definitions, as being 'defensive' or 'direct'. Defensive coping involves 'protecting self by getting away from threatening inputs and either mental or physical escape from the traumatic situation. One either flees from the problem and in future avoids going near the stress inducing situation, or blocks out the threatening inputs and denies the inputs are stressful'. Direct coping involves taking stock of' a situation, identifying an ultimate goal or adjustment, and coming up with a new approach.

The social impact of tourism

In their seminal work on tourism impact, Mathieson and Wall contended that 'social impacts of tourism were, until recently, a neglected area of study'. They noted that early studies, such as those by Young, Jafari, and Turner and Ash, had been very broad in coverage, providing lists of impacts. The 1970s had also seen a spate of studies of host attitudes to tourists (and their impacts), such as those undertaken by Knox, Thomason et al., and Pearce.

Other early studies examined the social impacts of tourism in a specific location, including East Africa, Spain, the Caribbean, Bali, and the Pacific Islands. More recent studies, in a similar vein, have been those by Boissevain on Malta, Sethna on selected Caribbean countries, Belisle and Hoy on Santa Marta, Colombia, on Hawaii, Milman and Pizam on Central Florida, Brayley and Var on Canada, and Ross on the Australian city of Cairns.

When categorising the nature of tourism impact, Kendall and Var found that the social impacts of tourism may include congestion, crowding, noise, litter, property destruction, pollution, environmental degradation, ad hoc development, loss of wildlife, more and better leisure facilities and parks and gardens, and an increase in employment and business opportunities. Allen et al, added that the consequences of tourism., as found by impact studies by Pizam, Rothman, Cooke, Loukissas, and Getz, include increases in prices, congestion, noise, and crime; disruption of family relationships and structure; and resentment by local residents.

These impacts should not be considered universal, and Certain impacts will be felt more readily than others. Long-term, slow-developing impacts are less likely to directly affect individuals in their everyday activities and are less likely to generate an accompanying resident coping response. Pigram's study on attitudes, perceptions, and implications regarding tourism in the NSW resort of Coffs Harbour, devoted one of its six sections to the social impact of tourism. He found that the seasonal nature of tourism had broad implications for Coffs Harbour, with short-term effects including 'interference with the daily activities of local residents'. In the study, residents were asked to indicate 'the perceived degree of tourist interference on such daily activities as driving in town, shopping, and a range of recreational and leisure activities. They were also asked to indicate any perceived change in the levels of enjoyment associated with these activities'.

Pigram found that 'the greatest perceived hindrances created by tourists were on driving in town (76% of residents), shopping (60%), use of the beach (25%), and dining in restaurants (21%)'; however, he did not examine how residents change their behaviour in response to these impacts as the study reported in this paper proposed to do.

An emerging area of tourism social impact research

has consisted of attempts to ascertain how residents differ in their perceptions of, and attitudes toward, tourism impacts. Research has sought to identify the extent to which differences in these perceptions and attitudes can be attributed to variables such as demographic characteristics or the level of tourism development in the community.

According to Long et al. many social impacts studies have focused on identifying differences in attitudes toward tourism among different types of local residents'. They state that the types of local residents have been identified on a number of bases:

(1) Pizam, Belisle and Hoy, Liu and Var, Milman and Pizam, Husbands, and Brayley and Var segmented residents on the basis of socio-demographic characteristics, such as socioeconomic status and culture, and generally found that such characteristics do not to any significant degree explain variations in resident attitudes.

(2) Belisle and Hoy and Sheldon and Var found, when they segmented residents on the basis of place of residence, that generally 'the perception of tourism impact varies with the distance a person [the resident] lives from the tourist zone'. More specifically, 'the perceived impact of tourism decreases as the distance between the individual's home and the tourism sector of the community increases'.

(3) Another basis on which residents have been segmented is that of economic dependence on tourism. Pizam, Milman and Pizam, Thomason et al, and Murphy used this basis and generally found that the favourability of attitudes toward tourism increases with the individual's economic dependence on tourism.

Allen et al. and Long et al. suggested that differences in socio-demographic characteristics, place of residence, and level of economic dependence on tourism 'provide little explanation, apart from economic dependency, of the variations among residential groups [and individuals']' perceptions of tourism's impacts. They therefore proposed, 'levels of' tourism development in the community' as a better basis for explaining differences in residents' perceptions. They therefore sought to determine the relationships between levels of tourism development and residents' general satisfaction with community life. Their findings were that 'the perception of tourism impacts would increase with increasing levels of tourism development'. These findings were supported in a study by Ross, who investigated 'the relationships between specific impacts on community facilities, global judgements of tourism's impacts on a community, and overall satisfaction with community life'.

The most recent studies of social impacts have criticised the nature of the research which has been conducted. Ap states that this research 'has provided a knowledge base that is exploratory in nature and primarily descriptive'. Birtles goes so far as to say, 'I am, as a scholar, profoundly dissatisfied with this material. It is going nowhere in an epistemological sense...', and Mathieson and Wall noted that 'most of these [social impacts] works have a poorly developed conceptual basis'. Possibly as a result of this, 'there is limited understanding of why residents respond to the impacts of tourism as they do, and under what conditions residents react to these impacts'.

With this in mind, these recent studies have attempted to develop acceptable and useful theoretical bases for examining and understanding residents' perceptions of tourism's social impacts. In attempting to answer questions such as, 'Do residents oppose tourism developments in a select or all-or-none fashion?' and 'What kinds of residents oppose or support tourism and how can we explain this opposition or support?', Pearce et at. and Birtles proposed the use of an equity-social representational perspective, while Ap proposed a social exchange process model.

Doxey theorised that a destination community regressed in their reaction to tourism from initial euphoria through apathy and irritation to antagonism as the adverse impacts of tourism increased. He termed this the 'Index of Tourist Irritation'. This was a unidirectional model which represented an aggregate approach, focusing on attitudes at the community level.

Another unidirectional, community-wide conceptualisation was proposed by Butler in the form of the tourist-area life cycle model. Butler contended that residents' attitudes to tourism go from approval to opposition as a destination grows and the adverse impacts of tourism become more perceptible.

In contrast to these contributions, Butler recognised that it is more likely that a range of attitudes toward tourism and its impacts, and a corresponding range of strategies for coping with these impacts, could coexist in a given destination. He thus developed a framework to attempt to cover the whole range of attitudes and resultant behaviour (strategies) likely to occur in a region. This framework consisted of a four cell typology encompassing:

- Attitude: favourable

  Behaviour: aggressive promotion and support of tourism activity;
- Attitude: favourable Behaviour: slight acceptance of and support for tourism, activity;

- Attitude: unfavourable
- Behaviour: silent acceptance of but opposition to tourism activity;
- Attitude: unfavourable
- Behaviour: aggressive opposition to tourism activity.

Dogan also recognised that 'combinations of strategies may exist simultaneously' in host reactions to the impacts of tourism. Dogan's research was quite extensive, first reviewing the major sociocultural consequences of international tourism, then identifying the primary kinds of strategies which have been developed by hosts affected by these impacts.

Dogan found that on a macro-level (that is, across whole communities) there are several possible reactions on the part of residents to adjust themselves to the socio cultural changes resulting from tourism. Which reaction is adopted depends on residents' perceptions: 'To the extent that the impacts of tourism are perceived as positive, their [the residents'] reaction takes the form of acceptance of the change; to the extent that it is perceived as negative, their reaction becomes more of a resistance'. Thus, five types of response to tourism were identified: *resistance, retreatism, boundary maintenance, revitalisation,* and *adoption.*

Resistance was suggested to occur in places where, as a result of numerous intense and broad negative tourism impacts, 'widespread enmity and aggression against tourists and touristic facilities' occurs. Retreatism involves the community 'closing into itself, avoiding contact with the foreigners, revival of old traditions, and increasing cultural and ethnic consciousness', Boundary maintenance 'involves establishing a well-defined boundary between the foreign and the local cultures'. Revitalisation was identified by Dogan as the community adopting a strategy whereby they preserve, display, adorn, and boast of their cultural resources to tourists, thus accepting some forms of tourism. Adoption as a strategy entails 'an active effort for the demolishment [sic] of the traditional social structure and for the adoption of Western culture symbolised by tourism'.

As Ap and Crompton noted in their investigation of resident response strategies in a small Texan community, Dogan's was a study of international tourism to third world countries, and as such its applicability to their study was limited. The 'clash of cultures in the Texan communities was much less pronounced than in the international context in which Dogan formulated his framework' 'Ap and Crompton, and because 'the strategies reported here are more a function of residents' reactions to tourism numbers and the behaviour of individual tourists than of the existence of a cultural gap which underpinned Dogan's conceptualization'. Thus, the relevance of Dogan's study is limited to the idea that residents may adopt forms of individual adjustment equating to those found for whole communities, and to the observation by Dogan that those affected by tourism would make their attempts at coping based on their values, interests, and cultures.

Ap and Crompton's research was that most closely related to the present study. They derived a continuum of strategies based on empirical observation. This continuum consisted of four broad resident response strategies. The first was embracement, which Ap and Crompton described as enthusiastic and effusive welcoming and praise of tourism. They suggested that this strategy mirrored the 'favourable, aggressive promotion' strategy in Butler's framework. The second strategy Ap and Crompton termed tolerance, which embodied, residents internalizing inconveniences or costs and being sufficiently cognizant of [tourism's] benefits to accept it "warts and all", without changing manifest behaviour to adjust to it'. This strategy was compared with Butler's favourable, slight acceptance description. The third strategy on the continuum was adjustment, which was cited as consisting of rescheduling activities to escape crowds or using local knowledge to avoid inconveniences caused by visitors. Interestingly, Ap and Crompton suggested that those who adopted the strategy of adjustment were apparently uninterested in tourism, and merely accepted it as a part of resort-town life and accommodated it, 'without expressing any feelings towards it'. The fourth strategy proposed was that of withdrawal, which could be either physical (moving out of town) or psychological (keep quiet and don't get involved with tourists). Ap and Crompton placed their withdrawal strategy between Butler's two 'unfavourable' categories ('silent acceptance of, but opposition to, tourist activity' and 'aggressive opposition to tourism activity').

The present study differs from the work of Doxey, Butler, and Dogan which proposed models of resident attitudes to tourism and conceptualisations which were concerned with host communities on a macro-level, rather than with individual residents and their adaptations and adjustments. Ap and Crompton's study differed less in these respects because it had a more individual orientation; however, their continuum of resident responses included both attitudinal and behavioural elements. The following study was concerned with behavioural adaptations. It addressed attitudes toward these modifications to everyday behaviour not toward the tourism impact which stimulated it.

An exploratory study was conducted which took the form of a focus group discussion with six female residents of Byron Bay in northern NSW. Byron Bay is the most easterly point on the mainland of Australia and is a popular tourist resort. It has a pattern of visitation which exhibits seasonal peaks during the Christmas, New Year and Easter school holiday periods.

It was decided to adopt an approach to the discussion which incorporated elements of a 'nominal group technique' (NGT), in which sessions offer a degree of structure with interaction only occurring after individuals have spent time writing down responses to a moderator's question. It has been claimed that the NGT technique is superior to unstructured focus groups in balancing participation and affording an equal status to all participants. Hence, NGT groups impose no restrictions on the number, heterogeneity, or previous acquaintanceship of the participants'.

The group members ranged between 30 and 50 years of age. They all lived in Byron Bay and the meeting was held in the home of one of the participants. It was thought that this venue would provide a comfortable, supportive environment which would encourage informality with participants openly discussing issues in their own language of everyday experience. It is important to emphasise that the objective was to identify types of responsive behaviour, not to determine the significance of possible causal factors such as place of residence in relation to the focus of tourism activity or the extent to which the resident is economically dependent on tourism.

The focus group was conducted in May 1993, at a time when residents would have 'returned to normal' after the busy Easter holiday, but when any modifications to their behaviour during this period should have been easy to recall. A brief explanation of the study was provided and then each participant was asked to write a list of any changes in the way they had behaved during the peak tourist season. The moderator asked each participant, in turn, to describe the first item on her list and provided an opportunity for group discussion. The process continued until the items on each list had been discussed, without duplication. At this point, each participant was asked to describe her attitude toward the behaviours she had described. The discussion, which lasted about three hours, was recorded using an unobtrusive, miniature audio recorder.

The results of the discussion revealed that each individual made a number of changes to her behaviour. No difficulty was experienced in being able to recall these changes and there was a high degree of similarity in the way residents coped. The nature of the discussion indicated that many of the coping strategies comprised a language of common experience within the group.

The impact of tourism forced changes to shopping. Behaviour, leisure activities and in terms of an ability to move, at will, in the area. It was apparent from both the placing on respondents' lists and from the discussion that coping with domestic activities, particularly grocery shopping, was considered to be the must significant.

It would seem that coping takes three forms: reorganisation, retreat and reaffirmation. The main strategy employed by local residents during peak periods of tourist activity involved a *reorganisation* of daily activities. However some people temporarily retreated from normal life and there was some evidence of a need to *reaffirm* one's identity as a resident of the host community.

The stimulus for most of the responses was a desire to avoid congestion and crowding at locations such as supermarkets and car parks, on certain roads and at recreational sites such as favourite beaches. It was apparent that people are made more conscious of their everyday behaviour as any reorganisation involves actively planning changes in timing and locations. There appears to be a reduced opportunity for spontaneity as behaviour becomes more deliberate and rational.

People cope by leaving home earlier, taking an alternative route or using a different mode of transport. These actions seem to be consistent with McConnell's 'direct' forms of coping. Prerequisites for the success of these strategies are local knowledge and an understanding of tourist behaviour. A predictability in the latter means that residents are not taken by surprise; they are able to take a small road, to a car park which they know will not be used by tourists at a particular time. Although the majority of this behaviour involved attempts to avoid the crowds, there was some support for Ap and Crompton's concept of embracement'. The discussion revealed agreement that, on occasions, it was enjoyable to walk in the streets and go to locations where tourists create a sense of vitality and an invigorating environment.

The most extreme type of reaction was when residents felt unable to continue their normal activities. They were not reorganised, they ceased during the peak season and residents retreated to their homes. These were 'defensive' forms of coping. A sense of 'imprisonment' was expressed with a suggestion that there were 'no escape routes' at the height of the season. The nature of the 'invasion' seemed to be at its worst when the residents were unable to relate to the behaviour of the tourists. The extent of this reaction seemed to be proportional to the difference between the residents' self-image and their perception of the type of tourists.

An interesting finding was the desire to be recognised as a local resident. For instance, people did not want to be confused with the tourists when shopping. This is an indirect impact of the host-guest relationship, but involves communication between local residents. It concerns a desire to be acknowledged as a permanent member of the community and clearly, there is scope for frustration with this problem to be at its greatest when temporary shop assistants, employed during the peak season, are unable to recognise regulars who have a usual order. Residents wish their identity to be confirmed when interacting with other local people and a suggestion of the need for a locals only queue seemed to be more of an "ample of Dogan's 'boundary maintenance' than of a desire for preferential treatment.

The attitude of participants to the changes in their behaviour was not as negative as one might have expected them to be based on the nature and scale of the changes. Overall there was a high degree of tolerance, possibly associated with an expressed recognition that there is a price to pay for living in a pleasant environment which inevitably attracts large numbers of tourists at particular times of the year. It was also suggested that it is good to be shaken out of one's routine and to be more organised. However, there was considerable resentment and anger expressed by those who felt forced to adopt 'antisocial' behaviour as a 'prisoner' in their own homes, especially if it, was necessary to adopt this 'siege mentality' for longer than had been expected.

It could be suggested that residents appear to be prepared to modify their behaviour during the peak tourism season if the timing, duration and intensity of the impact is as expected. There was evidence that residents were finding it harder to cope because the peak season was lasting longer than used to be the case. This created a greater degree of uncertainty, making it harder to predict when life would return to normal.

Expectations and attitudes toward coping seemed to

be based on a combination of specific and general prior experience of the nature of the impact of tourism in Byron Bay and a predisposition toward tourist behaviour which may have been gained elsewhere. For instance, it was found that a perceived increase in the intensity of tourism was more readily accepted by residents who had previously lived in Sydney. They interpreted their local experience within a different framework and an understanding of the personal context which shapes reactions to the impact of tourism is clearly very important.

A simplified pattern of daily activities in the host community suggests that residents may shop in the morning and go to the beach in the afternoon. During the peak tourist season, interaction between host and guest will occur when both choose to use the same shops and beaches, at the same time. The degree of tourism impact may be a product of the perceived distance between the residents' self-image, within the context of their normal way of life, in zone A-B, and their beliefs about the tourists and their culture in zone E, as manifested by the behaviour of the tourists in zone C-D. The movement of the tourists from their home area to the destination (E to D) equates to the stage of 'emancipation' and their behaviour at the destination (T in zone D-C) to that of 'animation' in Jafari's tourism model.

Some residents may dramactically change their normal behaviour by retreating to their homes during the peak period of tourism activity. A shopping trip may be used to stock-up on grocery items in order to extend the period of time they are able to stay at home. The shopping trip may be conducted in such a way to reaffirm one's identity as a local resident.

The perceived need to adapt one's behaviour during the peak season would be a function of a wide range of contact situations occurring throughout the destination. Thus, the social impact of tourism would comprise a composite variable which reflects the degree to which residents perceive their space to have been invaded.

A cumulative model which portrays resident behaviour over an extended period would indicate that residents have maximum scope to freely determine their behaviour before the arrival and after the departure of tourists. It would show that coping strategies may be only employed during a part of the season, when tourism impact is at its greatest. It would also suggest that the duration between the expected end of the peak season and when it actually ends may affect residents' ability to cope. This may subsequently have a negative affect on resident attitudes toward tourism.

At alternative model could illustrate a different end to the period of coping in which a sense of inertia is exhibited. This would occur when residents continue in a pattern of reorganised activities longer than is necessary to avoid contact with tourists. An example of support for this proposition would be if residents are sufficiently happy with any new shopping venues that another type of stimulus is required before they will return to the shops which they normally use. In this case, there would be a time lag between the end of the peak tourist season and reversion to routine.

